Dying to Live shows the extraordinary healing that comes from listening to God and being close to God. I highly recommend it to those who need inspiration for healing on all levels—physically, emotionally or spiritually.

—Peggy Huddleston
Author, *Prepare for Surgery, Heal Faster:*
A Guide of Mind-Body Techniques

The pain we don't address in our feelings and understanding will finally be expressed in our bodies. We are called then to listen to our bodies and follow what is revealed toward healing. In *Dying to Live*, Joan McHugh gives a moving illustration of that truth by inviting us to share her own harrowing journey to health. From one death-threatening illness to another, her faith and prayer led her to many ways of healing and a gradual revelation of the inner pain she had kept hidden. From scleroderma to lymphoma of the stomach and lung, breast cancer, the removal of her thymus gland, the loss of two molars and a total knee replacement, Joan went through a gauntlet of illnesses that revealed her deep sense of abandonment and self-rejection. Besides the medical interventions she underwent, she was led to inner conversion and forgiveness of her parents, husband and most of all herself. At the same time, her faith led her to excellent medical specialists and healers, from Drs. Bernie Siegel and Carl Simonton to the baths of love in the waters of Lourdes. She learned to surrender to God through it all and to unite her life with Our Eucharistic Lord, whose passion and resurrection show the way to transforming love.

—Rev. Robert T. Sears, S.J., Ph.D.

When I finish reading a section of a book by Joan Carter McHugh, I want to read it again. This memoir is unique among those journeying towards wholeness, for the author stays close to Jesus. She does not stray into the occult or New Age to find answers to her serious physical and emotional problems. In *Dying to Live*, Joan and Jesus work together, making their path through the narrow way, in a spiritual journey we are all called to take.

—Gail Parry, D.D.S.

D1462535

Joan McHugh's story starts with the sudden onset of a series of very serious illnesses that threaten her life, her relationships and her faith. Her life seemed like two separate tracks running parallel to each other. One track involved coping with a series of serious life-threatening illnesses that included scleroderma, lymphoma of the stomach and lung and cancer of the breast, by seeking the best expert medical advice and treatment. The other track involved the struggle of coping with her relationships and work in spite of her strong spiritual beliefs, sacramental practices, spiritual direction and healing prayer.

Her faith gradually guides her to the union of these parallel tracks of life, when she discovers in the midst of pain, suffering, darkness and disappointments, the relationship between her illness and her spiritual brokenness. This leads to healing of her body and soul as she discovers herself to be a lovable person of dignity and worth with unique gifts and talents. She is renewed and energized.

In the journey of life, we each have a unique story to tell. It always ends in healing when we search for the love that satisfies and discover who we are—our true authentic self. It is a story in which we can each identify some part of ourselves. This is an authentic witness of hope in finding the agape love that heals and sets us free to become one's true self. It is a story that must be read.

—Ken Fung, M.D. Ph.D.

Dying to Live
Faith: My Path to Health

Joan Carter McHugh

Lake Forest, Illinois

Published by Witness Ministries
825 S. Waukegan Road, PMB 200
Lake Forest, IL 60045

FIRST EDITION

Witness trade paperback: ISBN: 978-1-892835-10-9

Designed by Catholic Creative Services, Inc.

Visit Joan Carter McHugh's website at www.witnessministries.org

This book is for:

My many doctors, especially Myles Cunningham, M.D.

My mentors, Fr. Bob Sears, S.J., Irma Gendreau, P.F.M., Peggy
Huddleston, M.T.S., Cheryl Nguyen and Fr. Bob Faricy, S.J.

Beloved authors such as Bernie Siegel, M.D.,
from whom I learned so much

Anne Tschanz, a Witness worker bee and loyal companion
on the spiritual journey

Kandy Stroud

Anne Marie Lynch

Colleen Ambrose

Fathers Joe Whalen, M.S., Larry Hennessey, Bob DeGrandis, S.S.J., Dick
McHugh, S.J., and Dick Norman, S.J.

Mary Higgins Clark

Herb Roemmele

Rich McHugh for hours and hours of expert editing

Tom, Jr., and Sinead, Tommy III, Ryan, Aidan, Eva and Gavin McHugh
Katie, Greg, Ellie and Erin Ranke
Danny, Pippa, and Oscar McHugh
Rich and "Danie D"

All future grandchildren

My husband, Tommy, a pillar of unconditional love and support

Also by Joan Carter McHugh

Leaping in Faith: Stories of Answered Prayer

Feast of Faith: Confessions of a Eucharistic Pilgrim

My Daily Eucharist I

My Daily Eucharist II

Eucharist, God Among Us:
Essays and Images of the Eucharist in Sacred History

The Mass: Its Rituals, Roots and Relevance in Our Lives

The Real Presence: An Historical Perspective on the Holy Eucharist (DVD)

Eucharist: Legacy of Love, The Early Church (DVD)

Contents

The biblical understanding of wholeness is succinctly described in the first chapter of James. We are instructed there to consider it *pure joy* whenever we are in the middle of suffering, because that will lead to wholeness. Suffering tests our faith and builds our endurance, so that we can be mature and complete—not divided, but whole. James cautions that we must ask God for wisdom during this stormy process. It takes *total faith* to believe that God will bring us through the storms, or we will be unable to "receive anything" from God; without total faith in God we remain "double-minded"—divided (verse 8). Wholeness comes as we let Him lead us through the storms. We are to welcome suffering because it brings down the walls in our fragmented life so that we can become mature and complete (verse 4). It is God's intent to bring redemption to the wounded and fragmented places in our lives so that our weaknesses can be transformed into strengths. That can happen when we honestly address our pain. Suffering can lead to wholeness if we embrace it. It will take endurance and time, but the benefits are well worth it.

—James Friesen, E. James Wilder, Anne Bierling, Rick Koepcke, Maribeth Poole, *The Life Model, Living from the Heart Jesus Gave You*

Prologue

IN SEPTEMBER 2007, I flew to Kennebunk, Maine, to participate in a five-day seminar entitled *Who Am I?* I only knew one person, Allie Maggini from Cincinnati, a close friend from college days who had told me about it over the phone that summer. She said, basically, that it had to do with finding out who we are. The "who we are" bit caught my attention. I have been trying to answer that question since my childhood.

Called "Personality and Human Relations" ("Personnalité èt Relations Humaines" or PRH for short), the workshop was developed by a Catholic priest named André Rochais, in Poitiers, France, in 1970 to help people chart a path to their inner self so that they could gain access to the beauty and dignity of their own being. The blurb in the literature explained it as a process that enables each person to discover the depth of who they are and who they are becoming, to find his or her contemplative core and original goodness. That sounded great to me! Founder André Rochais described it as an "approach to personal growth, primarily a journey of self-knowledge and of taking charge of one's life in order to become who one truly is, to know for what purpose one was created, and in order to give meaning to one's life."[1] I liked the fact that the program didn't tell participants what to think, or what they should believe, or how they should feel, but rather it promised to lead them to a level beyond thinking and feeling to *what dwells in them.*

At the time of the workshop, I was thinking about writing this book. After each session, we took time to reflect on the lecture, and then responded to questions in our notebooks. One of the questions was, "If it were possible, what would I like to live or do," 1) that I have a very strong feeling about, 2) that would let me give the best of myself, and 3)

1

that would bring me deep happiness. In this "dream," the question went, "what are my deep aspirations that I have not yet lived?" This is what I wrote:

My dream is to write a spiritual memoir of my recent past, sharing how the Lord guided me to healing, step-by-step, in body, mind and spirit. In this book I can "be my-self" by expressing my faith and my values fully. It will enable me to relive the gifts God has given me in an authentic way. I love sharing my faith and my hope in God. It fulfills me. It is a passion—to share who I am at a very deep level so that God can touch and heal others through me.

I have thought about writing a spiritual memoir for over a year. It feels like the desire is coming from my being because if I start to think about the book or to read a "how to" book on writing spiritual memoirs, a gusher of enthusiasm and ideas well up inside of me. My "I" tells me that I can do it and that I'm a good writer, that I have a story to tell which will nourish others spiritually. My sensibility is alive with purpose and joy and my body is energized when I start to work on it.

Yes, my deep conscience says to me, "Go girl, others need to find the hope and healing you experienced."

WRITING IS IN MY DNA. One time many years ago while on a retreat I climbed a hill, looking for a spot to enjoy the view and to pray for God's direction for my life. *God, please let me know what Your will is for my life. Please show me because I really don't know what to do or how best to serve You.*

I was absent-mindedly feeling the grass under my fingertips when I moved a small rock. Underneath was a black pen with a red cross on it. *I want you to write* it said to me. It was a God-incidence! I *knew* He was directing me to do what was deepest in my own heart. While it was my hand that moved the rock, I felt sure that God guided me to it. It seemed to confirm my writing ability, a gift that I wanted to use to share my faith. I still have the pen. It is a metaphor for my relationship with God who always seems to be there when I need Him.

I started working on *Dying to Live: Faith, My Path to Health* as soon as I got home from the *Who Am I?* workshop that September. The first year I really didn't know what I was doing. I was writing a lot of things as if I were Mother Teresa trying to teach others about the spiritual journey. One day my son, Richard, who is an excellent writer, said to me, "Mom, what you really need to do is just tell your story. No teaching or preaching. Just tell it like it is."

So that is what I have tried to do. At first I was hesitant, couching things in proper language and keeping a respectable distance from my readers. But my writing soon took on a life of its own, forcing me to open up and be brutally honest. Along the way I asked myself, *What good is a memoir if it doesn't reflect the absolute truth of one's life?* My style of full disclosure might surprise people. Perhaps it will turn some readers off, and those who know me well may be shocked to learn things about me that they never knew. So be it. I hope that I can still count on their respect and love.

JUST LOOKING AT ME you would never guess that I have had: scleroderma, a chronic, progressive and usually fatal autoimmune disease, MALT lymphoma that originated in the stomach and spread to the lung, the removal of my thymus gland and breast cancer. Medically speaking I shouldn't be alive. People with scleroderma are lucky if they make it through the first ten years. After that, the odds are still great that they will either die or be disfigured by this killer disease. Underneath, or perhaps driving the illnesses, was a depression that I didn't even know I had because I had become so adept at denying and projecting my negative feelings on others, that I couldn't see that the source of the pain was inside myself.

I have come to believe that physical illness manifested itself last—after emotional and spiritual sickness had taken root. It came, I believe, in order to wake me up to a problem within myself—an inability to acknowledge negative feelings since childhood, which is when I think I disconnected from my true self. Emotional and spiritual imprints of disease were lodged in the memory of childhood physical and sexual abuse when self-rejection and self-hate bored themselves into my psyche—and into my body—which eventually became sick. As a child I barricaded myself behind a wall to protect myself from hurt. My system of repression kept me safe, but it also sealed me in, causing depression that I alternately blamed on the illnesses and/or on others, usually my husband. I didn't know that I had built a wall, or that I was hiding. It took illness to unlock the door of denial, allowing me to access my subconscious where I had stored painful memories and toxic feelings of abandonment, shame and anger that were literally killing me.

MINE IS A STORY of healing from the inside out. It begins in 1994 with the onset of scleroderma and ends in the present time, with a clean bill of health. Today I am thriving—in body and soul—at least most of the time. I am not a heroine, or someone especially favored by fate. Besides, I don't believe in fate. I believe in God. I am a wife and mom who wants to live a long and healthy life and watch my grandchildren grow up to lead happy, healthy and productive lives. I have a devoted husband whom I believe was hand-picked by heaven for me, four over-the-top fabulous kids, a life privileged (at least according to everyday standards) with a good Catholic education, a beautiful home and a talent for writing. The setting that holds all these diamonds in place is my faith in a caring God whom I credit for all this. In the course of my life I've lost love and I've lost hope, but I've never lost faith. It is the cornerstone of my life.

I invite you to journey with me through the last fifteen years on a roller coaster ride through the ups and downs of illness, and through the darkness of depression that often immobilized me in pain. These problems looked like insurmountable mountains that were blocking my path. At times I had to scale inner mountains of fear, self-pity, anger and even despair. Like my favorite childhood book, *The Little Engine that Could,* I chugged along in fits and starts relying on a divine Engineer who skillfully steered me to people and resources, usually just when I needed them, that helped me at every junction: counselors and spiritual directors, Christian authors, doctors, medicine, dreams, priests, friends, strangers, nutritional programs and most especially the Sacraments of the Eucharist and Reconciliation.

I know God can heal instantly. In my case I think He wanted me to step out in faith and really trust Him with my life. I had lessons to learn and things to do in order to grow, to become the person He created me to be. Mainly I had to learn how to love myself and to do what I needed to reclaim my inner child whom I silenced at a young age. For me, illness was a catalyst that led me to recover myself—my true self—who was yearning to live and be set free.

This is a story about the power of belief and how it opens the door to healing just as it did in the time of Christ. In the Gospels deep faith results in healing. Jesus usually prefaced His cures with statements such as, "Believe that you have it already and it will be yours" (Mk 11:24) or, "As you have believed, let it be done for you" (Mt 8:13). When a father brought his epileptic son to Jesus and His disciples, he pleaded, "if you can do anything, have pity on us and help us." Jesus replied, "If you can! All things are possible to him who believes" (Mk 9:22-23). The father said, "I believe; help my unbelief" (Mk 9:24). I like the way Jesus said, "If you can!" as if to say, *Of course I can heal this child.*

Faith, I'm learning, is to count on our prayers being heard—and answered. It is my deepest belief and the central message of this book that God will heal and transform our lives just as He did when He walked among us 2,000 years ago.

And therein is the source of our joy—and our salvation.

1

First Signs of Illness

The way in which a man accepts his fate and all the suffering it entails, the way in which he takes up his cross, gives him ample opportunity—even under the most difficult circumstances—to add a deeper meaning to his life.

—Victor Frankl, *Man's Search for Meaning*

WHEN I STEPPED ONTO a plane at O'Hare Airport in Chicago bound for Caracas in August 1994, I was one person; when I boarded a flight two weeks later to go home, I was another. Illness showed up at my doorstep unannounced and, like an army with an endless supply of reinforcements, it was relentless in pursuing the enemy: me. The problems were not only physical. Down the road I uncovered a hidden-in-plain-sight emotional obstacle—depression—that changed my strategy and the course of my life.

My husband Tom and I were joining a group of people from Boston on a pilgrimage to Venezuela led by Fr. Joe Whalen, a good friend we had met the previous year at a Marian Eucharistic Conference in Chicago. At the closing Mass he gave such a spellbinding testimony during the homily that I tracked him down afterwards and asked to interview him for our magazine, *Witness*, a quarterly journal of personal stories of healing and conversion.

Father Joe was a recovering alcoholic who had been married for twenty-five years, divorced and became a La Salette Missionary at age 68. A charismatic, outgoing, lovable person, he was a reconciler, bringing the healing love of Christ to others that he had experienced so powerfully himself. After

6

editing his life story I flew to Boston to present him with it, and I asked him to pose on the banks of the bay where he used to dig for clams as a teenager in Quincy, his hometown, for the cover photo. He was wearing a blue and red California Angels jacket and baseball cap, "props" he used to witness his devotion to Saint Raphael and the Archangels. Fifteen years later, friends of Father Joe still reprint this story that now circulates all over the world.

I was excited to go on this pilgrimage, if only to be with Father Joe and to enjoy the companionship of like-minded people of faith on a spiritual journey. (Going on trips ranks second on my list of favorite things to do. First is eating out.) We were headed to a jungle area known as Betania on the outskirts of Caracas, where the Blessed Virgin Mary was reportedly appearing to a mystic, the late Maria Esperanza. This short, gracious lady, whom we had the privilege of meeting one afternoon, had wanted to be a nun but married and had seven children. Her mystical life began when she was 5 with a vision of St. Thérèsè of Lisieux and was followed by visions of numerous saints, the Sacred Heart of Jesus and the Blessed Mother. Maria Esperanza became known for her healings, visions, the stigmata and bilocation, gifts like those of Saint Padre Pio, who is now considered by some to be the greatest mystic in the Church.

At that point in my life I didn't have a particular devotion to Mary, probably because I didn't have a very good relationship with my own mother. I thought that Jesus was all I needed. I also carried around painful memories of not being invited into Our Lady's Sodality in high school. (A Jesuit priest in Rome founded sodalities in the sixteenth century. They were communities of students who dedicated themselves to Christian virtue and piety in honor of the Blessed Virgin Mary under whose protection they placed themselves.) Each year when the nuns slipped the trademark blue satin ribbon holding a large silver medal over the heads of my friends, awarding them the honor of being a Child of Mary, I was secretly crushed. It triggered a core pain that has followed me through most of my life: feeling left out, as if I didn't really matter.

My husband had invited his two elderly first cousins to join us on the trip. While they caught up on family news in the gate area at O'Hare Airport before boarding the flight to Caracas, I wandered off to get a magazine. In a weak moment, I bought—and ate—a Nestlé's Crunch Bar, something I almost never do because I'm always trying to lose weight. We were on vacation, so I gave in to my penchant for chocolate and savored every delectable bite.

An hour into the flight to Caracas my hands started to tingle, as if they were going to sleep. No amount of rubbing stopped the tingling. I remembered my mother in the last year of her life clenching and unclenching her fists asking, "Joanie, why do my hands always tingle?" I didn't know what to say to her then, nor did I know why my hands were tingling now. Many months later I concluded that my mother and I shared an illness that was probably genetic. But I'm getting ahead of myself. On the plane I blamed the Nestlé's Crunch Bar. *No more sugar for me.* I intuited that sugar had a deadly effect on my body, a truth that would become clear to me in the near future.

During our ten-day pilgrimage, everyone was concerned about my physical condition and offered an array of ideas as to what the tingling could mean. Most thought it was carpel tunnel syndrome resulting from too much typing at the computer. But some thought it could be a form of rheumatism or possibly an allergy. They laid hands on me and said Rosaries for my recovery. Father Joe prayed over me many times and blessed my swollen hands with his Saint Raphael healing oil.

I awakened each night around 2 or 3 A.M. with piercing pains in the middle of my palms. Tylenol helped me get back to sleep, but not without a lot of concern as to what this could possibly be. I had been reading several biographies of Padre Pio, now Saint Padre Pio, the priest from San Giovanni Rotundo, Italy, who bore the bloody wounds of Christ in his hands, feet and side until the day he died. A fleeting—and impossible—thought crossed my mind: was the power of suggestion so powerful that just from reading about the stigmata, I could experience it? I knew that God chose very small, unworthy and holy people to bear his wounds. Me? Small and unworthy, yes, but holy? Not by a long shot.

Soon I would learn that these pains were the beginning of a different kind of stigmata, one of illness, that would mark my life with physical, emotional and spiritual suffering for years to come.

EACH MORNING WE LEFT our first class hotel in Caracas to take the long bus ride around narrow mountain roads that dropped us off near a football-sized gravel field surrounded by jungle. In one corner of this vast area was a crude outdoor chapel that seated a few hundred people. Behind it was a grotto with a very colorful statue of Our Lady, hundreds of burning candles and a slow dripping waterfall where we filled our bottles with holy water. Word had it that Our Lady provided this water for healing, and also that she had appeared to people in a grove of trees behind the chapel.

Father Joe had arranged for Tom's cousin, Sister Ellen, to be a reader at one of the daily Masses. Her smile was contagious. She had been a hospital administrator in Buffalo and held many important jobs in her order. But you would never know it. Sister Ellen, who had entered the convent at 17, was one of the most humble and happy religious I ever met. At the beginning of Mass, Father introduced her, saying that on this very day sixty years ago, she made her profession as a Sister of Mercy. Father asked her if she would like to say something. Without a moment's hesitation she said she'd like to renew her vows, which she did—from memory. Everyone applauded. It was a joyous celebration of her life and ministry dedicated to the poor and sick.

We stayed quite late in the field on our last night, the Feast of the Assumption, anticipating Our Lady's appearance. (Nothing certain is known about Mary's death, but Catholics have believed in her bodily assumption into heaven since the fourth or fifth century). The buzz was that if she were ever going to appear, this would be the most likely night. Father Joe was always on his feet hearing confessions and blessing everyone around him with his ever-present Saint Raphael oil. The sky was blanketed with the brightest stars I had ever seen. After a few hours, some of our group came running toward us saying that they had seen her—Our Lady appeared briefly to some people in an area behind the grotto. Her silent presence left them breathless with excitement. They were very believable. As much as I would have liked to have seen Our Lady, the joy I felt in their experience lessened my own disappointment. As far as I was concerned, we had already witnessed a miracle: thousands of people camping out on lawn chairs from all over the world singing, praying and sharing their faith with one another. It was an unforgettable spiritual happening.

But my physical condition was deteriorating rapidly. Walking to and from the buses on the dusty gravel roads was very difficult. I needed to sit down often and felt a general weakness and lack of strength, especially in my legs. My hands and feet were permanently puffy. I resisted asking for a wheelchair in the airport on our trip home, not wanting to admit how sick I felt. I couldn't keep up with the group and had to hang back and let them go ahead of me. The long walk to the gate was almost unbearable, forcing me to stop to look at magazines—but really to find a seat.

This was a far different me from the one who spent eight hours a day on tennis courts as a teenager or who walked from one end of Florence to the other and back when I lived there after college. Stamina and energy were never a problem, in fact they were my strengths. Now I didn't have either.

I ruminated about the possible cause of my condition and wondered if it was an allergic reaction to the herbs I had been taking for the last four months to lose weight. They promised everything from appetite control to energy boosting to cellular nutrition. The list of impossible-to-pronounce ingredients included esoteric names of things like tree roots in Asia. *Stop the pills and this will go away*, I thought. I carried those bottles of herbal pills around with me for almost a year, asking every doctor I saw if these could be responsible for my condition. They told me to throw the bottles away.

I ALSO RECALLED THE polio I had as a child wondering if polio compromised my immune system and set me up for this physical malaise. One night some years ago, I was flipping through the TV channels and caught the end of a panel discussion about post-polio syndrome and the serious health consequences that polio survivors often experience years after recovering from their initial attack of the virus. The symptoms include progressive muscle weakness, fatigue, and even muscle atrophy—all now strangely familiar.

In 1947 a polio epidemic devastated the country. The disease swept kids up in a tidal wave, indiscriminately, in droves. I was one of them. Thankfully—and miraculously—I survived the disease, without any visible scars. I didn't end up with a shrunken limb like a girl who was a year behind me at the Convent of the Sacred Heart, or in an iron lung like Roger, my friend and neighbor who lived across the street from our summer home in New Jersey. He was also one of the lucky ones—he lived.

Now I questioned if my debilitating new condition could have anything to do with polio. My symptoms were so similar, especially the muscle weakness and fatigue. In addition to my suspicion about herbs, I asked every doctor I saw for the next year if I was suffering from post-polio syndrome. Not one of them knew.

Polio was a virus, an intestinal infection spread by contact with fecal waste. Children in swimming pools were prime targets for the disease. Since I spent almost every hour of my waking life at the beach and in the pool during the summer, it was a likely place of contagion. Doctors became proficient at inserting long needles into children's spines to draw fluid that would indicate the presence of the virus.

Polio's origins actually date back to the Old Testament. Egyptian paintings and carvings depict otherwise healthy people with withered limbs, walking with canes at a young age. One stone carving from 1500 B.C. shows a priest leaning on a staff, one leg smaller and shorter than the other, his foot pointed in a manner resembling a polio victim. Theory has it that the Roman Emperor Claudius was stricken as a child, and this caused him to walk with a limp for the rest of his life.

Closer to our own time there was a large outbreak of polio in Brooklyn, New York, in 1916. It claimed 6,000 lives and left 27,000 people paralyzed. New York City also suffered thousands of fatalities and cases of paralysis, mostly young children under the age of 5. In 1921 polio permanently paralyzed 39-year-old Franklin Delano Roosevelt, a robust and athletic young man in the prime of his life. He demonstrated indomitable courage, fighting to regain the use of his legs, particularly through swimming. But he never did. Eleven years later he would become the thirty-second President of the United States. If a man like Roosevelt could be stricken, then no one was immune. By the 1940s and into the early 1950s the outbreak of polio in the United States was widespread.

No wonder my parents were so worried. In the summer before second grade the doctor came to our house late at night saying that I had all the symptoms—headache, fever, nausea, diarrhea, muscle stiffness—and recommended that my parents call an ambulance and send me to the hospital. I remember being more afraid of getting in an ambulance than of having polio. I begged them not to turn on the sirens. They didn't.

I laid on a gurney in a basement hallway of Fitkin Memorial Hospital in Long Branch, New Jersey, with my mom and dad standing anxiously beside me. I felt their fear. Someone wheeled me into a procedure room with lots of lights and people in white coats. I was totally awake the entire time I was in the room, aware of sights and sounds and waiting for them to do something to me. All the stories I've heard over the years about long needles suggest that they inserted something into my back. To this day, I recall waiting for something to happen and it never did. I don't believe they ever gave me a spinal tap.

"She's got it. We'll take her," they said to my distraught parents. Those were their exact words. Whatever "it" was, I had it and they admitted me to a ward with about six other kids. I was quarantined so my parents had to stand in an extra-wide doorway and talk to me at a distance. It was all strange and very frightening.

I spent a month in Fitkin Hospital. It was a long, painful separation from my parents and my world of friends, swimming and riding my bike on the slate sidewalks in front of our summer home near the ocean. The nights were the worst. I slept in an oxygen tent and feared the crabby nurses, who appeared by my bed unexpectedly at all hours of the night to stab me in my bottom. Literally.

I cried every night. Sometimes I screamed. No one came. That's when I turned to God. "Look down upon me good and gentle Jesus, while before Thy face I humbly kneel. Fix deep in my heart lively sentiments of faith, hope and charity." I knew this prayer by heart because my mother and I had been saying it every night for a few years from the time I was about 3 years old, when she allowed me to snuggle under the covers of their bed to say our nightly prayers.

I don't know which I liked better, being in my parents' bed or the mystery of this special ritual. The "Prayer Before a Crucifix" was inscribed on the left side of a two-inch hinged plastic case. The other side bore a relief of Christ on the Cross. Each night I held this special artifact and said words that I didn't understand; but they somehow spoke to my heart because I pictured God as a kindly father, with a big white beard, up in the sky. I seemed to know that He was real, that He heard me, and that He cared about me. I still have the little white plastic case that I look at every day because it sits with other treasures on a wooden file cabinet that faces my desk. A three-foot tall statue of the Sacred Heart of Jesus, with His arms outstretched to embrace the world, stands amidst many small statues of saints that I've collected from all over the world.

Please God, get me out of here. Help me. I want to go home, I prayed from inside the clear plastic walls of my oxygen tent. After a few weeks I moved to a children's ward with lots of kids. Life was a little bit better although I hated almost everything, especially the food. I was a picky eater and ate very little. We ate meals at long low tables and could move around in a large room. I still slept in a crib-like bed and somehow endured the nurses' nightly visitations.

There was a public pay phone in the hall just outside my ward. I asked someone to show me how to use the phone. After they walked me through it, I took the dime out of my pocket that I had been saving for this emergency and called home. I had memorized my phone number and shocked my mother who answered. I think my call unnerved her and she put my brother on the phone. Howie assured me that if I did what I was supposed to do I would get better quickly and be able to come home soon. Making contact with home appeased me for a few minutes.

One day the pastor of our parish stopped by. I didn't really know Father Everett, but I felt comforted by his interest in me. He handed me a small black leather case with "My Rosary" embossed in gold letters on the front. In it were black rosary beads. He taught me about the Mother of God and urged me to pray to her. I clung to the rosary case as if it were a genie in a bottle that had power to get me out of the hospital. I still have the rosary in the little black case. Perhaps he was the one who planted the seeds of devotion to Our Lady that would blossom many years later on a pilgrimage to Medjugorje in Bosnia-Herzegovina, where I realized that Our Lady is much more powerful than a genie in a bottle: I learned that the Mother of God holds the keys to the heart of her Son.

Another vivid memory I have is of the daily physical therapy sessions in the basement of the hospital where physical therapists stretched every muscle in our bodies. One exercise in particular was extremely difficult. Sitting upright on a rubber mat with our legs straight out in front of us, we had to make our head touch our knees without bending them. This was almost impossible and the only reason I worked as hard as I could to accomplish it was that they told us we couldn't leave the hospital until we did it. Enduring physical torture twice a day was my ticket home. I did it no matter how much it hurt.

Even then I was a fighter. My favorite childhood book, *The Little Engine that Could,* a story I had read a gazillion times, prepared me to deal with this seemingly insurmountable problem. It is about a happy little train whose wheels get stuck, preventing him from bringing the dolls and toys in his boxcars to the girls and boys on the other side of the mountain. Other engines come along and pass him by until a shiny blue engine offers to help. This little engine had never been over the mountain, but his kindness and determination urge him on as he puffs and chugs his way along saying, "I think I can, I think I can." When he finally makes it over the mountain and arrives at his destination, he makes a lot of children very happy.

I think *The Little Engine* is a metaphor for our spiritual journey.

I had an inner drive to keep going—no matter what. I *believed* I could scale this mountain of illness, saying, "I will get out of this hospital, I will get better, I will go home." Faith fueled my engine. The nuns used to teach us to pray as if everything depended on God, and act as if everything depended on us. I tried to do that.

One morning a nurse confided to me that she thought I would be going home soon. I think she was one of the few nurses who liked me. I couldn't sleep a wink that night in anticipation of getting out of the hospital and going back to my normal life. When it was time to leave she helped me gather my few belongings and walked me to the front door of the hospital where my parents and my best friend, Mary Jane, awaited me. Mary Jane was a few years older than I and lived in a house around the corner. We adored each other and played together every day. (One day we made walkie-talkies using hundreds of yards of string tied to soup cans at either end. We strung the line between our houses and tried to talk to each other. It didn't work). The day I walked out of Fitkin Memorial Hospital was the happiest of my life. At least I was able to walk and I had my arms and legs—unlike so many others who were less fortunate. I seem to remember a doctor or a physical therapist telling me that my left side was now smaller than my right side. When I measure my wrists or ankles, there is a slight difference in size. But it is not noticeable and as far as I know, I left the hospital without any physical setbacks. I probably will never know what polio did to my immune system.

This was my first experience with suffering related to illness, one that inscribed a lesson in my 6 year-old memory which I would recall many times in the future: that illness can awaken us to a wider vision of life's meaning and possibilities.

WHEN I WENT INTO the hospital I was a spoiled brat. When I came home a month later, I was no longer the center of the universe. Polio gave me new eyes to see—and appreciate—the world through different lenses. I became aware of others and thankful for the love of my parents and friends. After dinner I sat on the front porch of our Victorian house overlooking the ocean and had a conversation with God. To this day I remember my litany of gratitude. *Thank you God for your love and your care. Thank you for giving me life, and for my parents, my brother, Gertrude (my nanny who lived with us), for my friends, my house, my bike, the pool, the ocean, the sun, the stars and for the world. I love you God.* Then Gertrude brought me a piece of chocolate cake that she had baked just for my homecoming. I'll never forget the sweet taste of her cake; to this day I still compare every piece of chocolate cake I eat to hers. Nothing ever compares.

She and I had only recently met when she came to work for us at the beginning of that summer, in June of 1947. Gertrude lived with us six days a week during the summer, and went home to nearby Asbury Park on Sundays where her elderly mother lived with some other relatives.

I think Gertrude was part American Indian. She was short and black and a no-nonsense type of person, at least with me, a willful and demanding child from a well-to-do family who was used to getting away with murder. One day we squared off in the kitchen, she telling me that my behavior was out of line and she would have none of it. She stood her ground and I stomped away in my usual manner to pout and punish her by not speaking to her.

After I came home from the hospital she treated me like a queen. I felt her love and respected the boundaries she set, so that I learned to behave with good manners, if only to please her.

Underneath her tough exterior was a woman of deep faith, compassion, kindness, generosity and love that won the adulation of our relatives and my parents' friends who visited on weekends. Gertrude's room was on the third floor of our three-story home. After dinner I would often go up to talk to her and would find her sitting in a rocker by an open window, with the ocean breeze blowing the sheer curtains and Gertrude deeply engrossed in her big black Bible. I would enter under some pretense and end up on her bed in a pool of tears, pouring out my heartaches that were for her ears alone. I can't remember exactly what my problems were but I sense that the dark moods I often suffered from feeling rejected, unloved, or not worthwhile were the early warning signs of depression that I never associated with myself until sometime after midlife.

I played a lot of tennis as a teenager, I think to prove myself to the world. Wimbledon champion Doris Hart was my coach for a few years. I worked my way up the tennis ladder, winning tournaments beginning with the Thirteen and Under—all the way to Women's—which I ultimately lost. I didn't suffer defeat well. Whenever I lost a tournament I fell apart and sought out Gertrude who pieced me back together again, with such tenderness. Sitting on the edge of the bed next to me, she would put her hand under my chin to raise my face, look me sternly in the eye and say, "Remember Who You Are, Miss Joan." "Miss Joan," she would say, "Who are you?" and I would sheepishly stammer "Joan Carter." After repeating this four or five times, she concluded saying, "Now Miss Joan, hold your head up high and don't ever forget who you are." I didn't really know who

I was or have a clue as to why "Joan Carter" was special, but I always left Gertrude's room feeling a little less depressed than when I first went in to see her.

Gertrude was like a mother to me, loving me in ways that my own mother couldn't. On the night Tommy gave me an engagement ring in Central Park, when I got home at midnight, I went straight to Gertrude's room to wake her up to share my news. I told my parents the next morning. One night soon after that when Tommy came to the apartment to take me out to dinner, he went in the kitchen to see Gertrude. I knew that she liked him by the way that she laughed at his humor, but that night I found out just how much she liked him. She said something that I can still remember forty-plus years later: "Oh, Mr. McHugh, I am so glad that you asked Miss Joan to marry you. I was hoping that would happen because she needs someone strong like you to keep her under control." Gertrude knew me better than I knew myself. I still miss her after all these years. There isn't a day that goes by that I don't think about her or pray to her.

Gertrude is so deeply embedded in the story of my growing up, that when I write about polio or anything else that happened during the years she lived with us, she is always in picture. There is one picture she was not a part of, and that is my wedding. Oh, she was there when I dressed and the photographer took pictures in our apartment before we headed to church. She even came to the church and then went back home because we didn't invite her to the reception. I remember telling my parents that I wanted to invite her to the reception but they didn't feel it was her place and they said that she would be uncomfortable herself. I gave in and regret it to his day. I was happy she came to the church, but when I think about her walking back to our apartment by herself I could cry. The one person I loved the most in the world was not there, and I still feel a sharp pain of remorse whenever I think about it.

EIGHT YEARS AFTER MY HOSPITALIZATION with polio Dr. Jonas Salk developed a vaccine against the disease. It was 1955 and Salk became known as "The Man Who Saved the Children." Although he had many detractors, he endeared himself to the general public by refusing to patent the vaccine and made the cover of *Time*. Less than ten years later, another doctor, Albert Sabin, developed an oral vaccine that effectively eliminated polio from the United States. (Today only four countries are still trying to eradicate it: Nigeria, India, Pakistan and Afghanistan.)

I recently met a man at a conference whose sister had polio around the same time I did. He gave me her number and when I phoned her in Texas, we told each other our polio stories. It was the first time I had ever spoken with anyone who had serious repercussions from the disease. This soft-spoken woman with a gentle spirit and strong faith is ten years younger than I am. She contracted polio three years after I did, in 1950, at the tail end of an epidemic and before Dr. Salk's vaccine. She was 4 years old. The disease affected her respiratory system and she was put in an iron lung. She was completely paralyzed.

Today this valiant woman is considered a partial quadriplegic. She has limited use of her arms and uses a power chair to get around. She is married and has an appealing attitude of gratitude for her many blessings. Although I've often felt so thankful that I was spared paralysis or even death, my gratitude was mostly in my head. After speaking with this woman, I felt very vulnerable. The full realization of what could have been my life hit me hard.

ON MY RETURN FROM South America, physical paralysis was threatening me. Now like *The Little Engine*, I was getting stuck on the tracks, wondering how I would scale this mountain. Arriving home was difficult enough; solving this physical dilemma would be another problem. I continued to question if polio had anything to do with my strange new condition, but I had no way of knowing. Weak, tired, sore, and generally not myself, I tried to ignore my physical symptoms, which were definitely slowing me down but not stopping me. My fingers and feet were swelling—and my body would have liked to just go to bed. Instead, I made it work harder than ever. I could barely hold a pen, much less write legibly. Nevertheless I poured myself into my writing projects, hoping that I could will my body back to life.

I sensed that I was in a fight for my life.

2

Diagnosis

I thank God for my handicaps—for through them I have found myself, my work and my God.

—Helen Keller

ABOUT A MONTH AFTER our return from South America I could no longer ignore my hands, which were so swollen and claw-like I could barely hold a pen. My feet were swollen too, and one morning when I was walking up the path to daily Mass at our parish church, I realized how little strength I had and how out of breath I was. When I got home from Mass I finally called our family doctor.

He could tell I was in bad shape but I could see that he really didn't know what was wrong. I asked for his notes (which are impossible to read) and the results from several blood tests that he ordered. Aside from high cholesterol and a SED rate of 3 (the amount of inflammation in the blood), which was minimal, the tests were fairly normal.

Between late September and December of 1994 I made the rounds of doctors. First I saw a neurologist, then a rheumatologist, gynecologist, cardiologist, a specialist in infectious disease and finally another rheumatologist for a second opinion. None of them knew for sure what I had, but they were giving me their educated opinions. I knew something was seriously wrong by the sheer number of questions they asked.

The neurologist tested me for carpel tunnel syndrome because of the tingling and weakness in my hands. I really didn't feel that this was my problem and was surprised when the report came back "abnormal" indicating a mild right and borderline left carpal tunnel syndrome. For a few weeks I wore wrist splints that immobilized my hands, but I lost interest in them because they didn't seem to do anything for me.

After examining me, the rheumatologist mentioned the word "autoimmune" and told me he thought I might be developing rheumatoid arthritis. I had already tried and discontinued several anti-inflammatory drugs because my stomach couldn't tolerate them, so he put me on another one, as well as on 5 mg. of prednisone, and recommended physical therapy. In a letter to our family doctor he described me as "an overweight, middle-aged woman." I didn't really like him and, apparently, he didn't think much of me either!

When I saw him three weeks later, he thought that I was developing a connective tissue disease with an outside chance that this was "scleroderma." I had never heard of the word—or the disease—and when I pressed him for details, he seemed reluctant to go there, as if he really didn't want me to have it. He said it was premature to discuss it because it was unlikely that I had "scleroderma." So I let it go.

He noted in his correspondence that I was "doing poorly" and that I had stopped the prednisone and physical therapy. I resisted taking Plaquenil (a drug used to treat malaria that can make you go blind) and instead wanted to follow "nontraditional remedies such as purging her system of toxins that a chiropractor friend of hers advised." That sounds like me. He recommended that I see a doctor at the Medical College of Wisconsin for a second opinion.

The infectious disease doctor thought I might have Lyme disease, until the tests came back negative. Then I had an echocardiogram for my heart that showed "no acute chest disease," meaning it was normal. It was worth doing if only to hear good news for a change: I had a very healthy heart.

By now every joint in my body was sore, my knees were painful and swollen, and I was constantly exhausted, stiff and out of breath.

IN BETWEEN DOCTOR VISITS I flew to Sea Island, Georgia. I think I was trying to escape. I desperately wanted to be near the ocean, always a healing place for me, and sensed that a week of sun and relaxation would help me. I had a feeling that the salt water would reduce the swelling and bring me back to normal. My husband couldn't get away, but urged me to go. I flew to Jacksonville, Florida, rented a car and drove north.

I must have picked this resort out of a hat after reading an article about it, thinking that it was in the south where it would still be warm in October. Little did I know that it was hurricane season and it would be rainy and cold the entire week. So much for the sun and saltwater! I had a few massages that eased the pain and discomfort in my arms and legs, but spent most of the time in my room reading and sleeping.

One afternoon I got directions to the nearest Catholic Church, where I went to spend some time in prayer. I felt great comfort sitting in a dark-ened church beside the tabernacle, knowing Jesus was present. I needed to know that I wasn't alone and that God was with me and would help me. My faith in the Real Presence of Jesus in the Eucharist had sustained me in times of trouble since my childhood, when I first learned about this sacred mystery.

In second grade Mother Ranney prepared us to receive our First Holy Communion by cutting up tiny squares of graham crackers that she ap-plied to our tongues. We were to let them sit for ten minutes, the amount of time Jesus would be with us. They were supposed to dissolve on our tongues (no chewing allowed) while we welcomed God into our hearts. My mother bought me some graham crackers that I carefully cut up into squares after school. Then I solemnly gave them to myself, pretending that I was receiving Jesus. On the actual day of my First Communion, I was ready—and eager—to receive God.

My mother fostered my religious rituals. When I was 9 or 10, she bought me a small plastic and rather ornate Gothic-type altar for my room. I could plug it in and when I turned the lights off in my room, my ivory colored altar glowed in the dark. I thought I was in heaven! If I had to guess, I would say that I looked forward to Jesus coming to my altar and into my heart like a hungry child looks upon food. I needed to be filled. I was starved—even as a child—for love. With the wisdom of hindsight, I think I was born with an emotional hole in my heart that I looked to Jesus to fill. The memories I have of my childhood are scant, but I know I drank a bottle until I was five and wet my bed for more years than I would like to admit. When I came home from grade school, my wet sheets were often hanging over the door to my room, drying. I also bit my nails. I think I was neurotic in the real sense of that word, crying at the drop of a hat and always anxious.

My faith in God filled a need in me to bond with Someone who loved me. Even though I knew deep down that my parents loved and cared for me, I was unable to return that love and instead relied on God to help me. Faith was as natural to me as breathing. I never questioned it, doubted it, or thought it strange that some people didn't have it. I believed therefore I was.

My faith grew up with me. By the time I got to high school, I was depending on God a lot. During junior year when I was on the varsity basketball team, we were at an "away" game at one of our Sacred Heart sister schools. I was a forward, which in the 1950s meant that you could take two giant steps before passing the ball. As I drove toward the basket for a shot, I twisted my knee and cringed in pain. I had to sit out the rest of the game.

I hobbled to the water cooler in the hall and saw the chapel doors nearby. Since I was out of the game I had time to go in and "make a visit" as we used to say. It was a huge chapel, very long and narrow. Way up front on the left was a golden tabernacle. I sat in the last row and recollected myself. My eyes focused on the tabernacle and the red vigil light hanging next to it, indicating that Christ was "home."

I drew enormous comfort believing in Christ's presence in the con-secrated hosts reserved in the tabernacle. I began talking to Him. Soon I was sharing all my problems. There were many, as I recall, not the least of which was my mother's mental and emotional suffering. Added to that were personal anxieties, especially my ever-present sense of loneliness and inferiority and my struggle for recognition and approval. There were petty rejections, upsets over dating issues and struggles to measure up—socially and academically—in school.

How much time elapsed I don't remember. What I do remember is the intimacy I felt with Jesus. Although I didn't hear Him speak any words to me, He did touch my heart with a felt sense of love. It was as if He took all my problems into Himself, deep into His own heart, where I knew they would be resolved. He turned my darkness into light. He gave me hope. My tears eventually stopped and I thanked Him for being there for me, for listening, for caring, for helping me.

When I got up to go and was leaving the chapel, I had a thought that made me feel euphoric: *I have just had a conversation with the Son of God and He is a personal friend of mine.*

I continue these conversations today in much the same way as I did in that chapel in high school. On that rainy afternoon at St. William's

Church in Sea Island, Georgia, I felt as if the Lord was telling me to thank Him for this cross of illness and to carry it for others—like He did. I sensed that if I united my suffering to His, He would heal me, as well as others. I asked Him for the strength to put my life in His hands and to trust in His caring love. I wrote words that seemed to come from Him: *Give Me every ounce of your will in every minute of every day.* "How do I do that?" I asked. *As soon as you wake in the morning tell me that you are Mine and that you give Me yourself, your time, your energy for the next twenty-four hours for Me to do with as I please. Give it to Me like a gift, special, wrapped with love, and I will take your gift and use it to save souls.* "How will I know what is coming from You during the day?" *That is the easy part,* He said. *Once you have made this act of submission, then everything is in My control. You don't even have to question. Just follow.*

When I left the church, the weather hadn't changed, but I had. The world—and my future—looked brighter even though I was still in the dark regarding my illness. I wasn't alone. God was with me and I knew I needed to stay close to Him and to discern His guidance.

I *always* questioned these conversations, wondering if God was *really* talking to me or if I was just speaking to myself with words I wanted to hear and thoughts I wanted to believe. I never heard an audible voice, but thoughts and images came to me spontaneously.

There were at least three times in my life when I felt as if God spoke directly to me. One happened many years ago on the final morning of a charismatic retreat that Tommy and I attended. I awakened out of a sound sleep at 5 A.M. with words ringing in my ears. It wasn't that I *heard* the words, it was more like the words silently impressed themselves in my mind. I was groggy, but sensed that I should get up and write the message down. They were: "Go out now and minister unto others, giving them healing, love, kindness, gentleness and mercy. You have new power that comes from My Heart. Use it." They were more than words. They were filled with love, promise, encouragement, affirmation, and direction—all of the above. It was the Holy Spirit, who was commissioning me to do His work. I was sure of it. I have never forgotten the message and whenever I recall it, I feel close to the Lord.

Another "mystical" experience happened during my adolescence at our summer home in New Jersey. I had gone to bed and was still awake, lying there looking out the window at the moon reflecting on the ocean. It was a beautiful scene. I think I was praying when I saw a face come out of the moon and come towards me. It was pulsating. I stared into the night trying to make out the face, when I saw that it was the face of Christ. He was wearing the crown of thorns and He was suffering. I couldn't believe that I was actually seeing the face of Christ. I closed my eyes and rubbed them thinking that I was dreaming. But the vision was still there. I was not imagining it. I was in awe, just looking at Him. But then I began to feel afraid. I froze in my bed and couldn't move from fear. After that, the vision receded slowly back into the moon. I was convinced that I really saw the face of Christ but I couldn't imagine why He would honor me with such an experience. Whenever I think about it, I wish that I had not become nervous and wonder if the vision would have stayed with me. I feel sorry that, if it was Christ, I turned Him away. Every time I recall this vision, I feel God's love for me.

Another experience took place on a ski trip to Devil's Head, Wisconsin, when our children were young. On the drive there, I was reading Saint John of the Cross, hoping that he could shed some light and bring comfort to the darkness I was experiencing in my life. I also was searching for a way to share my faith in a ministerial capacity, but my children were small and I was totally occupied with them. One night I awakened with these words resounding in my head: "Do not be afraid to follow the good intentions of thine." I felt that it might be a message from God, but I didn't know for sure. I still don't know, but I never forgot it and when I remember it, I feel blessed.

When I returned from Sea Island, carpenters were constructing a cathedral ceiling addition next to our family room for an office/chapel for Witness Ministries, a publishing venture that we began after our pilgrimage to the Eucharistic shrines in Italy in 1992 (I had always dreamed of having a prayer room or chapel, but we needed a place to work. So we designed a beautiful space that would serve both needs). The noise and chaos would have driven most people to distraction, but I was so busy researching a book of reflections on the Eucharist that I barely noticed it.

With our kids grown and out of the house, I was grateful for the passion I felt for my faith that I poured into my writing. It not only gave me a reason to get up every morning, but it lifted me out of my problems and into another world—a spiritual one that energized me and nourished my soul. I started working on the Eucharist book after a phone conversation I had with my son, Danny. When he called home from college one evening, he asked about my next writing project. I told him that I had been checking out the religion section of bookstores, looking for a book of quotes on the Eucharist but, as far as I could tell, none existed. I knew that a treasure trove of writing on the Eucharist existed in 2,000 years of Church history and I also knew that I would enjoy owning such a book of short, poignant reflections. I was thinking about assembling one, taking quotes from the diaries of saints and popes, and stories from people in all walks of life who lived—and died—believing in the Real Presence of Christ in the Eucharist. Small self-help books such as "Healing the Inner Child" were extremely popular, and I could envision one on the Eucharist in that style.

After listening to my idea Danny said, "Mom, I think you should do that book, and do it right away. For Catholics and Christians who love the Eucharist, it will be a best-seller."

"Really, you think so?"

"Mom," he answered, "I don't think so, I know so."

How did he know? For someone so young and who didn't even go to church, Danny spoke with the authority of a theologian. The first thing I did when I got off the phone was look through books in my library to find spiritually nourishing selections on the Eucharist.

I took off like a long distance runner and never lost speed. I actually think that my positive attitude and focus charged my cells with life-giving energy that boosted my immune system.

Fourteen years later, *My Daily Eucharist* is in its tenth printing, and is now available in Spanish.

NEXT TO GOD, MY family and my work, books are my greatest comfort and joy. On weekends I collapsed in the blue leather wing chair recliner in our family room with a stack of books beside me and a roaring fire in the fireplace. The books came into my life in all sorts of ways that I can't even remember now, but each one had a special lesson to teach me. The authors were like best friends who walked with me on my journey of self-discovery and healing. They taught me things that helped me grow spiritually and they expanded my vision to see the role I could play in regaining my health, physically, emotionally and spiritually.

In my office there is a large bookcase with "tons" of books I've enjoyed—stacked according to topic. But on the wall behind my desk are my favorites that I can't live without. They are placed randomly on three shelves in a large French provincial cupboard designed to display dishes. You can be sure that when I share the name of a book or the lessons I've learned from an author, that book is on my special shelf. If I lose one or can't find it, I'll turn everything in the house upside down until I find it. Sometimes I think they are alive.

There are four Bibles on that shelf. From the very beginning of my illness, I had a hunger to read Scripture in order to draw closer to Jesus. I wanted to know Him in His comings and goings, in His teaching and miracles, but mainly I wanted to insert myself into the Judea of His time and to walk with Him alongside His disciples. I had always wanted to be a disciple but now I wanted to be one of "His own" (Jn 13:1), a term Saint John used to describe the intimate relationship Jesus had with His disciples. I reread the Gospels, paying particular interest to the healings Jesus performed. There was one lesson that spoke to me over and over again: it was Jesus' teaching about faith. His questions and statements about faith echoed throughout His miracles when He asked people what they wanted Him to do for them. "Master, I want to receive my sight," blind Bartimaeus said. "Go your way" Jesus said, "Your faith has made you well" (Mk 10:51-52). Or when He was explaining to Peter about the fig tree that withered after He cursed it, He said, "Whatever you ask in prayer, believe that you receive it, and you will" (Mk 11:24).

Jesus cured so many people and in almost every case He related their healing to their faith. The centurion, whose servant lay at home paralyzed, told Jesus, "only say the word and my servant will be healed" (Mt 8:8), and Scripture says that the Lord "marveled" because "not even in Israel have I found such faith" (Mt 8:10). I dwelt on these passages: *Believe what you pray for. It is your faith that heals you.* I didn't know it at the time, but in the early days of my illness, I see now how the Lord was trying to build up my faith to rely on Him to guide me.

ON DECEMBER 23, 1994, four months after the onset of my mysterious and debilitating symptoms, Tommy and I drove north about an hour and a half to the Medical College of Wisconsin. We had an appointment with the director of the Arthritis Institute, who invited his doctor-son to participate in the exam. They spent two hours with us.

Both doctors studied me carefully, especially my hands and the beds around the fingernails. Everything was sore and hard to move, even my legs and hips. I could only make a 50% fist on either hand. My skin was "tight" and I had developed Raynaud's phenomenon, a condition in which the fingers and toes turn white and blue because of sensitivity to hot and cold. They thought I might have a mixed connective tissue disease or scleroderma. There was that word again.

At one point the elder doctor said rather offhandedly, "Of course this could be related to problems in a marriage." I didn't think the underlying stress of our relationship was evident. His remark stung.

And it brought up a core worry. Was there a connection between my physical symptoms and the angst that I tried to disguise and conceal? Were the issues that I tried so hard to hide manifesting themselves in physical ailments? And why did the doctor bring up my marriage? Was my marriage creating stress that was making me sick? The doctors were compassionate, which was comforting on one level, but it was also scary. Was I *that* sick?

When I got dressed and met with them in their office, the senior doctor gave me his educated guess: "scleroderma." I still had no idea what it was. He explained that it was a chronic, often progressive autoimmune disease that can affect the skin, joints, blood vessels and internal organs. In scleroderma the body produces too much of a protein called collagen that reduces circulation and causes a hardening of the skin and/or internal organs. The hardening prohibits the body from functioning and it can be fatal.

I was dumbstruck. I went from thinking I might have rheumatoid arthritis, a disease my Aunt Helen successfully lived with for many years, to a rare disease that is often fatal and that has no cure. I was back on 5 mg. of prednisone, a steroid I didn't really want to take because it had so many negative side effects, and 30 mg. of Procardia, a calcium channel blocker that relaxes and widens the blood vessels. In a follow-up letter to my original rheumatologist, the Wisconsin doctor described me as "a delightful 53 year old woman." That was a lot better than "an overweight, middle-aged woman," the label my original rheumatologist pinned on me. He summed up my case saying, "she is certainly an interesting problem."

It was two days before Christmas. I tried to keep a lid on my emotions, which were all over the map. I wanted to be strong but then I'd remember that there would be no presents under the tree and I'd start to cry. About a week before Christmas I had gone to the mall to shop but I could only make it as far as the bench in the entranceway and had to sit down. Shopping was out of the question. It would be the first time *ever* that there would be no gifts for my kids—or my husband—to open on Christmas morning. That was almost more painful than having scleroderma.

Danny had done some research at Columbia's Health Science Library in New York and called that evening. He was coming home the next day and seemed reluctant to share his findings. I pressed him for details. *Mom, this is serious. Scleroderma is in the same ballpark as lupus and multiple sclerosis in which the body's immune system attacks its own tissues. The word "scleroderma" comes from two Greek words: "sclero" meaning hard, and "derma" meaning skin. There are two types: localized and systemic. Let's hope you have the localized one because the other one can damage internal organs including the lungs, heart, kidneys, esophagus and gastrointestinal tract. Seems like scleroderma is chronic and can even be fatal.*

I was glad Danny couldn't see me, because I was crying.

3

Inner Disunity

"And if a house is divided against itself, that house will not be able to stand."

—Mark 3:25

BEFORE ILLNESS APPEARED ON my doorstep, I was in a good place in my life—for once—having survived some rough storms, and knew that if I could weather them, I could endure anything. My dad, whom I adored, had recently died and one of our children was very sick. At the same time I was getting burned out from the work of publishing *Witness Magazine,* a nine-year labor of love that was now more labor than love. The decision to let it die a natural death was difficult but necessary. All of this stress put a strain on our marriage, causing me lot of sleepless nights.

In 1992, Tommy and I went to Italy for our 25th wedding anniversary where we trod in the footsteps of beloved saints. Before the trip I sat in a church, asking God to free me from never-ending pain. I opened a Bible at random to a passage from Exodus in which the Lord was speaking to the Israelites, telling them that He was going to free them from slavery and to lead them into a new land that He would give them as their own posses-sion. It made me cry. Those words held out a promise. I thought the Lord would use the trip to Italy to free me from the bondage of emotional pain and recurring unhappiness.

On that trip so long ago, I prayed my way through Italy, shedding copious tears in magnificent Gothic cathedrals and in crumbling ancient chapels. My prayers for healing led me into places in myself that I had closed off, trying to forget the past. Only when I returned home and was writing a book about that trip, did the memory of a long ago abortion surface (before I was married), forcing me to dredge it up and surrender it to Christ's healing forgiveness.

I devoted a chapter to the healing of the abortion in *Feast of Faith, Confessions of a Eucharistic Pilgrim*.[1] In it, I tell how I was led to confess the sin and take steps to face the hidden trauma and to heal the wound. I thought that this was the fulfillment of the prophecy the Lord gave me when I opened the Bible in church before the trip, the prophecy in which He promised to rescue the Israelites—and me—from bondage. I took it to mean the bondage of sin.

While I was writing this book, I was reflecting on that hurtful experience and realized that the sin of the abortion, combined with the stress of living with that buried secret for thirty years, created a negative spiritual environment that I'm quite certain contributed to my eventually becoming ill. At least that's what the late Dr. Serafina Anfuso, a wise marriage and family therapist, told me. She said that the hidden sin and deception was blocking my spiritual path, preventing the healing for which I was so desperately searching. Tied to it like barnacles on a rock were the shame and guilt, the sense of abandonment and emptiness, the depression and anger, and the denial and the conflict of living with this deep dark secret.

The abortion happened in 1964 when I was 23 and living in Italy. Young and naive, I was swept off my feet by an Italian lawyer when the unthinkable happened and I found myself pregnant by a man I wasn't sure I loved or wanted to marry.

Knowing full well that life begins at the moment of conception, I told myself that because I was barely pregnant, the baby wasn't developed yet; it was only a blob of protoplasm. (I now know that at four to six weeks old that "blob" already has a beating heart, the foundations of the brain, an established spinal cord and nervous system, and the beginnings of arms, legs, eyes and ears.)

I had a moment before the procedure (a "D & C," otherwise knows as a dilation and curettage) to reflect on what I was about to do. I was terrified that a moment of passion with someone I barely knew and with whom I had never discussed the future, would force me to spend the rest of my life with him. All my faith and years of Catholic education went down the drain. Afterwards, the guilt I felt in betraying my values and conscience sent me in search of a priest to whom I poured out my heart and confessed my sin. After that, I so completely blocked the abortion from my memory that it seemed as if it had happened to someone else.

Serafina told me that an aching sense of loss created a deep wound and a void that no one could fill. The intimacy I craved with my husband was impossible, she said, as long as this secret existed between us. It was divisive and created deception and division in our relationship that prevented real intimacy. She explained that keeping such a secret from my husband prevented truth from flowing between us. It was like we were each standing on the precipice of a mountain with a deep crevice separating us. As long as the deception and the secret existed, she said, we could never bond in true intimacy.

"Why not?" I asked, hoping to let sleeping dogs lie. "Because intimacy presupposes connection, and you and Tommy are disconnected at your core." I will paraphrase her reasoning here: The unfinished business of the abortion created a division between me and myself, first, she said, because my heart was not connected emotionally to my missing child. I could see that. Then, she continued, a second division existed between myself and the father of the child. Inasmuch as I acted independently in regard to our child and made the decision without his knowledge, I needed to bring this to prayer and ask the Lord to forgive me and to release the father of the child from the hurt and separation that this wound caused him. I could also see that. And thirdly, she said, there was a division between me and my husband because of the secret.

All of this made sense. Serafina explained that healing is a process, the first step of which I took by sharing this with her. There would be other steps. First, she wanted me to share the abortion with my husband, saying that the health of our marriage rested on the establishment of truth between us. I believed this. I also trusted the promise of the Lord who told His disciples that the truth would set us free (John 8:33). Then, Serafina said, I also owed my grown children the truth, because inasmuch as our marital relationship was hurt by this, so was the family. And, Serafina explained, they also needed to know that they had two siblings in heaven, one child from a miscarriage that happened before our fourth child was born, and one from the abortion that happened before I was married.

The other steps she wanted me to follow were to name my lost children, to embrace them in a guided imagery session, and then to have a Mass offered for their complete healing and salvation.

I followed Serafina's steps like a schoolgirl completing homework assignments. Sharing with my husband, and later with my children, was not easy, but it was healing. Tommy said he would have preferred that the abortion didn't happen, but in the end he appreciated my openness and honesty. My children were stunned at first, seeing a side of their mom that they never knew. The sharing elicited a frank dialogue during which Tom Jr. wanted to know why I had told them this. What came to me to say was that when I die, I want to leave them more than furniture and things. "I want to leave you a legacy of love," I said, "and that legacy is the truth of my life." That was the best gift I had to give. I told them I gave it to them with unconditional love.

Each child hugged me. I could feel their gratitude—and love. The whole experience brought deep inner peace and a feeling of freedom, as if a huge weight had just dropped from my shoulders. I felt cleansed and forgiven, and, best of all, I forgave myself. (For more detailed explanation of this, please read chapter 22 in *Feast of Faith, Confessions of a Eucharistic Pilgrim.*)

Looking back on that experience fifteen years later, I see how God's forgiveness released me from my own crippling guilt and freed me to get on with my life. I thought I was "done," so to speak, with the inner work of repentance and on the road to wholeness—and holiness. The problems around that period eventually resolved themselves. Our child regained his health, and eventually I was able to let go of my dad after he came to me in a powerful dream. The trip to Italy spawned a new Eucharistic apostolate that replaced the work of publishing *Witness Magazine*, and our marriage got back on track. At 53, I hoped to slip peacefully into midlife and to live happily ever after.

I had no idea that the promise God made to me in that church before our trip to Italy many years ago—to free me from bondage—was just the beginning of His plan to set me free. With the gift of hindsight, I can see how He answered my prayers for healing by showing me the inner wall I erected to hide from the shame—and sin—of abortion. It blocked me from loving—others as well as myself—not to mention God! It had to be dismantled if I were to live a Christian, spiritual life, and become my true self that God created in His image and likeness.

The healing of the abortion took place in 1994, the same year I went to South America and became ill. I pick up the story now, after the Wisconsin doctor diagnosed me with scleroderma.

THE REMARK THAT THE Wisconsin doctor made about my marriage unnerved me. I was pretty broken physically, but worried now that my emotional life was contributing to my illness. I thought I had come to terms with the root of my pain when I acknowledged the abortion to my family and received God's forgiveness, but that just cleared the decks to allow me to go deeper into the source of my pain, which was still a mystery to me.

I have almost no memory of the Christmas of 1994. But I do remember my family being very supportive. We cut back on Christmas gifts, and they took over the shopping, purchasing the presents I could not buy. They even cooked Christmas dinner. The fact that I have no journal entries or records other than doctors' notes tells me how shut down I must have been. I did find a photo of our family at the dinner table. I'm wearing my traditional sprig of red berries in my hair, but I look tired. I can tell that I'm trying to put on a happy face but inwardly I'm desolate. These family dinners were always events in themselves because everyone had a lot to say about everything. I'm always happiest when around my children, as I was this night when we gathered as a family for Christmas dinner. Rich was home from Santa Clara University in California where he still managed to pursue his passion: hockey. Danny flew in from New York where he was a junior at Columbia's School of General Studies majoring in literature writing, and Katie drove out from Chicago where she was a trial attorney at a law firm. Our eldest son, Tom Jr., a Boston College graduate who had just received his M.S. in real estate from the University of Wisconsin and had recently married Sinead, was not there because he was visiting his new in-laws for Christmas.

AFTER CHRISTMAS A BROCHURE came in the mail advertising a ten-day charismatic healing retreat given by Fr. Peter McCall and Maryanne Lacy, who had a thriving healing ministry in the Bronx. It was in St. Croix, which meant warmth and ocean, and it involved prayer and healing. For me it sounded like a win-win situation. I signed up to go.

Grace Gibson, a long time friend and a fellow member of the Association of Christian Therapists which was sponsoring the retreat, was looking for a traveling companion. We were kindred spirits who often roomed together at ACT conferences. I looked forward to these yearly events mainly because of the wonderful people who gathered from all parts of the country: doctors, nurses, dentists, psychologists, psychiatrists, counselors, social workers, chaplains, clergy, religious and lay people like myself—all of whom had one focus: to minister the healing love of Jesus to their patients and clients.

In St. Croix we had plenty of time to relax and swim, which was healing in itself. Someone took a picture of me standing in the ocean. My swollen hands were resting on the water—they looked like baseball mitts. I remember before the trip hoping that the cold ocean water would bring the swelling down and normalize my hands and feet. It didn't.

At the retreat house, word had spread about my scleroderma and everyone wanted to know what it was and how he or she could help me. Father Peter, Maryanne, and another priest from New York, Fr. Bob McGuire, S.J., prayed over my swollen hands many times. Each day Father Bob approached me after breakfast to inquire how I was feeling. A tall, rather imposing figure who ran the Spirit Life Center on Long Island, Father Bob was as gentle and compassionate as a child.

At breakfast with Maryanne one morning I asked her if she thought that I had brought this sickness on myself through my own sin and guilt. She said "no" but I wasn't convinced. In her personal testimony she had told of her own healing from breast cancer by letting go of bitterness and deep resentments during long hours of prayer in front of the Blessed Sacrament. Her story inspired me to spend more time in prayer.

One night before Mass, Father Peter and Maryanne were praying over people. When Maryanne was praying for me, she put her hand on my heart and I began to wail and sob loudly. The pain came from some deep, unknown place within. Although I didn't know its source, it was the continuation, as far as I can determine, of a deep inner healing.

The next day, which happened to be the Feast of Our Lady of Lourdes, I took some time to write in my prayer journal. I wrote that I felt divided from others, and from myself, and asked the Lord to show me the root of my disease. Later that morning I chatted at the water cooler with a man named Mel who told me that he was experiencing arthritic type problems similar to mine. He shared that the Lord told him it was due to disunity within him.

I thought about his remark all day.

Was God sending me a message through Mel that my disease was about inner disunity? I thought that the healing from the abortion sealed the division in myself and restored my integrity. I believe it did, on one level. But, if truth were known, there were other cracks in the foundation of my inner house that threw me off balance. I was living with a great deal of stress that I was trying to hide. On the outside I behaved as if I didn't have a care in the world. On the inside I often felt empty and unhappy. There was a disconnect between the outer and the inner me that had existed for as long as I could remember—probably since my early childhood.

THE FIRST TIME I got in touch with this disunity was when my children were in grade school. I was a young married wife and mother who had everything to be happy about but I often felt emotionally desolate. One time when the pain was too much to bear, I fled to a nearby Carmelite retreat house for five days. I didn't know if the pain was due to my marriage or if it was inside of me—a question I would ask myself hundreds of times in the ensuing years—but I explained to my patient husband that it was either the retreat house or a psych ward. I labeled my mother's bouts with depression "nervous breakdowns." Mine I called a midlife crisis.

When I first arrived the priest assigned to be my spiritual director asked me to fill out a questionnaire. After writing one or two answers, I imploded in pain and spent my allotted time sobbing on the bed. When I met with him before dinner I told him that I wasted the afternoon imagining myself as a 5 year-old at the beach, chasing sea gulls and filling her pail to make sand castles at the water's edge. He asked me to describe her. "Happy, spontaneous, full of life and fun, playful and irrepressible" (My dad always described me to others as an "irrepressible" child) I said, mourning her loss. He listened quietly then told me that the Lord had been speaking to me from memory, calling me to reclaim that child. I started to cry again. "That's impossible," I said, "she's gone, dead. She's been replaced by me." Then I asked how could I become a child again and he said that this was the way to find God: to *become* that child. My homework was to meditate on a certain passages of Scripture in which Jesus used a child to teach His disciples who is the greatest in the kingdom of heaven. He called a child into their midst and said: "Unless you change and become like little children you will not enter the kingdom of God" (Mt 18:3).

I was beginning to understand. Through that experience I felt God's nearness, His presence and His direction. I felt that God heard the cries of my heart and was showing me the path to healing. Before leaving the retreat, I sat in the chapel that had once been the living room of a magnificent private home, and for a long time just kept saying "thank you" to God over and over again. Now I was crying tears of joy, not pain. I didn't know the next steps to take, but that didn't worry me. I trusted that the Lord would show me.

When I got home my children asked me what I did on the retreat. Not really knowing how to explain everything, I pulled the image of an egg out of the air and shared that I was like the egg. At the retreat, I told them that when my egg cracked, out came a golden yoke, which was the heart and soul of the egg. The yoke was the real me, I said to their disbelieving ears, my inner child who was hiding in a lot of pain.

"Why was she in a lot of pain?" they asked sincerely.

I explained that when she was little she didn't know how to be truthful when things bothered her. She thought her negative feelings were a sign of weakness and that she shouldn't even admit them. So she hid them. She stuffed them down inside herself, where she thought they would just disappear. They didn't go away but stayed down there where they took on a life of their own, making a ruckus because they wanted to come out. They were part of her real self that she ignored and tried to pretend was dead. But their cries got louder as her real self wanted to break out and breathe free.

This confused them. "What will her real self look like?" they asked. "Spontaneous, loving, happy, playful and peaceful," I said.

"But you are that way now," they protested. "Yes," I agreed, "that's true, but there is another side of your mom who is often unhappy." I realized that they really didn't really know the mom who battled dark moods and periods of intense emotional pain that made me feel trapped and hopeless. I was trying to hold it all together so I kept that side of me pretty well hidden.

The retreat was a watershed moment in my spiritual life. Underneath the emotional trauma of being 50 and very unhappy, I found an inner child whom I had ignored and who was desperate for love. It would take many long and pain-filled years to realize that the dark cloud of depression that I always hated in my mother actually hovered inside my own heart from the time I was in grade school.

That retreat I made when my children were small started me on a search for my authentic self, the carefree, joyful person who is free to give and receive love unconditionally, who forgives easily and holds no one but herself accountable for her sins and wounds. I saw, perhaps for the first time, that my adult pain, which I usually thought my husband was causing, was actually buried inside the broken heart of my inner child, the one

I silenced by making her hide her feelings and pretend she was someone else.

After that retreat I could never again blame my unhappiness totally on my husband—although God knows I tried. I needed to get in touch with the part of me that I lost in my childhood.

Finding my inner child was one thing. Freeing her would take many years and a lot of hard work.

That retreat took place many years ago, in the early 1980s. It was a fork in the road pointing me down a new path: to find my inner child, my real self, a search that still drives me to workshops and retreats such as the one I attended on St. Croix.

AT THE END OF FEBRUARY 1995, I returned home from ten glorious days in St. Croix with a great tan but even more swollen from scleroderma. But I felt new peace from trying to put my life completely in God's hands. I decided to pray more and to trust that the Holy Spirit would lead me where I needed to go.

It just so happened that the same priest who gave the retreat on St. Croix was giving a talk to ACT members not far from where I lived, at the University of St. Mary of the Lake Seminary in Mundelein, Illinois. Although I didn't feel up to it, I forced myself to go and was so glad I did. I liked Father Peter and trusted the way he combined psychology with religion. He spoke about illness and healing saying that we need our roots healed because Jesus wants to heal the *cause* of our problems. Although he had talked about this on the retreat in St. Croix, I guess I hadn't been listening. Now I took notes: "Healing is not what we do as much as what we undo. We have set up roadblocks in ourselves with our negative patterns of thinking and behaving. When we ask Jesus to take away our symptoms, we are asking Him to be our enabler. He wants to do so much more than that for us, freeing us from the block that is often the cause of the disease."

Father Peter was making a connection between our physical and emotional selves. I left the Seminary that day with a sense that I should begin to look *inside* as well as outside to find healing for my new illness. It was a path I knew I was going to take.

IF THE TRUTH WERE known, I *was* living two lives and had to admit that my inner life could be the block that was causing my disease. On one hand I was happily and deeply involved in Witness Ministries, promoting devotion to the Eucharist through my writing and speaking. My calendar was full with two or three Eucharistic presentations each month in the Chicago area. Several were out of state; one at St. Sabina's Church in Dearborn Heights, Michigan, and one was a conference on the Real Presence in Colorado Springs. Then there was an upcoming trip to Jackson Hole, Wyoming.

On the other hand I was quite weak, physically and emotionally, yet I kept up a hectic schedule, too hectic for someone in my condition. Was I behaving compulsively to fill an inner emptiness or to avoid facing a pervasive unhappiness that erupted periodically in my relationship with my husband? I brooded over that.

There was a story on the news one night about a guy who pulled up to a gas station to fill his gas tank when the ground fell out from under him and swallowed the car whole. Somehow the man escaped from falling into the hole. This is a good analogy to describe what often happened to me emotionally. I would be going about my day when some small incident, usually something my husband said or did, would upset me. Negative voices inside my head started chattering, suggesting that if only he would change, I wouldn't feel this way and I could be happy. Eventually I would fall into an emotional sinkhole where I felt trapped, despairing that I would ever find a way out. I automatically blamed my husband for the pain I was feeling (I didn't always tell him but I thought it or wrote it in my journal) and saw separation and divorce as an escape route. But down deep I didn't really want that because I believe that God willed our marriage. And I was also raised as a good Catholic girl for whom divorce was out of the question.

Besides, I loved my husband. I saw stars when I first met Tom McHugh. He had something so special that attracted me to him. He was sure of himself, a good conversationalist, witty, he didn't take himself too seriously, and he had a serious side of faith and compassion. I loved this man deeply and continue to thank God for him, for our four exceptional children, eight grandchildren and for a life of extraordinary blessings. After thirty years of marriage I couldn't conceive of living without him. But there were days when I couldn't bear to live with him.

What exactly did the Wisconsin doctor mean when he suggested that the scleroderma could be related to problems in a marriage? His remark still bothered me. And so did Father Peter's lecture. The signs were all around me. I suspected that had a lot of "undoing" to do. Deep down I felt like a hypocrite, behaving like one person on the outside and another on the inside.

IN THE EARLY YEARS I dragged my husband to Marriage Encounters, hoping that they would help me find the intimacy I craved. They were weekends that taught couples how to share feelings with each other through a system of written dialogue. We would write the answer to a question in our notebooks, such as "How do I feel about the way we handle disagreements?" Then we would exchange notebooks and verbally share our reactions. They stressed that we were not to have intellectual debates, but to share feelings.

I cried the entire weekend. Even though I felt hope in learning the technique of dialogue, it acted like a trigger that released not only feelings pertaining to the subject at hand, but those from my childhood and adolescence that were stored in my unconscious, just waiting to be released. I think some of the lead couples worried about me because I cried so much. I was all mixed up, thinking that the tears were related to the unhappiness I suffered in my marriage, but in reality, they were related to pain that had been dammed up, probably since my birth. One hole in the dam was enough to unleash a flood.

My husband, on the other hand, was not used to sharing feelings and wrote to me as if I were his business partner. I remember in one letter he used the word "heretofore." We were quite a couple! Underneath his macho mask was a little boy who was terrified of sharing his feelings. Tommy was and is a very sensitive person, but on that weekend I needed a bulldozer to dig up his feelings.

The Encounters taught us—ever so gradually—how to be more honest and open with our feelings, both positive and negative. The deeper communication sensitized us to each other by making us more understanding and forgiving. I remember realizing on that first weekend that, in seven years of marriage, we had never had a fight. We each dealt with anger in the same way: the silent treatment. We didn't know how to fight nor did we realize how unhealthy this behavior was for our relationship. It took each of us many years before we could express our anger. In one of the talks on our first Encounter weekend, the presenting couple spoke about the masks that we wear in order to camouflage our real feelings. They said the hardest to deal with was "the mask of no mask," which of course was the one I wore.

Despite the great tools of communication we learned on these weekends, they barely made a dent in the arsenal of defense mechanisms that I used to hide behind. Denial and projection were so imbedded in my personality that I simply didn't have a voice when it came to sharing hurts and negative feelings. To paraphrase the words of Scripture, it was much easier to judge, to see the speck in my husband's eye, than to take the log out of mine.

Multi-colored spiral notebooks took the brunt of the anger, resentments, despair and self-pity that I didn't know what else to do with and was too afraid—or embarrassed—to verbalize. I've often thought of setting them ablaze in a bonfire in the backyard to symbolically get rid of the junk in my life. I didn't. Down the road a counselor would change my attitude about the "garbage" in the journals, suggesting that my storehouse of negative feelings was like a compost heap; the "garbage" (our negative feelings) acts as fertilizer she said, to help our garden grow. I was shocked to learn that I wouldn't have to get rid of it, but that I'd have to transform it.

In boxes beside my desk, these journals held the dark secrets of my soul that I needed to revisit in order to chart the course of my "undoing," and to write this book.

4

Finding Help—and Hope

Dr. Siegel told of two oncologists chatting about a study they were participating in to test a combination of four chemotherapy drugs, which had the initials EPHO.

One doctor's patients were doing spectacularly well; three quarters of them were responding to the drugs. But only a quarter of the other doctor's patients were improving. Then the first doctor explained that he had simply rearranged the letters of the drugs so they spelled HOPE.

—Dr. Robert Buckman
The New York Times, December 6, 1998

ONE COLD FEBRUARY AFTERNOON when I was feeling pretty down, Kandy phoned from Washington, D.C. We had been best friends for years, the maid of honor in each other's wedding, and shared a lifetime of memories, starting in first grade at the Convent of the Sacred Heart in New York City. She had read something in one of her holistic newsletters about scleroderma that she thought might interest me. I asked her to fax it. I was hungry for information.

The blurb that she faxed advertised a book and had a phone number. I called the number and spent an hour on the phone with Pat Ganger, a woman in Delaware, Ohio, who was diagnosed with systemic scleroderma in 1983. This was the first time I had had any contact with a person who had scleroderma. She described the disease in frightening detail, explaining how the body eats itself up, little by little, including the internal organs, unless you are lucky and have the localized form. Even then, she said, it can still disfigure and paralyze you. She is convinced that she would have

40

died within the first ten years (as a majority of scleroderma patients do) if she hadn't found Dr. Thomas Brown's therapy. He promulgated the infectious theory of rheumatic diseases before he died in 1989, treating thousands of patients who had rheumatoid arthritis, scleroderma and lupus with an antibiotic remedy that put them in remission. When Pat Ganger started his antibiotic protocol six years after she contracted scleroderma, it put her disease in complete remission and today she is living a full and active life, giving back to others all that she has received. She suggested I order *The New Arthritis Breakthrough*[1] by Henry Scammell, which explains the whole story.

I thanked her for sharing so honestly with me and also for giving me hope. As soon as I hung up the phone I ordered the book. When it came I devoured it in one sitting. The author Scammell managed to break down the medical and scientific language for lay readers, making the concepts very understandable.

As a young doctor, Thomas Brown became interested in the infectious theory of inflammatory diseases, especially rheumatoid arthritis. He had a long and distinguished career as a medical doctor in Washington, D.C., serving as Chairman of the Arthritis Institute of the National Hospital, as medical consultant to the White House, and as former Chairman of the Department of Medicine at George Washington University. In other words, his credentials were solid gold.

In 1988, the year before he died, he appeared on *Good Morning America* to promote his book, *The Road Back*, simply stating its two central concepts. The first is that every inflammatory, or rheumatoid, form of arthritis starts with an infection. The second is that all those rheumatoid forms can be treated effectively with safe, easy and inexpensive antibiotic therapy. His theory was controversial to say the least, especially his view that mycoplasma (a microorganism that is a cross between a bacteria and a virus) could be responsible for the infection. His thinking was controversial but it had been around for decades.

Brown tested his protocol on the swollen joints of his rheumatoid patients, injecting them with a form of tetracycline, believing that he was attacking the cause of the infection. In case after case, their symptoms lessened. Some went into remission. Before he died in 1989, thousands of patients were helped and many doctors across the country learned the protocol. Yet in his obituary that appeared in newspapers around the country, one spokeswoman from The National Institute of Health wrote "most experts agree that it hasn't been proven that antibiotics are an effective treatment of rheumatoid arthritis."[2]

For years the medical establishment tried to debunk his antibiotic theory. One reason was because doctors were promoting Cortisone (popularly known as prednisone), claiming that this steroid could bring healing, even possibly a cure. After the medical community invested millions of dollars in this wonder drug, the "wonder" wore off and according to author Scammell, Cortisone "became the most heavily traveled dead end street in the history of modern medicine."[3]

Doctor Brown's theory lives on—along with thousands of his patients—and is constantly under scientific scrutiny in double-blind studies under the sponsorship of the National Institutes of Health and other prestigious medical establishments.

Doctor Brown's theory made sense to me, and it was backed by numerous case histories and it offered hope. I wanted to try the antibiotic protocol, believing that I had much to gain and nothing to lose.

"Joan, you believe everything you read," Tommy said when I finished the book and told him I wanted to try the antibiotics. He is a born skeptic and a lawyer to boot, and has to test everything. "Then you read it," I snapped. He read it and it didn't take him long to agree with me. I booked an appointment several months out in April with Dr. Joseph Mercola in Schaumburg, Illinois, who was mentioned in the book.

ABOUT A MONTH BEFORE my appointment with Mercola, I checked into the Mayo Clinic in Rochester, Minnesota, hoping that "Mayo" meant "miracle." I had waited several months for this appointment and was so curious to find out what one of the top hospitals in the country could do for me. The Mayo experience was difficult—and disappointing. I don't know what I thought would happen, but nothing did. In the five days I was there, I had every test imaginable, all leading to an appointment with two rheumatologists on the fifth and final day. Negotiating the long hallways was almost impossible. I could hardly walk ten feet. It was so difficult that I'd sit on any bench or chair to rest between appointments. Things were looking bleak.

Two different rheumatologists examined me. There was no question that I had scleroderma, they said; the only uncertainty that remained was to determine how extensive it was. The first doctor, a petite Chinese woman, held my swollen hands in hers and said with utmost compassion, "I am so sorry." The other doctor also examined me and together they came up with a program. They upped my prednisone to 8 mg., put me on Plaquenil (a drug that my first rheumatologist put me on which I quit because it can cause blindness) and Procardia (a drug used for heart patients which relaxes artery muscles and dilates coronary arteries and other arteries of the body), a daily aspirin, and wished me good luck.

They offered no solutions. The only good news was that they found no evidence of lung, esophageal or renal involvement. To me this was huge.

In April, a few weeks after the Mayo Clinic visit, we flew to California to spend Easter break with Rich who was a freshman at Santa Clara University. Tommy booked us into the resort at Pebble Beach so they could play golf. I was looking forward to this vacation, to the warm weather and beautiful surroundings, but especially to spending time with our youngest son.

We spent Easter in Santa Clara where we attended Good Friday devotions and Easter Sunday Mass at a beautiful old Franciscan mission church. Then we drove to Pebble Beach for a few days of golf and relaxation. The condos were situated on a hill, which meant we had to unload the luggage on the street below. The path leading to the condo was up a rather steep incline that I could barely make. After depositing the bags in the front hall, Tommy went to park the car. Rich grabbed two suitcases and flew up the stairs to our suite on the second floor. I just stood there and started to cry. I couldn't make it up the stairs.

When Rich came back down, I hated to see the frightened look on his face. We both realized how sick I was. When my husband came along, the three of us just stood there in shock until Rich decided there must be an elevator. Thankfully, there was. Up we went and there I stayed all afternoon. They were worried and insisted on keeping me company. I literally had to push them out the door so that they could get in a round of golf and I could sleep.

I drew the blinds and tried to rest—and cried—all afternoon. The severity of what I was dealing with hit me hard. I was 54 going on 104.

We stayed at the resort for a few days and I recall taking a drive along the picturesque Monterey coast one afternoon and ending up in Carmel, a quaint town where we parked to have lunch. It was a shopper's paradise. One store window was more beautiful and appealing than the next. I managed about two shops and couldn't go any further. Walking and standing was just too difficult. But on another day I was able to spend some time in the Pro Shop at Pebble Beach where I found golf shirts for my husband and our kids with the Pebble Beach emblem on them. (Wherever we went on business trips I always found my way to the store in the hotel to buy our kids toys or, when they got older, clothes. Now I do it for the grandchildren.) The other memory I have of Pebble Beach is our long lunches in the Grill Room and dinners in an elegant restaurant at the resort. It was totally enjoyable to be able to spend such quality time with Rich, who filled us in on his travel adventures in Mexico.

WHEN TOMMY AND I arrived back home in Chicago we went to a talk on scleroderma at a local community hospital. The auditorium was filled with people who were in varying stages of this killer disease. The doctor giving the lecture explained scleroderma, and the medicines commonly used to treat it, most of which I knew something about from the reading I had done. I waited expectantly to hear about the infectious theory of rheumatic diseases and Dr. Thomas Brown's breakthrough in treating people with antibiotics. The speaker never mentioned either.

At the end he fielded questions from the audience. As I recall, most of them were about transplants that people either had or were considering having due to scleroderma—of their kidneys or lungs. It was sobering.

We liked the presenting rheumatologist, Thomas Palella, M.D., whose heartfelt efforts on behalf of people suffering from this disease was apparent. I had never focused on his name, and probably forgot it as soon as we left the lecture. Thirteen years later when I was working on this memoir, digging through my records to sort out my medical history, I found the flyer from 1995 inviting us to the talk on scleroderma. I couldn't believe the coincidence: Dr. Thomas Palella is the same doctor who gave the talk years ago and who now belongs to our parish and who Tommy knows because they attend a men's prayer group together. But it wasn't until I was looking through my medical records and saw the invitation from 1995 that I realized that he was one and the same person.

In 1995 as people filed out of the auditorium, the severity of this disease overwhelmed us. People were in wheelchairs and some of their faces were disfigured. Many wore black gloves to protect their hands from the cold. It was one thing to read about scleroderma, but quite another to the see the effects of it on living people. I understood why they wore gloves because I had some experience with Raynaud's phenomenon, watching my fingers turn blue in a hot bath or in cold weather. It is a condition brought on by exposure to hot or cold or emotional events. First the fingers or toes turn white because of a diminished blood supply, and then they turn blue because of a prolonged lack of oxygen. When the blood vessels finally re-open, the fingers or toes turn red.

On the drive home neither of us spoke. It was as if we had just come out of a horror film and were still in shock. I think Tommy suffered more than I did. I don't know if I was in denial or had a gift of inner peace, but the terrible scene didn't affect me as deeply as it did my husband. I was so focused on Dr. Thomas Brown's success and my upcoming visit to a doctor who would administer the antibiotic protocol, that it shielded me from panic because I had an escape route.

I had hope.

My long-awaited appointment with Dr. Joseph Mercola finally arrived. The reason I even knew about him was because his name was mentioned in *The New Arthritis Breakthrough,* where I first learned about the antibiotic protocol for treating rheumatic diseases. Dr. Mercola had used Minocycline with great success in the treatment of a young patient with juvenile rheumatoid arthritis. Instead of the months or years that it was supposed to take for patients to respond, Mercola's little girl improved in a matter of days and within weeks she was completely cured. Mercola continued using the antibiotic protocol on hundreds of rheumatoid arthritics and he developed a reputation as one of the most experienced antibiotic therapists in the country.

I couldn't wait to meet him. An old friend just happened to call the night before and offered to drive me to the appointment in Schaumburg the next morning, about an hour away. I was so grateful because Tommy was out of town and I could barely walk, let alone drive. I liked this doctor instantly. He was young, upbeat and so knowledgeable about Dr. Thomas Brown who originated the infection theory and the antibiotic protocol. I felt excited and so hopeful.

After filling out a lengthy questionnaire, Dr. Mercola spent an hour with me asking tons of questions and noting it all on his computer. I was very swollen and sick. He joked around a bit and gave me the impression that all would be well. I watched as he typed into the computer: *Patient is having difficulty with pain in both hips that radiates into both legs, muscle weakness in both legs for four days. Also experiences swollen hands and right arm, tingling in both hands, redness on both legs, a tightness in face and neck and moderate fatigue most of the day, lack of endurance and stamina for eight months. Four days ago developed severe incapacitating pain, which limits her walking.* At the end he recorded: *Was under much stress from personal crisis in her life the previous year. Was also under much pressure from a book deadline.*

Then he hooked me up to an I.V. attached to a small bag of clindamycin (900 mg.) that dripped into a vein in my arm. It took less than five minutes. In addition he prescribed an oral dose of minocycline (100 mg.) that I was to take three times per week. Also known as Cleocin and Minocin, these drugs were from the tetracycline family. Clindamycin is used to treat infections and certain diseases including malaria, and minocycline is used to treat a wide variety of bacterial infections. Minocycline kills mysoplasma, the organism that Dr. Brown had identified as the prime suspect in rheumatoid arthritis, and most other connective tissue disease, as the cause of the inflammation and pain. Dr. Mercola also discontinued the Plaquenil I had been taking since before Christmas, and he started to wean me off prednisone. I was grateful for that.

Then we discussed my diet and he changed my eating habits severely. He recommended chicken, turkey, buffalo, venison and lamb. He also told me to avoid processed, cured, smoked or dried meats such as bacon, sausage, ham, hot dogs or luncheon meats—all my favorites! Vegetables were most important, he said, but they should be raw or steamed and preferably organic. He urged me to drink freshly processed vegetable juice and green tea and, other than those, the only drink I could have was bottled water. I was to limit grains and avoid margarine, trans fats and milk, which meant no ice cream or cheese. He suggested that I eat cottage cheese (which I've never liked) and plain yogurt. No fruit juices or corn products and, if I had to have fruit, I could have one serving of apples, plums or strawberries. Sugar was an absolute no-no and that included fruits which were high in glucose. I had to eliminate all shellfish and not eat my favorite baked potatoes, as these would raise insulin levels too high. And, under no circumstances, could I ever have French fries, because they were filled with 100% trans fatty acids. I didn't know how I would live without them!

But that wasn't all. Mercola also wanted me to take two tablespoons of flaxseed oil everyday. It was impossible to swallow, so I devised a cocktail and mixed it in a few ounces of V8 juice. Flaxseed oil, I learned, is considered the king among oils probably because it plays a healing role in nearly every system of the body. It is also nature's richest source of omega-3 fatty acids and I'm quite certain he gave it to me to boost my immune system. That plus some acidophilus was my daily program. As I understood it, the acidophilus was supposed to replace all the good bacteria that the antibiotics killed.

On the night of my first visit to Mercola I slept peacefully for the first time that I could remember. The next morning when I put my feet on the floor and stood up, I felt different. Usually the blood would rush to my swollen feet and it would be painful to walk to the bathroom. On this morning, there was less pain and I knew the medicine was working.

5

Illness and Emotions

It is our central premise that an illness is not purely a physical problem but rather a problem of the whole person, that it includes not only body but mind and emotions. We believe that emotional and mental states play a significant role both in susceptibility to disease, including cancer, and in recovery from all disease.

—O. Carl Simonton, M.D.
Getting Well Again: A Step-by-Step,
Self-Help Guide to Overcoming Cancer for Patients and Their Families

FOR THE FIRST TIME in months I felt like I was on the road to recovery—at least physically. The diet was difficult, but I stuck to it religiously. The better I felt, the easier it was to stay on it. Emotionally I wasn't quite sure what was going on. I had a chronic physical disease but underneath there was also a chronic unhappiness tucked in a corner of my heart that erupted periodically and held me hostage.

There is a chapter in *The New Arthritis Breakthrough* in which Dr. Thomas Brown discusses the psychological components of people suffering from rheumatoid arthritis, scleroderma and lupus. Titled, "Depression and Other Psychological Parameters," in it he claims that depression goes hand in hand with these diseases. He says that it is "organic" and comes in short episodes, lasting anywhere from a few hours to a few days. Brown describes it as a family disease because the husband or wife of the arthritic patient is a victim of the same depression, only secondhand. People suffering from the depression that accompanies these autoimmune diseases cannot just will it to stop, he says. Brown claims that the psychological problems are the result of an immunologic defect and will improve when the cause of

48

the disease is addressed—namely when people receive the antibiotics, the medicine should not only heal the root of the physical disease but it should also eliminate the depression.

I actually skimmed this chapter because I didn't think it applied to me. Depression was something my mother had, not I. I had been to counseling off and on for over ten years, and never once did I relate my emotional blackouts to depression. (And, for what it's worth, I'm still not sure if depression is the result of a chemical imbalance in the brain or if it is a psychological disorder resulting from the repression of traumatic memories.)

ONE DAY I PICKED up *Spontaneous Healing, How to Discover and Enhance Your Body's Natural Ability to Maintain and Heal Itself*, a New York Times bestseller by Dr. Andrew Weil, M.D., a respected guru of integrative medicine. There were three or four references for scleroderma so I bought the book and read it with interest. Weil made several connections between the emotions and scleroderma. One of them was "diseases of the skin (and gastrointestinal tract) should be assumed to have an emotional basis until proved otherwise, because these systems are the most frequent sites of expression of stress-induced imbalances."[1] On another page he wrote: "Autoimmunity has an inherent tendency to wax and wane, with the ups and downs often mirroring emotional highs and lows."[2]

This upset me. Was the moment of my "undoing" at hand, when, as Father Peter suggested, I would have to expose my inner anxieties, negative thoughts and feelings known only to my journals and God? These negative undercurrents, he said, were roadblocks that could make us sick. Now Andrew Weil was saying the same thing in different words. In one of his newsletters he also reported findings from a study he did on three hundred people aged 70 and over. They were the sorts who continually dwelt on negative thoughts and they had higher white blood cell counts, as if their bodies were trying to fight off infection.

I knew that my life was Exhibit A for "stress induced imbalance" and, according to Weil, it was making me sick. Scleroderma is a disease in which the body turns against itself. The immune system produces an abnormal amount of antibodies that mistakenly attack the healthy tissues, resulting in a hardening and swelling of the blood vessels. Was it possible that I contracted scleroderma because of my "dysfunctional" emotional system? By swallowing pain for so many years I contracted a disease that was trying to swallow me. I sensed that the jig was up, that I'd actually have to deal with the buried stress that Weil suggested was at the bottom of scleroderma. I was afraid of the intensity of my hidden emotions because I didn't know if our marriage could stand the kind of honesty that fessing up would require.

WHEN I GREW UP in the 1950s psychosomatic medicine had come of age. I clearly remember wondering if my mother's psychological problems were mind over matter. I was intrigued with the idea that the mind could have such an influence over the body as to make it sick. All things psychological interested me then—as they do now—and although I didn't understand the mechanics of it, the cause and effect idea intrigued me.

Freud had laid the groundwork for it by treating his patients who suffered from hysteria by encouraging them to let out their repressed pain. He concluded that when they opened up and confessed traumatic memories, their physical symptoms went away and their bodies no longer had to express it for them. This was at the end of the nineteenth century and, according to Anne Harrington who wrote a fascinating history of mind-body medicine, Freud's conclusions were a secular variant on a much older Judeo-Christian understanding of the healing that happens through confession. For centuries Christians believed in the words of the Bible: "Confess your sins to one another, and pray to one another, that you may be healed" (James 5:16).

But according to author Harrington, it took the work of Franz Alexander (1891-1964), a Hungarian American psychoanalyst and physician, to explore the physiology of emotions and to reach some conclusions. "He made two claims on the origin of psychosomatic disorders: 1. There is a specific relationship between chronic repressed emotional conflicts and specific diseases; but 2. Disease itself is not caused directly by the repressed emotions, but rather by the fact that chronic repression of different specific emotions has the effect of chronically stimulating or activating different specific vegetative organs in one's body—the heart, lungs, circulation, gut and more—until they finally begin to malfunction."[3] This doctor combined psychoanalysis with data from the medical laboratory and included it all in a popular textbook in the 1950s.

Today new research has replaced some of his theories (asthma, for instance is a disease caused by allergens, not anxieties), and the mind-body approach to medicine has been relegated in large measure to the world of alternative, feminist and holistic medicine.[4]

This brings me full circle to where I started this narrative: with Dr. Andrew Weil, an alternative medicine doctor who linked diseases of the skin to emotions. A new discipline has evolved today in the world of alternative healing, called "energy medicine," that integrates sound, electricity, magnetism and light into one amazing system. When I heard about a conference being held on energy medicine in Chicago, I felt drawn to it and signed up. It seems that some medical doctors are recycling the psychosomatic debate, saying that our minds and our emotions are closely connected through a sort of chemical communication. There are neuroscientists today who go so far as to say that the mind and body are one, that our cells are conscious and communicate with each other, thus allowing our thoughts and emotions to alter our body chemistry.

Speakers at the energy medicine workshop presented the idea that we are in the midst of a paradigm shift in medicine. In the old way we treated ourselves like a clock, they said; when it broke we just replaced the broken parts to fix it. Now we know we are more than our individual parts, they say, and we are connected by sophisticated systems that work together to keep us in balance. We are a product not only of genetics, but also of our environment—external as well as internal. The bottom line of this is that a growing number of doctors and psychologists today believe that emotional stress can cause imbalance or blockage, that it can create inflammation and produce disease—at least according to the presenters at this workshop.

I wondered how this actually plays itself out in the body.

BEING SICK SEEMED TO force issues to the surface. I had a lot of extra down time because I needed to rest and recharge my batteries. Sometimes in the late afternoon I went to church where I found comfort in God's presence in the Blessed Sacrament. Whatever was bothering me surfaced sooner or later—usually with tears. I could let my hair down with God, whom I believed had my best interests at heart and would help me find my way out of this dilemma. Another way I like to think of it is "Jesus has my back." (Cheryl Nguyen coined that phrase during a retreat she gave with Fr. Robert Faricy, S.J. and I have loved it ever since.)

It was debilitating to be so physically incapacitated and unable to do normal things such as walking ten steps without effort. I think it threw me off balance emotionally. My joy was gone and I was always on edge, reacting to everyone, especially my husband, with anger or hurt. I was losing my grip and worried that I was becoming just like my mother who lived with chronic unhappiness that she blamed on my father.

I had lived with an emotional heartache my whole life—but I had always been able to manage it or to pray it away. Now it was hanging on and crying for attention. Was it, I worried, something I inherited from my mother, from her dysfunctional patterns of behavior that were now becoming mine? Was it genetic?

I grew up with a great deal of pain because of the relationship I had—or rather didn't have—with my mother. Photos that were taken of me around age 3 with my mom and dad tell the story. In the one with my mom, I am standing next to her, ramrod straight, pouting. In the photo with my dad, I have my arm wrapped around his leg for dear life in a sort of love-hug. My body language spoke volumes.

My dad told me on many occasions, "Your mother was a very beautiful woman." I always wondered why he said that to me, considering the nature of their relationship. I knew early on that they were as different as day and night and that they really didn't have much in common. They lived in separate worlds and I was forever trying to bridge the tension and unspoken hostility at home so that we could be a normal, happy family.

My mother *was* a beautiful young woman, judging from the photos she pasted in an oversized scrapbook that she began after their honeymoon, in St. Augustine, Florida. From the bits and pieces I gathered of her family background, she had a very repressed childhood and adolescence, a prologue, I think, to her lifelong bouts of depression and mental illness. My mom was gifted with artistic and musical talent and her strict Italian parents groomed her for a career as a concert pianist. She told me on several occasions that she had to practice the piano every day of her young life and never had any kind of a social life as a teenager or young adult. My dad was the first person she dated, and then only with a chaperone, my grandmother!

My dad was proud of her musical talent. He often bragged that when they were engaged, he saw her perform at Carnegie Hall in 1928 on the same stage as Paderewski, who was then reputed to be the greatest pianist in the world. But that wasn't exactly correct. When I was getting ready to write this book, I did some research and found out that she did play at Carnegie Hall in May 1928, but not with Paderewski. She performed in a gala concert that featured several arias by the Metropolitan Opera tenor Beniamino Gigli who was then the rage. The program also included two sopranos, a violinist and my mom, Sabina Borgia, at the piano. Just after intermission she played an etude by Chopin (Op. 25, No. 1) and "The

Hungarian Rhapsody" by Liszt. The next day, *The New York Times* reviewed the evening under the headline "Ovation Given to Gigli." Sabina Borgia was mentioned by name as a pianist and one of the "assisting artists." I loved reading this because it showed a passionate side of my mom that was never apparent at home. I felt so proud of her accomplishments and, now in retrospect, I mourned the missed opportunities for sharing this with her.

My mom gave other concerts in New York, their programs proudly pasted in her scrapbook. One was in the main ballroom of the Hotel Majestic, a review of which appeared in an Italian newspaper: *The most admired among the players was the charming Miss Sabina Borgia, who gave a new exhibition of her skill at the piano and of her continuous progress, rendering to perfection the most difficult compositions of Scarlatti, Schumann and of that "colossus" who was Franz Liszt, of whom she played with deep sentiment the superb and delicate creation.... Miss Borgia received numerous ovations.*

Hand in hand with her musical talent was her extraordinary creative ability, which was legendary in our family. My mom gave elaborate birthday parties for me when I was 5 and 6 years old and later for my brother's children. She designed extravagant centerpieces for the dining room table around certain themes: one year a circus, complete with a musical ferris wheel, clowns she made from clay, dancers and bunches of balloons. Another year she created an Alice in Wonderland garden using a huge Bonsai tree as a perch for the Cheshire cat that she made out of clay with grey and black stripes, whiskers and huge eyes. Alice, standing nearby in her blue dress with a white apron, waved to him, while the March Hare stuck his head out from behind a bush. Huge puffy clouds of cotton hung on unseen wires from the chandelier in our dining room and fake flowers bloomed everywhere. It was spectacular! We had party favors and hats and I wore a white organdy dress and black patent leather shoes. On these occasions, my mother curled my long hair in ringlets, I think with a curling iron.

My mom showed love for me through these endeavors and in many other ways I am sure, although as a child and adolescent, I wasn't open to her love. She had the heart and sensitivity of a saint, giving away groceries or money to people who helped her. I didn't understand my mom, or relate to her because we were like oil and water. I recoiled from her I think because I was afraid of her depression and her negativity. She was a "bird alone" (to borrow a phrase my friend Velma likes to use), staying home virtually all the time. She didn't have friends or go out to lunch like my friends' moms did, or have any kind of a social life. My poor mom was always brooding about something, mostly in the kitchen.

We seemed to bring out the worst in each other. While my father was a larger-than-life, outgoing, enthusiastic and extroverted person who always encouraged me, my mom was introverted and afraid and usually tried to curtail my freedom. We were exact opposites and our differences created arguments, especially as I grew older. She projected her fears onto me, always worrying over something. While in my father's eyes I could do no wrong, with my mother I was never right. Her lack of trust extended to every area of my life and her negative outlook worked on me like sandpaper, so that after awhile, I just stopped communicating with her.

I think that my mom was born carrying some heavy baggage, emotional issues such as depression and mental illness that were generational. (To this day I don't know what mental illness my mother suffered from, whether it was schizophrenia or bipolar disorder or something else.) She then lived a life of repression and emotional abuse that she suffered while growing up and in her married life. My dad had a tendency to be sarcastic. At the dinner table he sometimes made fun of her inability to find her way downtown in a subway or some such thing. She laughed off these abusive attacks, then privately vented her anger to me in the kitchen. These episodes stung me to the core. I hurt for her and disliked my father for being so mean. Yet I never said anything to him about it and neither did she. This kind of verbal abuse left a deep scar inside of me.

In high school I stayed up late at night reading psychology books, trying to figure out what was wrong and how to help my mom. One day when I came home from school and opened my closet door, my whole room came tumbling out. My mom had jammed every movable object in my bedroom into my walk-in closet. I don't know why she did that, but it signaled that she was not in her right mind. She also had a tendency to put personal things in garbage bags that she gave to the back elevator man to throw in the incinerator. One time she threw out her 14 carat gold watch that my dad and I bought her for Christmas. The reason I know this is because she told me after the fact. I knew that my mom's suffering was extreme. She was like a bird with a broken wing, handicapped and unable to help herself. I could sense that she had been very hurt and was trying to deal with it the best way she could. Many nights I cried myself to sleep. The tears were for her, but for myself as well, because I wanted—and knew I would never have—a "normal" mother.

It wasn't until I saw "One Flew Over the Cuckoo's Nest", after I had been married about ten years, that I understood what my mother must have suffered when my dad admitted her to The Reese Pavilion in New York City. (It was a separate wing of St. Vincent's Hospital). My mother would often beg me, "Joanie, please don't let them give me shock treatments." I didn't know what they were and thought they were good for her because she always came home in her right mind. While we were watching "One Flew Over the Cuckoo's Nest," what I saw was so painful I couldn't watch the rest of it. I ran upstairs to my bedroom and sobbed. I got a taste of my mother's pain and I couldn't bear it.

A FEW YEARS AFTER we moved to Illinois in the early 1970s, I flew to New York one January to stay with my mom for two weeks. Dorothy, our faithful housekeeper, was taking a well-deserved vacation and my father was making his yearly trip to the Breakers in Palm Beach to play in the Winter Golf League. When I opened the apartment door and saw her, she didn't even look like herself, she was so old and thin. "Look at me," she said, "don't I look awful?" "No" I lied, "you look fine Mommy." I wanted to protect her from herself but I also wanted to stay in control lest I burst into tears. Slipping automatically into my detached caretaker role, I tried to stay upbeat and make her tasty meals. She had so little enjoyment in her life and nothing to look forward to. Her gratitude for a delicious spaghetti dinner that I made was so effusive it made me throw my arms around her, something I hadn't done since I was little. "Oh, Mommy," I said, "you are so brave," I blurted through my tears.

While I was staying with her I phoned the doctor and asked him to come over. In those days they made house calls. In addition to advanced emphysema and a weak heart condition, she suffered from many physical ailments, and among them, I believe, was an undiagnosed autoimmune disease. In retrospect I think she might have had scleroderma. Her legs were so swollen they were four times larger than usual. She had a severe case of edema. I remember talking to the doctor in the kitchen and being dissatisfied with his casual assessment. To simply remove salt from her diet was a palliative, I felt, and not a cure for her serious condition. My memory of all this is a bit fuzzy, but I think I wanted my mom to be hospitalized but my dad didn't think her condition warranted it.

When I returned to Chicago Tommy asked me how long I thought my mom had to live. "Three months," I said, not really knowing how I knew.

Almost to the day, three months later, my brother Howie called one morning, telling me that he thought our mother was dying and that I should come to New York right away. He spent the day with her. By the time I organized babysitters, packed and got on a plane to New York, it was late in the afternoon when I arrived at the apartment. As the plane was approaching La Guardia, I heard someone call out "Mommy." I turned around to see who it was and it didn't appear as if anyone had said anything. It crossed my mind that she might have been dying at that moment. My brother said that my mom was battling all day, resisting whatever was happening to her, calling out and saying things like "I don't want to see him." It spooked my brother.

When I finally arrived at the apartment my brother said, "Mom died about forty-five minutes ago." I looked at my watch and realized that was when I was on the plane and heard someone call out, "Mommy."

Was someone welcoming her to heaven?

I didn't cry. I just felt real sad—and relieved that she was out of her suffering. My poor mom died before her 70th birthday. I think she died of a broken heart. Although a doctor signed her death certificate, I don't recall knowing the cause of her death.

My dad walked in from the Golf Club while the undertakers were still there. Without even saying hello to Howie or me he went right into his bedroom and shut the door. When he came out a few minutes later he made himself a Johnny Walker Red label with crushed ice in a gold-rimmed cocktail glass, and sat in his usual chair in the living room. Then he wept.

6

The Roots of Illness

The real killer in the world today is not heart disease, cancer, stroke or immune system failure, but repression which limits our ability to react to events and inhibits the expression of feelings. It is the foundation of many diseases, emotional and physical, and it often literally kills.

—Arthur Janov,
Why You Get Sick, How You Get Well, The Healing Power of Feelings

I LOOKED FORWARD TO my weekly appointments with Dr. Mercola. Under his regimen I was getting better. His assessment after one week: "major improvement." *Patient stated that the swelling in hands has greatly improved. Also is very pleased that there has been very little pain in joints. Patient has had increased energy. Myalgias* [muscle pains] *are diminishing and nearly gone. Has decreased Prednisone to 5 mg without any problems.* I was on my way to regaining my health. The very fact that I was feeling so much better was proof enough for me that the antibiotics—and diet—were working.

Each week we discussed my strict diet and my menus; he was pleased. "Food is medicine," Mercola said, not once but all the time. (I credited him with making up that clever statement until I read later that the Greek physician, Hippocrates, popularized that phrase more than 2,000 years ago.) Breakfast was the hardest meal because so few foods were allowed; I solved the dilemma by eating broiled chicken drumsticks (sans skin) and sliced zucchini. Grains (cereal and bread) were to be avoided as much as possible and fruit was limited because of the sugar, so I just eliminated it. Each week after we chatted for a few minutes, Dr. Mercola hooked me up to the IV and gave me 900 mg. of Cleocin. In addition I took 100 mg.

of oral Minocin three times a week. He discontinued the Plaquenil and started to wean me off prednisone. I was grateful for that.

I would have to skip the following week's appointment because we were going out of town. I worried about missing an antibiotic treatment because I was beginning to feel better and didn't want to regress. Dr. Mercola reminded me to stay on the diet, a feat that would not be easy on the road. I packed the flax oil and some small cans of V8 juice in my carry-on bag (this was in the days when we could carry liquids on board), promising to follow this dietary program to the letter.

IN EARLY MAY 1995 we headed to the East Coast to attend a family wedding after which we planned to meet up with Fr. Joe Whalen, our friend and spiritual director from the pilgrimage to South America. I welcomed the spiritual replenishment that this trip promised. We caught up with Father Joe in Auriesville, New York, at the Shrine of the North American Martyrs where Maria Esperanza, the visionary we had met in South America, was scheduled to be the keynote speaker at a Marian Eucharistic Conference.

The Shrine at Auriesville is a center of devotion to the Mother of God where, according to tradition, the first recorded recitation of the Rosary in North America took place on September 29, 1642. It was also the birthplace of Blessed Kateri Tekakwitha. When I was at Sacred Heart elementary school in New York some of my friends went to Camp Tekakwitha in Maine every summer. The name always sounded so strange to me until one day, when I was doing research for *My Daily Eucharist,* I learned that the camp was named after a valiant Indian woman, the daughter of a Mohawk warrior who converted to Catholicism. Kateri had a deep love of the Eucharist and used to trudge through the snow in the middle of the night and stand at the church door until it opened for Mass. She was only 24 when she died. I included a reflection of Kateri in *My Daily Eucharist II,* on July 14, her feast day.

Particularly appealing to me about Auriesville was the fact that America's first and only canonized martyrs were buried within walking distance of the shrine: the Jesuit saints Rene Goupil and Isaac Jogues as well as the lay missioner, St. John Lalande. I wanted to absorb the atmosphere where Isaac Jogues and his heroic companions endured untold tortures trying to bring Christianity to the Indians. When I was doing research for *My Daily Eucharist* I was drawn to the unbreakable faith of these young priests, especially to Isaac Jogues who had a deep devotion to the Eucharist. Several of his fingers had been eaten or burned off so that he could no longer celebrate Mass. When he was about to be burned to death, some Calvinists rescued him and secured his passage on a sailing ship to New Amsterdam (New York), where he then boarded a lugger (a small sailing vessel) to Paris. He landed in Brittany in a state of utter destitution and was nursed back to health by his fellow Jesuits in France. While there he asked the Pope for permission to celebrate Mass with his mutilated hands (his thumb and index finger were so distorted he couldn't hold the Sacred Host). Pope Urban VIII was deeply touched by the story of his captivity and responded, "It would be shameful that a martyr of Christ not be allowed to drink the Blood of Christ."[1] St. Isaac Jogues celebrated his first Mass in twenty months, and then asked to return to Canada where he was eventually martyred.

Although walking was extremely difficult, I was able to negotiate a rather steep downward path to visit the graves of the Jesuit martyrs. It was a pastoral scene next to a babbling brook. It was so peaceful and beautiful that it was difficult to picture the imprisonment and barbaric tortures the missionaries endured. I began feeling very vulnerable and started to weep. The thought of these brave young men undergoing such extreme suffering for Christ moved me to tears. My physical problems seemed so inconsequential by comparison. I thanked these brave souls for their witness to the Gospel and asked them to shore up my faith and endurance.

Hundreds of people attended the conference in Auriesville. Maria Esperanza gave the keynote address, a passionate call to reconciliation through faith—with our families and with all peoples. She spoke about Our Lady and Our Lord from an intimate perspective, as well as several saints, some of whom had actually appeared to her. She spoke about Jesus revealing His Sacred Heart to St. Margaret Mary Alacoque in France, and how He recently appeared to many people in Betania, showing His Sacred Heart on fire with love for souls. I had been reading biographies of saints since high school and was familiar with the saints she spoke about, but the fact that Our Lord and Our Lady were reportedly appearing to people today was thrilling to me. She also mentioned that when she was struggling with the decision to come to Auriesville, Blessed Kateri appeared to her in the middle of the night urging her to visit "her land."

The size of the crowds made it impossible to approach Maria, so Tommy, Father Joe and I headed for the gift shop. While browsing among the Indian artifacts someone said, "Maria is here." She, her husband and their interpreter were standing about five feet from us. She and her husband, Geo, spoke with Father Joe for a few minutes and then they prayed with him. Father Joe wore a big smile and looked adorable with his white hair and beard and his trademark bright blue and red Angels baseball jacket.

Remembering that I had not been well on our pilgrimage to South America, a lady who had been on that trip introduced us to Maria. I had secretly wished to have a moment with this renowned mystic, never dreaming that someone would actually introduce me to her. In addition to having the stigmata (the bleeding wounds of Christ), Maria Esperanza reportedly had gifts of healing, levitation, bilocation, and prophecy. I felt her caring presence as soon as our eyes met. I was taken with her—as I am with all mystics—who seem to have a direct line to God. I told her that I had an unusual, often fatal disease called scleroderma, and asked for her prayers. After a minute or two her eyes teared up. I didn't understand. Seeing my concern, the interpreter said that Maria was touched by my spirituality. (I didn't understand this because I see myself as a very flawed human being.) Then, as if looking into my soul, she told me that the scleroderma resulted from a sexual abuse incident I suffered when I was 12; she said it was a great shock to my system that my body still carries. While I was trying to wrap my mind around this disclosure, she said something equally startling: "You are going to be completely healed through a wonderful doctor."

I was incredulous—and speechless. My first thought was: *she really is a mystic.* My second was: *Thank you God. This is the happiest moment of my life.* I felt as if I had been serving a life sentence behind bars and someone just gave me a key to get out. Tommy was standing slightly behind Maria's left shoulder deep in thought. Without seeing him Maria said, "You have a very supportive husband."

Sexual abuse at 12. I could still see and feel the horrible experience as if it happened yesterday. I was sitting on the couch in our living room in our Manhattan apartment on East 86 Street where I lived until I got married. Next to me was "Uncle Jim," a gregarious friend of my dad's who drank heavily. My dad was sitting about five feet away in "his" chair facing the couch. I had just taken a bath and put on my nightgown and a new robe. I loved the robe because it zipped down the front and it made me feel grownup. "Uncle Jim" put his arm around me. Then he moved his arm down behind me—in slow motion. I froze. *What is happening? Should I jump up and run to my bedroom? Does my dad see this? Will he say something?* In a matter of seconds—an eternity—his hand was under me where it found its way into me.

I felt paralyzed. Frightened. Shocked. Embarrassed. Ashamed. Guilty—all of the above. *Was my father watching? Why didn't he say something?* Our positioning on the couch was a bit awkward and I don't see how my father could have missed it. I wanted him to see it and to rescue me and at the same time I didn't. I had never felt anything like this before and was blaming myself for enjoying the pleasure of it. When I finally broke away (two minutes, five minutes?) I went to my room and locked the door—as if to barricade myself from the assault—and from the shame and anger that spilled out in tears.

Maria Esperanza's insight about this incident sounded plausible. It *was* a huge shock to my system. (I read recently about the work a German doctor has done regarding shock, stating that disease is a symptom of a biological conflict situation. When the conflict is resolved the illness disappears.) As a result of the experience, I think I froze emotionally. Instead of getting rid of the shock by letting out my rage, I swallowed it and stored it in my body. Years later, it erupted in a disease that gradually paralyzes the body, first through a hardening of the skin that can also effect the internal organs.

I kept this as a deep dark secret that I never told anyone, except my mother. For reasons that I can't remember now, I told her a few days later. She was very upset but I begged her not to tell my father. I don't know if she ever did. I also don't know why I wanted to protect him for not protecting me.

I FILED THE SEXUAL abuse incident away for forty-plus years until I dredged it up in 1993, the year before I got scleroderma, during a retreat at Our Lady of Guadalupe Abbey in Pecos, New Mexico. Sheila Fabricant and the Linn Brothers devoted a day to sexual abuse traumas. Resurrecting the memory of my experience, I wrote in my journal: *fear, guilt, violated, trapped, rage.* The deep inner work of the retreat enabled me to open to the rage inside of me. It oozed out like poison through every pore of my body; I sobbed at the awful memory. During the retreat I asked myself why I tried to protect my father for not protecting me. I *wanted* to believe that he didn't see what was happening on the couch, but I couldn't be sure. I also wondered if my pattern of feeling trapped when I'm in pain is traceable to that horrible experience when I felt so paralyzed.

When our openness is violated, we close up, one of the presenters said. This was truth. I blamed myself, thinking it might have been my fault, and I did close up. I erected a wall to keep others out, but mostly to protect myself from pain. This helps explain the boundaries I set with people, never wanting anyone to get too close. I also think I shut down my emerging sexuality, almost trying to deny my feminine identity. I'm not a psychologist, but I think the sexual abuse incident was a turning point in my life that caused me to split in two, so to speak. (In actuality I think that the split was already there. This just deepened it.) I squelched my real self, silencing her pain with denial, fearing the power of her dark feelings. Repression, in a sense, helped me because I wasn't strong enough to deal with the trauma. I disconnected from my truth and adopted a persona, a "false self" that carried me all the way to mid-life—until I got sick. Eventually, the tension between the two selves and the energy it took to keep silencing the negative feelings caused pain that I could no longer handle. And I think it made me sick.

The few minutes I spent with Maria Esperanza were like golden moments that light up my life whenever I recall them. I believed her insight into the sexual abuse incident; it pierced a veil of mystery surrounding the origins of scleroderma—at least for me—showing me the possible psychological root of this dread disease. And the good news she gave me that I would be completely cured through a "wonderful" doctor was a gift that keeps on giving. Every time I think about it I thank God. The only question I have ever had is which "wonderful" doctor would be instrumental in effecting my healing. I had yet to meet him.

THE TRIP TO AURIESVILLE and the meeting with Maria Esperanza stirred up so many memories, especially of my dad. At the time he had only been dead about five years; sometimes it felt like five minutes. I don't think I ever *really* blamed him for what happened on the couch, for not speaking up. If I did, I let the pain go because I loved him so much.

If I ever missed him, it was now, when I was sick with something so serious. As a trial lawyer, he tried so many cases involving doctors that he often said he could have become a doctor himself, because he became so well-read in the world of medicine. He laughingly referred to himself as "Dr. Carter." He was sincerely interested in everything and anything to do with medicine. Perhaps that's where my interest comes from. He used to come home excited about new theories he'd read about in the world of nutrition. One time he asked my mother to buy jars of honey so he could put a teaspoon of it in his tea every night; he was convinced that it was a healing agent that helped fight disease. He got hooked on Chinese food because he thought it was good for the waistline. At the time, I looked askance at all his theories and never paid any attention to them. Ironically, I have become just like him, investigating every cutting edge nutritional program on the market. If my dad were alive today, I know he would have some helpful insights about my condition. I missed him more than ever.

I never asked him about the sexual abuse incident and I'll never know if he saw it or didn't see it. It doesn't matter; I don't hold it against him. I adored my dad and looked to him for encouragement and support. The truth is, I needed him. He was all I had, because my mother was usually preoccupied with her own problems and wasn't there for me. So I put all my eggs in his basket. I had, and still have, a deep bond with him that will never be severed.

Part of the reason why I adored my dad was because he believed in me. He always saw the best in me, taking my side in arguments or disagreements I had with my mom. On top of that he was fun. I think we brought out the child in each other. When I was too young to drive, he bought a pistachio green Thunderbird two-seater convertible sports car which he drove around the half-acre lawn of our house in New Jersey. Actually he made tracks in the lawn, infuriating my mother. He would switch places with me and taught me to drive. Only trouble was, it was a stick shift. No matter how many times I ground the gears, my dad never lost his patience. I was only 13 or 14.

When he was 57 he bought a Cessna airplane and learned to fly. When he got his license I was his first passenger. (I think my mother only flew with him once, after which she said, "Never again.") One Saturday morning he asked me if I wanted to fly to Portland, Maine, so he could check out a ballfield where he played baseball as a young rookie. After seeing the location of the old ballfield, we had lunch in town and then flew home. I went on many excursions with my dad, who affectionately referred to me as his copilot. He also taught me to fly and in the summer before senior year of high school, I took official instructions from a pilot at the Monmouth County Airport in New Jersey. After about seven hours, he got out of the plane and told me to "take 2-0 Mike for a spin." I was 15!

Then there was the monkey. I had seen the cutest little black and white marmoset swinging on branches in the window of a pet shop that I passed walking home from school everyday. I didn't know that my dad had always wanted a monkey, which is why he probably encouraged me to find out more details about "the chimp," as he called him. My dad was a pushover when it came to making his daughter happy. One beautiful spring evening Daddy suggested we walk across 86th Street to see "the chimp." I knew I had him. My mother threatened to leave if we came home with a monkey.

My dad was just as smitten as I was and plunked down some money for the monkey and a huge cage. He was so small my dad could hold him in his hand. When the owner delivered the monkey to our apartment, my mom locked herself in the bathroom. But eventually the little marmoset won her over and she ended up making diapers for him: pink and blue terry cloth on the inside, rubber on the outside with snaps and a hole for his long tail. We named him Chi Chi after the noise he made. Sometimes I took him for walks in my old doll carriage or for a ride on my bike. A crowd usually gathered when they saw the monkey in the carriage. At the pet store I bought a leash for him in case he decided to try to get away. He performed for people, jumping onto the hood of the carriage and behaving in such a cute way that people didn't want to leave! At night when my dad came home, Chi Chi would climb up on his lap and snuggle close to his neck. When my dad took a sip of his Johnny Walker red label, Chi Chi took a sip as well. Then he would chase Danny Boy, our Irish terrier, around the apartment, jumping up on his back, riding him like a jockey. Danny ran around the apartment trying to shake him off while Chi Chi held on for dear life. It was a scene out of a movie. Chi Chi lived with us for two years before he got pneumonia and died.

My dad was a Damon Runyon character who grew up in Richmond Hill, Long Island. A year before he was married, he was admitted to the New York bar in February 1928. He was 23. But he wasn't sure he wanted to practice law because his heart was in baseball. He had played varsity ball at the High School of Commerce in New York City with none other than Lou Gehrig. It was heady stuff for a kid from Long Island who didn't have a penny to his name and had no idea what he wanted to do in life. It seems he made a name for himself because a Jesuit priest from Fordham University offered him a scholarship to Fordham Law School if he played baseball for Fordham.

While playing for Fordham and prior to getting his LL.B., he got drafted into the big leagues: the Cincinnati Reds. He signed a contract with them in 1926 for $400 a month, but never got a chance at bat. That is what he told us. In his obituary in the New York Times, they reported that he played in five games as an infielder in 1926, according to The Baseball Encyclopedia.

He toured with the Reds, playing at Ebbets Field, the Polo Grounds, Boston and Philadelphia. For about three months, they used him as a pinch runner or hitter, Daddy said, but the recognized stars would shunt him off telling him to go shag balls. Cincinnati farmed him out to Peoria (he thought to gain experience) but he soon found out that they released him to them. Still not giving up, my dad played for Peoria, then signed on with the Bushwicks, a semi-pro team that played in Dexter Park, Brooklyn. That year, 1927, was the year the Yankees won the pennant and the World Series and that was the same year that Babe Ruth hit the sixty home runs.

Daddy became friends with Babe Ruth and he and my mom would often go to parties at their house. Babe always asked my mother to play the piano. If his wife stepped out to go to the powder room, he would call her back saying, "Honey, get your (bleep) down here quickly. Sabina is going to play!"

My dad opened a small law office with a friend on 57th Street in New York City. Jimmy Cagney, who worked down the street, used to stop by and taught my dad how to do the soft shoe on top of a desk. He eventually joined a law firm, Townley, Updike, Carter and Rodgers, and became a successful trial lawyer. He represented the New York Daily News, and had some colorful clients such as Elizabeth Arden who was always being sued. One case involved one of her racehorses that bit someone. She loved her horses and used to put Eight Hour cream on their cuts. She was a very gracious lady and a dynamo of a person, having built up her business from a small beauty salon she started in Canada. She trusted my dad and appointed him the executor of her estate. One time she invited my brother Howie and me up to her pink duplex apartment on Fifth Avenue. I wore white gloves. She served us tea and fruitcake. My brother ate it but I hid mine in my purse. When we got home Howie threw up.

When I toasted my dad at one of the lavish surprise birthday parties Howie and I gave him (one for his 75th and one for his 85th), I thanked him for who he was in my life, and for passing on to me some of his many gifts, integrity and honesty among them. (Others are his *joie de vivre*, his "can do" attitude, and his adventurous spirit.) Then, quite out of the blue, what popped in my mind were all the memories of flying and watching him perform, sometimes under great pressure and danger. So I thanked him for his guts—and for giving me a good dose of them.

In 1974 Daddy was inducted into the Fordham Athletic Hall of Fame.

I DON'T KNOW WHEN my dad fell away from his Catholic faith. He had served as an altar boy at Holy Rosary Church in New York City, but as long as I knew him, he never went to church, except during my high school years when I insisted that he accompany my mom and me to Christmas Eve midnight Mass. His lack of faith caused me much pain and heart-ache. Heated discussions about religion often took place around our din-ner table, where he would coax me and my high school friends into long debates about the divinity of Christ, the Resurrection, the Real Presence of Christ in the Eucharist, the Bible, the need for Confession, and on and on. While he played the devil's advocate, I never knew if he was enjoying our enthusiasm or probing his own mind, but we'd go around in circles and never get anywhere. Sensing my frustration, he'd throw back his head and laugh, saying, "You can't make a silk purse out of a sow's ear." He'd tell me he couldn't pretend to have faith. If he didn't have it, he didn't have it. Period.

I want to share the story surrounding his death, because it is so uplift-ing and inspiring. In the year before he died, I flew to New York on a regu-lar basis, at first to accompany him to his radiation treatments, then to buy his favorite groceries, and to just *be* with him in his time of suffering. And I prayed for him constantly. I arranged for a priest friend to drop in on him, hoping that it would spark his desire to get his spiritual life in order. They spent the whole time talking about baseball!

Back home a friend told me over coffee that she had prayed for God's mercy for her mother before she died. Prior to her death, her mother said to her, "Bea, I got your message." Bea had left no message. "What message, Mom, I don't remember leaving a message?" Her mom said, "Mercy." Bea knew that God heard her prayers.

From that moment on I prayed for God's mercy for my dad. I also asked the Lord to let me be with my dad when he died. Back home I made holy hours in the presence of the Blessed Sacrament, imploring God's mercy for my dad. Scenes from the past bubbled to the surface leading me to ask God's forgiveness for *myself,* for all the buried resentments and angers that I secretly held against my dad. There was a backside to the tapestry that displayed all the knots and loose ends—the unresolved hurts and incidents needing forgiveness. While I spent so much time praying for healing of my dad's spiritual blindness, the Lord was showing me that I was the one who was spiritually blind, seeing the speck in my father's eye but missing the beam in my own. Now I wanted to release all these judgments that took up precious space in my mind and heart.

Other memories surfaced, scenes of my life which played like a movie on the screen of my imagination, showing me how much I had been loved by my heavenly Father who showered me with earthly blessings. *"Every spiritual blessing in the heavens have we received from the Father through the Son"* (Eph 1:3-4).

My dad, I knew, didn't have the same advantages. He loved to reminisce about how he would chase after his two older brothers who took turns riding on an old bike they had found in the junkyard. The tires had long since been discarded and they were riding on the rims. My dad, who was the youngest, had to run hard to keep up with them just to get a five-minute ride. Daddy ran hard all his life. He always had to take care of himself because he didn't know that he had a Father God who would take care of him.

One day when my dad was suffering in the late stages of throat cancer, I went to Marytown to pray for him. Marytown is a Conventual Franciscan Friary that is also known as the National Shrine of St. Maximilian Kolbe. It houses a magnificent Chapel of Adoration that was constructed at the request of Cardinal Mundelein in the early part of the twentieth century. It is perhaps one of the most beautiful chapels in existence, resembling the magnificent Papal Basilica, St. Paul's Outside the Walls, in Rome. It is open for prayer and adoration of the Blessed Sacrament twenty-four hours a day. The huge complex also has a retreat house, a gift shop and conference rooms. I look upon it as an oasis where I can find spiritual nourishment whenever I need it. When my dad was so sick I went to the chapel to ask Lord to bathe him just as He was bathing me. My dad had never known Jesus' love. As a child, he was neglected and he buried his angers, too. I begged Jesus to bathe Daddy, to let him open his heart and feel God's love for him.

In the gift shop at Marytown I picked up a small Divine Mercy prayer booklet and opened it at random. My eyes fell on these words Our Lord spoke to Sister Faustina, now Saint Faustina of the Blessed Sacrament: "Encourage souls to say the Chaplet which I have given you. . .Whoever will recite it will receive great mercy at the hour of death. . .When they say this Chaplet in the presence of the dying, I will stand between My Father and the dying person, not as the just Judge but as the Merciful Savior. . . I desire to grant unimaginable graces to those souls who trust in My mercy. Through the Chaplet you will obtain everything, if what you ask for is compatible with My will."[2]

It was a divine directive that I would follow. In the early part of the twentieth century, Our Lord appeared to Sister Faustina Kowalska in Poland. He was clothed in a white garment. One hand was raised in blessing and from beneath the garment emanated two large rays, one red, the other pale. "The two rays denote blood and water, " Jesus said. "The pale ray stands for the Water which makes souls righteous. The red ray stands for the Blood which is the life of souls. . . ."[3] Our Lord wanted the image to be painted and honored by the establishment of a Feast of Divine Mercy on the first Sunday after Easter. He taught her the prayers for the chaplet saying, "By this novena I will grant every possible grace to souls."[4]

I bought five Divine Mercy booklets and five rosaries, one for each of the nurses, that I would give them on my next trip to New York in the hope that they would learn the Chaplet and say it at his bedside. A few days later, Daphne, my dad's favorite nurse, called on a Sunday morning, saying that my dad's blood pressure had dropped very low and that I better come. My husband was at his prayer group, so I left him a note, packed my bag and flew to New York. My dad was in a semi-coma, unable to speak, but I do believe he could hear. Two weeks prior I had brought my Walkman so he could listen to his favorite Mills Brothers singing "Lazy River." Seeing a tear trickle down his cheek, I knew he could hear.

Eternal Father, I offer you the Body and Blood, Soul and Divinity of Your dearly beloved Son, Our Lord Jesus Christ, in atonement for our sins and those of the whole world.[5] We sat in vigil beside his bed, praying the Chaplet around the clock. He was near death but still alive. I whispered my love in his ear and encouraged him to go to Jesus, assuring him that I would catch up later. On the third morning his breathing became erratic. Daphne signaled me that he was dying. She ran into the bathroom because she was afraid of death. I called her back, asking for her company and support. We continued the Chaplet in soft tones. I hugged and kissed my dad and marveled at the moment of death. He seemed to suck in air with such force that it jettisoned his spirit heavenward. He was gone.

I cried tears of joy. A spirit of joy and peace filled the room. *I knew that my dad was with the Lord.* Our merciful God granted me the desires of my heart; first to be present at my dad's death, and second, He ordained the timing of his departure to coincide with our praying the Chaplet of Mercy, assuring me that my dad was safely home. I felt like singing and dancing to celebrate Daddy's homecoming. Daphne said she had never experienced such a beautiful death.

Entrust yourself completely to Me at the hour of death, Our Lord told Sister Faustina, *and I will present you to My Father as My bride.*[6] I visualized Jesus presenting my dad to His Father, who was awaiting him with open arms. I saw him being scooped up in the Father's love, receiving the welcome that he always extended to me.

About a month after my dad's death I missed him deeply. We had always been in touch by phone. He usually called every night around 7:30 just to check in. If we were traveling or even out of the country, I would call him. One time we were in Ireland staying at Ashford Castle and I called him because I knew how much he loved Ireland. One evening I was standing in the kitchen and happened to glance at the digital clock on the oven; it was 7:30, the same time my dad used to phone. I thought, *I will never speak to my dad again.* I couldn't contain my grief and cried my eyes out. I prayed telling my dad how much I missed him.

That night I dreamed that I was on the phone with my son Tom Jr., when my dad interrupted, saying, "Joanie!" "Daddy, how are you?" I said incredulously. "Wonderful" came the reply in his familiar voice. "I'm so happy. They are treating me like royalty here." Click. He was gone.

The dream healed my grief. I knew my dad came to me in the dream to console me—and to tell me not to worry, because he was very happy. After that, I rejoiced in his new life.

7

The Gift of Faith

Nothing is more practical than finding God, that is, than falling in love in a quite absolute, final way. What you are in love with, what seizes your imagination, will affect everything. It will decide what will get you out of bed in the morning, what you will do with your evenings, how you will spend your weekends, what you read, who you know, what breaks your heart, and what amazes you with joy and gratitude. Fall in love, stay in love and it will decide everything.

—Pedro Arrupe, S.J.
Superior General of the Society of Jesus 1961-1983, *America,*
November 12, 2007

AFTER OUR TRIP EAST I resumed weekly doctor appointments to receive the intravenous antibiotics and a review of my diet. I was slowly losing weight and getting healthier by the day. After about three months I could clench both fists even though my hands and feet were still swollen. This was a huge victory; it would take almost a year before I could get my engagement and wedding ring off my finger. Dr. Mercola weaned me off prednisone and encouraged me to walk or use the treadmill a few times a week. It always made me feel better, probably because it released stress. Vigorous exercise, I've since read, stimulates the immune system and activates the body's natural defenses to battle with malignancy. Experiments with animals that are stressed show that if they don't have any exercise, their bodies degenerate.

Then one day Dr. Mercola gave me a hard sell about fruits and vegetables. I had never been too fond of either of them and certainly never ate the five to nine daily servings recommended by the American Medical

Association. Not only did he want me to eat them—raw—but he also suggested that I juice them. His pep talk went like this: *Buy some organic kale, parsley, carrots, broccoli (stems) and bok choy, or whatever else you like, throw them in a blender and drink them. It will give life to your cells and you will feel great.* Part of me wanted to wretch. I had a flashback to an "I Love Lucy" show when, for a TV commercial, she was trying to make a drink that contained a percentage of alcohol. With each take of her "vitameatavegamin" commercial, she got progressively drunker and funnier. It was a hilarious show that still makes me laugh—fifty years later!

But there was nothing funny about what Mercola was proposing. I bought a used Vitamixer from him, lugged the heavy machine home and stuffed some organic carrots, kale, celery and a bunch of other greens into the machine. Out came what I can best describe as "sludge." It was thick and lumpy and looked like mud. Forcing myself to take a taste made me sick. I drank a little and quit. When I told him that juicing vegetables wasn't for me, he gave me another pep talk so I went home and tried again.

In the meantime I read a story in a health magazine about a woman who was deathly sick with an autoimmune disease who juiced her way back to health. I learned that the raw vegetables and fruits deliver maximum nutrition to our cells and tissues in the form of *enzymes,* a protein that gives life to our cells. The magic word is *enzymes.* They contain antioxidants that are like foot soldiers in an army; they go to battle and fight the free radicals that are trying to damage our systems. These proteins help in the digestion of food; they stimulate the brain and provide cellular energy for repairing all tissues, organs and cells. They are only prevalent in raw foods, because heat, such as cooking or pasteurization, destroys them. These raw foods boost our immune systems, and if there were ever anyone who needed help with that, I did. I was beginning to "get it" and resolved to drink the sludge.

Next to family, my work—researching and writing about the Catholic faith and especially the Eucharist—was my salvation. Days were full and purposeful, thanks to my faith. My belief in a personal, caring God gave me a reason to live, to love and even perhaps to die. I wanted others to come to know Jesus as a living, real Person as I had experienced Him. I'm not sure where that fire came from. My father always said that I was a born saleswoman. When I'm convinced about something, my enthusiasm knows no bounds. So it is with my faith. I simply want to share with others the joy and meaning my relationship with God gives to my life.

In the fall Cathy and Jim McCarthy, friends with whom we served on a committee to promote Adoration of the Blessed Sacrament in the Chicago Archdiocese, invited me to give a slide presentation on the Eucharist at an event they organized at their parish. A distressing Gallup poll was taken in 1992 about Catholic attitudes toward Holy Communion. It found that only 30% of Catholics believed that when they receive Holy Communion they are really and truly receiving the Body and Blood, Soul and Divinity of the Lord Jesus Christ, under the appearance of bread and wine. This is known as the Real Presence.

When I grew up in the 1950s and '60s there was standing room only at Sunday Masses. Now, our churches are half-filled. This was difficult—and painful—to fathom, and it inspired people like the McCarthys to do something about it. Empty pews fueled my desire to reawaken Catholics to what they were missing.

Sixteen years of Catholic education, together with my own reading and research, led me into the Bible for a deeper understanding of God's relationship to His people and our salvation in Christ. I wanted to show God's paternal and maternal love for His children from the perspective of His *presence*, that He was and is a "hands on" God, reaching out to His children by means of signs, promises, disciplines, visions, teaching, prophecies—and ultimately, through the gift of Himself in the Person of Jesus Christ. Using spectacular slide images of the Great Masters, I retold the biblical story of our salvation from a Eucharistic perspective, illustrating the ways God has revealed Himself to His people, in the Old Testament, the New Testament and in the Church today, through the Sacrament of the Eucharist.

At the end of the slide show, the parishioners lit a fire under me to make a DVD of the program so that they could share this teaching with their families. The next morning I began production of *The Real Presence: An Historical Perspective of the Holy Eucharist*, which is still selling today, fourteen years later.

I CAN'T REMEMBER NOT having faith. Just as the French philosopher Descartes said *Cogito ergo sum* "I think therefore I am" I could say, "I believe, therefore I am." While my mother planted the seeds of faith in my toddler heart, it was the Sacred Heart nuns who watered those seeds through their teaching and example. The twelve years I spent at the Convent of the

Sacred Heart in New York were some of the happiest of my life. I'm sure my father sacrificed to send me to this school that attracted mostly well-to-do students whose families could afford the tuition. In the many retreats I've attended over the years I cringe when people criticize the nuns who taught them. Abuses did exist in many convents and schools (with nuns *and* priests), a terrible reality that I was spared. I don't have a single complaint about the Religious of the Sacred Heart of Jesus; not only do I not have a grievance, but I also have deep respect for these women who trained our minds and our wills in the practice of virtue (especially "order" and "courtesy," the practice of which earned the winner a medal each week). And last but perhaps first in importance, they inspired us to *want* to lead prayerful lives in the pursuit of holiness, according to the motto formulated by their foundress, St. Madeleine Sophie Barat: *One heart and one soul in the Heart of Jesus.*

While pictures of St. Madeleine Sophie adorned the walls of our classrooms and hallways, I never really knew much about this little woman (she was 4' and 11") until recently, when I read her biography. I'm so glad I did because it gave me a new appreciation for my faith-based education, which originated in the heart of a simple young French girl whose vision for education began during the French Revolution when she was in Paris and learned about the desecration of churches and the persecution of the Catholic Church. Her original idea was to gather young girls together in "a little community that night and day would adore the Heart of Jesus, whose love had been desecrated in the Eucharist."[1] Realizing that it would take more people than the few members of her community, she said to herself, "If we had young pupils whom we formed in the spirit of adoration and reparation, now, that would be different, and I saw hundreds, thousands of adorers before a perfect universal monstrance, raised above the Church."[2] Sophie's vision was noble. She wanted to "raise up a multitude of adorers from all the nations, to the very ends of the earth."[3] Sophie worked tirelessly to renew faith in the Real Presence of Jesus in the Blessed Sacrament and at the same time to fight Jansenism, which was turning people away from the Sacraments, particularly the Eucharist.

I think I was one of the thousands of adorers in Sophie's vision. My faith in the Real Presence of Christ in the Eucharist began when I received my First Holy Communion. My devotion arose, I am sure, from my need to bond with someone at a deep level. In hindsight I can see that my dysfunctional patterns of denying my real feelings and hiding from everyone, my parents especially, left me hungry for emotional connection. Meeting Christ face to face, so to speak, at Mass and in Communion, filled a void inside of me. My faith in Jesus gave me Someone to hold on to, to rely on, to guide me and to live for. It was also a support system that kept me on the straight and narrow, at least most of the time.

One nun, in particular, influenced me by the depth of her faith and her personal witness. I looked up to and feared Mother Beatrice Brennan, who was a dynamo, intellectually and spiritually, and who had the drive of the Energizer bunny. I can still see her flying through the corridors, her black veil swishing behind her. She was our principal during high school and taught us theology. During senior year she held up a copy of the New Testament saying: "If it weren't for this Book I wouldn't be in this habit." She also said that she had turned down the keys to a new car and a trip to Europe in order to enter the convent. After that I began to think about entering the convent. Sr. Beatrice Brennan also taught us the theology of the Mass. She, more than anyone else, helped me understand what the Mass really means. During junior and senior years she used diagrams on the board to show us how the priest stood *in persona Christi* to offer the Father the Body and Blood of His Son, on our behalf. The understanding that the Sacred Liturgy is a re-presentation of Christ's sacrifice on Calvary—and that His sacrifice is of infinite value—seared itself into my being, where it still inspires me fifty years later.

At graduation in 1959 we wore white dresses and long white veils, processing into the chapel behind a banner of the Sacred Heart of Jesus, singing, *Jesus be our king and leader, grant us in thy toils a part, are we not thy chosen soldiers, children of thy Sacred Heart.* The thought of leaving the world that had been like home to me for twelve years was more than painful; it was gut wrenching. When we walked into the chapel for the last time I had to stifle sobs that would have erupted into a wail. I felt as if my life were about to end. Afterwards someone took a picture of Kandy (my best friend) and me in our white graduation dresses standing in front of a life-sized oak statue of the Sacred Heart of Jesus, His welcoming arms outstretched to embrace the world. At our fortieth and recently at our fiftieth high school reunions, Kandy and I posed for the exact same picture. I keep these photos side by side on a bookshelf in my bedroom; they bring back the joy of my youth.

I had the gift of reconnecting with Sister Bea recently at my fiftieth high school reunion. Standing in the chapel saving seats for some of my classmates, I noticed an elderly woman with a walker steer her way down the center aisle of the chapel. I recognized her at once and flew over to greet her. My eyes teared up. I sat next to her at Mass and later at lunch. She was the same; wise, filled with light—and love. I felt it. She remembered me as shy and unsure of myself. I reminded her of what her teaching and example meant to me. "When did you decide to become a nun?" I asked. "When I was very young," she said. She lived on Long Island, in Astoria. Their little house had a view of the sound. She would go out on her balcony, smell the salt air and look at the water and the stars and "marvel at the immensity of God." Bea had a heart for the poor and worked with Dorothy Day, the founder of the Catholic Worker Movement, when Day started her soup kitchen. In those days Bea said the way to serve God was to become a nun, so she entered the convent after attending Manhattanville College. When the cloister ended in 1967 and the Sacred Heart nuns could travel, Bea went to Upper Egypt where she spent thirteen "marvelous years" establishing small village foundations and where she studied enough Arabic to teach kindergarten. We talked of many things. I shared a bit about my health problems and my past (she didn't know about my mother's mental illness) and my struggle to find inner peace. She quoted from a poem of Thomas Merton in which he descended into his own inner hell but emerged to find new life. Bea stressed our inner child's need to receive love. "What do you do with darkness?" I asked her. "Just sit in God's presence and He will fill you with Himself," was her response. After all these years, I felt a kindred spirit in a woman whom I once put on such a pedestal.

IF I HAD TO MAKE a list of ten things that give me the greatest joy in life, travel and faith would be in the top five. Combining the two is heaven. One of the great gifts we have experienced in our marriage has been our travels. My husband took his first trip to Europe on a freighter in his twenties, and later he circled the world, stopping in India to spend time with his brother, Dick, a Jesuit who has spent most of his life there. Together Tommy and I have been to Europe many times. In November 1995 we took a spontaneous trip to Rome for Thanksgiving. Our children were otherwise occupied with in-laws or travel, so we decided to take advantage of a newspaper ad that was too good to turn down: a one week stay at a hotel in Rome including airfare for under $700. We knew we wouldn't be in the lap of luxury, but as long as the hotel was clean, we felt we could make the best of it. We set about gathering the necessary papers from the Archdiocese of Chicago for a possible general audience with Pope John Paul II. Just before we left, we got a call from Bishop Abramowitz's office in Chicago. He was a personal friend of Pope John Paul II. A friend had put in a good word for us with him, telling him about our work to promote devotion to the Eucharist. We had met this affable bishop some years back when he confirmed our daughter Katie, after which he willingly posed for a family photo. Handing his staff to our youngest child, Richard, he said, "some day you will be a bishop!" (That has yet to happen!)

Just before our departure for Rome, my husband took the call from Bishop Abramowitz' secretary, who had arranged for us to attend a special Mass in the Vatican. She ended the conversation saying, "You will have a very good time in Rome." We both wondered what she meant by that.

I felt euphoric to be back in the Eternal City. It had only been three years since our twenty-fifth anniversary trip but it seemed like I had lived ten lives since then. I had been well back then, full of energy and stamina and able to walk from one end of Rome to the other. Now I could barely walk a block and had to sit down and rest often. My swollen hands were an ever-present reminder that I was ill. I went from being a young and energetic woman in the prime of life to walking like an old lady. But at least I could walk.

A priest we met at a Eucharistic conference in Chicago arranged for us to spend Thanksgiving at the Pontifical North American College, America's seminary in Rome. We didn't know a soul when we walked in, but by the time we left we had made many new friends. We attended noon Mass in their beautiful chapel where we sat behind rows of American seminarians dressed in their blacks. Then we dined at a table with a group of seminarians from the Chicago area. They welcomed us like old friends; it seemed as if our presence reminded them of their parents. We met the rector, Monsignor Timothy Dolan, who, at this writing, is now the Archbishop of New York. The dinner was home cooked—turkey and all the trimmings—and the conversation flowed freely. They were most interested in our Eucharistic endeavors and we promised to send them one of our books. After dinner these talented young men entertained a dining room full of guests with skits performed in groups according to their home state. They took obvious enjoyment in the production of these hilarious spoofs, one trying to outdo the other with extremely funny satire. The grand finale of our visit was a trip to the roof that afforded sweeping views of Rome. We took pictures of us with the Vatican in the background.

The next day we fanned out all over Rome to special sites that we wanted to research and photograph for our books and videos. Our work with the Eucharist heightened our interest in art and fueled our search to see as many Eucharistic paintings, sculptures and artifacts as time would allow. We devoted a day to visiting the catacombs, the underground maze-like burial chambers of the early Christians, where we saw an early second-century fresco called the *Fractio Panis* (Breaking of the Bread) in the "Greek chapel" in the Catacomb of Priscilla. Sister Madeleine, whose religious community cared for this shrine, obliged us by speaking in front of our Camcorder, sharing her expertise on this important Eucharistic fresco. She compressed a vast amount of information into two gripping minutes, underscoring the fact that this is the earliest representation in Christian art of the offering of the Mass. We included her presentation in the video we were making of the Eucharist in the Early Church.

On this trip I discovered the chapel of adoration in St. Peter's, concealed behind heavy velvet drapes. Pope John Paul II started perpetual adoration in the Vatican in 1981, urging every parish in the world to adopt this practice. Sitting in the pew amidst throngs of people from many countries around the world was humbling and gratifying. Almost two thousand years after His appearance on earth, I am in awe that I can be with Christ who is present now in a different but real way—in a golden monstrance high above an altar—where each and every person can have their own personal audience with Him. I felt so blessed to be there, to have faith and to be in love with a God who is always present and available to His children, not only spiritually, but in a human, bodily way.

AT THE TOP OF MY wish list—but not really connected to our work—was the desire to visit a church personally important to me, Trinita dei Monti, a monastery inhabited by the Religious of the Sacred Heart. I grew up gazing at a life-sized painting of the Blessed Mother, known as Mater Admirabilis, on a wall beside our chapel at school. It was a replica of the original painting in Trinita dei Monti, the Motherhouse of the Sacred Heart, above the Piazza di Spagna in Rome. The nuns taught us to pray to Mater for the grace to lead a prayerful life. I couldn't wait to see the original.

Resurrecting what was left of my bare-bones high school French, I asked the sister at the reception desk about the painting. She shrugged off the story of the miracle of the paint that I had heard about in school, saying that no such thing had ever happened, but we were welcome to go upstairs and see it. I didn't believe her.

The story goes that a young French girl who later became a Sacred Heart nun obtained permission from Mother Superior to paint a picture of the Blessed Mother on the wall in a niche adjacent to the cloister. (This was in 1844.) After spending months praying to Our Lady and preparing the surface of the wall, she painted the likeness of Mary. When she finished, she thought that the wet paint was too vivid and left it to dry under a protective drape. Some days later when she removed the drape, the paint appeared in the lovely subdued shades that we see today. The young French girl considered it a miracle. When Pope Pius IX visited the monastery, he asked what was hidden behind the curtain. As soon as he saw this beautiful fresco of the Blessed Mother the pope exclaimed, "Mater Admirabilis" (Mother most Admirable), the title that she bears to this day. After his visit, miracles began to happen when people prayed to Mater.

The painting was more beautiful than I had imagined. I loved seeing this image where many saints had stopped to pray, including St. Therese the Little Flower, and later, Sts. Madeleine Sophie Barat and Rose Philippine Duchesne, the latter of whom sailed across the ocean where she founded the first Sacred Heart schools in America. I basked in this sacred atmosphere and spent a long time praying for my children and many other intentions—my own health among them. I asked Mater for a miracle.

ONE DAY WE HEADED over to the Vatican office, eager to see if any tickets awaited us or, if not, we could try to arrange for an audience with the Pope. An Irish Christian Brother was sitting at a desk besieged with people claiming their tickets. He would dig into a file and when he found the tickets, the happy recipients would swoon with gratitude. We stood off to the side, patiently awaiting our turn. He was a bit exasperated by my husband's humor. We finally had our chance and asked for tickets. "It is not that simple," he said. "Do you have papers?" We assured him that Cardinal Bernardin's office in Chicago sent a letter on our behalf requesting an audience with the Holy Father. Then we lost our place to another group who came in looking for their tickets. This went on for close to an hour. My husband kept needling this good man who was more accustomed to people bowing and scraping than he was to someone tossing one-liners at him. "My good friend, I'm sure if you dig down deep enough in that box you will find our letter of recommendation from the Archdiocese of Chicago," Tommy would quip. After endless interruptions, the Christian Brother sorted through the box and found our papers. "Ecco ci!" he shouted with relief.

Our papers entitled us to a general audience with the Holy Father scheduled for the following Wednesday. "Is there any way we could arrange a semi-private audience?" I pressed. "We have a ministry in Chicago in which we publish books and give presentations on the Eucharist." Before he could reply I handed this overwrought man a copy of *My Daily Eucharist,* saying that I would love to present this to the Pope in person. "You and five thousand other people," he quipped. "Not a chance," he said with finality.

When John Paul II visited the States in 1979, I fell in love with this Pope. He was charismatic, funny, spontaneous, prayerful and brilliant. *Time* magazine dubbed him "John Paul, Superstar." Writing in the *New York Times*, columnist James Reston noted that with the possible exception of Alexander Solzhenitsyn, John Paul "condemned the moral anarchy, sexual license and material consumerism in this country more than any social critic. Yet somehow, despite his condemnation of our spiritual bewilderment, he has been received here with more applause than any religious or secular leader in the world."[4] Some people did not applaud, however, because they deemed his teaching out-of-touch and unfit for a pluralistic society.

I was especially drawn to John Paul II because of his great devotion to the Eucharist. He flew to Iowa in response to a letter he received from a farmer. In the most touching homily of his American visit, he reflected on God's bounty in the Eucharist saying: "Farmers everywhere provide bread for all humanity, but it is Christ alone who is the bread of life . . . . Even if all the physical hunger of the world were satisfied, even if everyone who is hungry were fed by his or her own labor or by the generosity of others, the deepest hunger of man would still exist . . . . Therefore I say, come, come all of you, to Christ. He is the bread of life. Come to Christ and you will never be hungry again."[5]

Our persistence at the Vatican ticket office paid off. Our Christian Brother friend handed us two tickets to a general audience and seemed pleased to present us with two additional tickets to an Eastern Rite Mass that the Holy Father would celebrate on Sunday in the Vatican. These, we assumed, were through the courtesy of Bishop Abramowitz, for which we were most grateful. Then he handed *My Daily Eucharist* back to me saying that there was no way I would be able to give this to the Holy Father, and even less of a possibility for a personal meeting with the Pope. "If you sit in the first few rows of a general audience," he said, "you might be able to say something to him; but you certainly wouldn't be able to give him anything. But take this paper and write a letter to Monsignor Dziwisz, the Holy Father's secretary, telling him what you do and what you want. When I come back from lunch I will personally give it to him." Handing us a large sheet of paper he said, "Here, leave it on my desk when you're finished." He then ushered us through some doors into what must have been the papal apartments and disappeared.

The furniture was elegant—dark polished oak—and every few minutes a monsignor or a bishop would walk by and nod to us as if we were dignitaries. I sat at a magnificent library table with pen and paper while Tommy circled around me dictating a letter to Monsignor Dziwisz. Basically we told him who we were, where we were from, our connection to Cardinal Bernardin and our good friend, Bishop Raymond Goedert in the Archdiocese of Chicago, a few sentences about our Eucharistic apostolate, and our wish to meet the Holy Father.

Two hours later, after a long lunch, our Christian Brother friend returned and I handed him the letter. I then asked if he would attach the book to the letter.

"THE BOOK AGAIN!" he cried incredulously.

"Please?" I begged.

He took the book and the letter and attached them to each other with a rubber band. "Thank you," I said, meaning it. I felt peaceful knowing that we had done everything possible to see Pope John Paul II. If Monsignor Dziwisz even looked at the book, I thought it might at least influence him to give us front row seats at a general audience.

Now it was in God's hands.

8

Physical and Emotional Pain

You will not grow if you sit in a beautiful flower garden, but you will grow if you are sick, if you are in pain, if you experience losses, and if you do not put your head in the sand, but take the pain as a gift to you with a very, very specific purpose.

—Dr. Elizabeth Kubler-Ross

WITH ONLY TWO DAYS left in Rome I made a hair appointment at 7:30 P.M. (in Italy hairdressers work at night). We planned to go out to dinner afterwards to our favorite trattoria around the corner from our hotel. Just as we were leaving the room, the phone rang. It startled us because we couldn't imagine who would be calling. Perhaps it was an emergency?

A male voice with a heavy Polish accent asked if I was Mrs. McHugh. "Yes," I said, not having the slightest clue who he was.

"This is Monsignor Dziwisz [pronounced Jeevits but we were pronouncing it Dee-sha-wits] and I would like to invite you to attend Mass in the Holy Father's private chapel tomorrow morning at 7:30."

Which one of our friends would play such a cruel joke on us, I thought to myself.

"Hello, are you there?" he said.

"Yes, monsignor, I am here and we would love to come to the Holy Father's Mass in the morning. Thank you for asking us."

Tommy was staring wild-eyed at me, unbelieving.

"Good" he said. "Meet downstairs under the colonnade by the administrative offices at 7:00 and someone will come to bring you upstairs."

Click.

I couldn't believe it. At dinner we were beside ourselves with excitement. What would we wear, what would we say, who else would be there, how did he get the phone number of this second-rate hotel, should we bring our cameras, and what about an extra book to hand to the Holy Father? And to top it all off, the timing of my hair appointment couldn't have been better. Now my hair would look great for the Holy Father!

Neither of us slept a wink. My husband was up and dressed at 5 A.M., ready to go. It was only a ten-minute ride to the Vatican, so if we left at 5:00, it meant that we'd be outside (it would be cold and damp for sure) standing under the colonnade for almost two hours. We compromised and left at 6:00. Some people had already gathered at the designated spot. One was a tall, thin man, dressed in scruffy clothes, who had a smile that could light up the world. We introduced ourselves. He was Fr. Ted Hochstatter, just back from working for Mother Teresa in Albania. He was as excited as we were—probably more so.

As many as twenty people gathered, and most of them were priests. Up we went in an elevator that opened into a large room where this august group formed a huge circle. A short priest stood in the middle. No one was talking and it was a bit awkward. I spontaneously walked over to the priest to thank him for including us in this assembly.

"What is your name?" he asked.

"We are Joan and Tom McHugh from Chicago, Father."

"I am Monsignor Dziwisz," he said, and "I would like to thank you for the book."

Ohmygosh. The full realization hit me. *The book got us in!* I was sure of it.

We filed into the Holy Father's private chapel where two gracious Polish nuns greeted us; they asked us to leave the camera outside the door before seating us in the last row. The Pope was already kneeling on his *prie deux* facing the altar, deep in prayer. I thought to myself that as the head of Christendom, he carried the burdens of the world—for Christ. There were only four lay people, and we were two of them. A stained glass ceiling formed a canopy of brilliant color over us; in the center was a large image of the Risen Christ surrounded by scenes of the Resurrection. I wanted the Mass to last all day. Pope John Paul II was deeply reverential and deliberate. There were long pauses between readings and prayers, especially during the Consecration. This man believed with all his mind and heart that Jesus Christ was in our midst in the Eucharist; his body language showed it. He addressed the priests during the homily. The majority of them were from England and five or six were from Africa. He spoke to them like father to son. He was friendly and funny. I found it all extremely touching and personal.

After Mass we filed out into a large ornate reception room. A line formed in a semi-circle. We were the next to the last in line, standing beside a diplomatic couple from Hong Kong. The Holy Father worked the line, listening intently as each one introduced himself. He gave out his special rosary. When he got to our friend Father Ted, he gave him two, saying out loud, "and one for Albania." (I assume it was because Father Ted just came from there). The priests cheered. The Holy Father was serious and jovial at the same time, kidding around with some of the priests. One of the African priests in line yelled out, "We love you Holy Father, we are all in your boat" which made the Pope laugh. I saw for myself what I had only read about: his humor that so endeared him to people.

I hadn't prepared anything to say. I thought I would just be open to the spirit. When the Holy Father stood in front of me, he looked at me and I looked at him. For the first time in my life, I was tongue-tied. He broke the silence, saying in his thick Polish accent, "Where are you from?" "Chicago, Your Holiness." "Sheekaggo" he said, making me laugh. We introduced ourselves and told him about our apostolate with the Eucharist, then handed him a copy of *My Daily Eucharist*. "Ah, the Eucharist is the strength of our Church," he said. Then he gave each of us a rosary, said a word or two to my husband, then he made the sign of the cross over us saying, "I bless your community."

It was over in a flash. He took a step toward the couple from Hong Kong, and then he turned back and looked at me. He just stood there staring at me as if he was thinking something and wanted to speak. It really seemed like he was he listening to an inner voice while still looking at me—or through me. I will never know what was going through his mind. I've wondered if he saw my illness and was praying for me. Whatever it was, there was a connection between us that I will treasure forever.

The Vatican photographer snapped lots of pictures. We have one framed in gold on our dining room wall. I am extending my hand to the Holy Father while explaining our Eucharistic apostolate. He is holding the rosaries he is about to give us in his hand and is listening intently. My hand is in mid-air, totally swollen with scleroderma.

OUR NEVER-TO-BE-FORGOTTEN personal meeting with Pope John Paul II was an early Christmas gift that would keep on giving for the rest of our lives. We arrived home in the first week of December 1995, in time to prepare for Christmas with our family.

One evening during Advent we attended a meeting at Marytown which our good friends, Frs. Patrick Greenough and Steven McKinley, organized to interest people in a trip to the Holy Land in February. Neither of us had ever been to the Holy Land and we both wanted to go. More than that, I felt a burning desire to visit the land of Jesus, as if going to the Lord's homeland would enable me to get closer to Him and be healed, like the people in Scripture.

But my health was an ongoing concern. Like the childhood game, "Mother, May I?" I took three steps forward and two steps backward. I kept my food choices under control (mostly) but tired of the flax oil drinks and cut back to two a week. One entry in Dr. Mercola's notes in early February 1996 reads: "Needs to decrease cookie intake." Sweets, he warned for the tenth time, fed the bacteria that were infesting my joints, causing swelling and weakness. Cookies were my downfall. I wasn't sleeping, and was always tired. I didn't feel like exercising—and didn't. I was still taking 900 mg. of intravenous Cleocin every few weeks as well as oral Minocin three times a week. It definitely reduced the swelling and discoloration of my hands and feet. But the scleroderma was still alive and kicking.

The Holy Land trip would be strenuous and I honestly didn't know if I'd have enough strength to keep up a hectic schedule. There would be a lot of walking involved and I worried about the food and staying on my diet. But I desperately wanted to visit the sacred sites where Jesus lived and taught, hoping that just by being there it would bring me closer to Him. The prospect of being in the land of Jesus overrode all my fears and we set off to an area of the world where neither of us had ever been.

AT THE END OF February 1996, we set out for the Holy Land. While going through security in O'Hare Airport before boarding the flight to Tel Aviv, I twisted my right knee and had to limp for the entire trip. My knee just gave out. It was impossible to put full weight on it because it was swollen and very painful. I didn't know if it was related to the scleroderma or if it was a random meniscus tear. A cane I bought in one of the markets in Jerusalem enabled me to get around. It was made of olive wood that oozed a sticky substance and became more of a problem than my knee.

The change of scene—and focus—was refreshing. It lifted me onto another plane, away from my illness and my ever-present emotional struggles. The hotels, the food and the company were all five star. I somehow managed to make healthy food choices and not get out of control with my diet. We grew to love our fellow pilgrims with whom we shared such special—and fun—experiences. Steve Shebenik, the music director from Marytown, played the organ in every church we visited. He sat a few rows in front of us on the bus. His droll sense of humor spilled over constantly in side remarks loud enough for us to hear. He often took aim at the shopping habits of one of the women. She carried five or six fishnet shopping bags that she filled with water bottles and so much paraphernalia that they often broke or fell, sending the rest of us scrambling for her stuff. Steve's timing was impeccable and the laughter was a great gift.

I was unprepared for how beautiful the scenery was, especially around the Sea of Galilee. I fell in love with Capernaum, the little town where Jesus lived when He was in Galilee. (Scripture describes it as "his own city"). It was poetically beautiful, perched on the banks of the Sea of Galilee, the home of Peter and Andrew, Jesus' first converts. We attended Mass in the church built over the ruins of the house thought to be that of Saint Peter, where the Lord cured Peter's mother-in-law. The remains of the stone walls showed the layout of the house. It did not take much to imagine Jesus staying here, where He ministered to the sick, such as the paralytic whose friends lowered him through the thatched roof. I saw the apostles as real people who lived in small houses with flat roofs and dirt floors, who cast their nets and moored their fishing boats a few feet away in the Sea of Galilee. Not far from Peter's house are the ruins of a synagogue built over the one in which Jesus gave His famous, "Bread of Life" discourse (John 6). Father Patrick obliged me by standing in the synagogue and giving a brief talk on camera about the Eucharist for a video I wanted to produce on the foundational story of the Eucharist in the Early Church.

On the bus ride to Jerusalem I was struck by the vast amount of desert in this region and the realization that Jesus and His disciples *walked* such great distances. It is estimated that they walked about five miles a day. On the bus Father Patrick stressed that Jesus walked "up" to Jerusalem. I never understood what that meant. Now it was clear as the bus chugged its way "up" to the this jewel of a city that was elevated about 2500 feet above sea level.

When we passed through a small intersection of dirt roads in Jericho, the bus driver stopped and pointed out a sycamore tree, no doubt similar to the one that the wealthy—and hated—tax collector Zacchaeus climbed to get a good look at Jesus. We stopped briefly to ponder the scene, imagining Jesus looking up into the branches addressing Zacchaeus by name, saying, "Zacchaeus, make haste and come down, for I must stay at your house to-day" (Lk 19:5). You could almost hear the crowd grumble, expressing their outrage. Zacchaeus must have been very touched by the love he felt from Jesus, because Scripture says he converted on the spot, offering to give half of his possessions to the poor and to repay whatever he had extorted four times over. What a charismatic figure Jesus was; He drew people to Himself so easily, empowering them to completely change their lives!

Following the route Jesus took when He carried His cross was difficult, especially with my bad knee. The cane helped me over the rough uneven stones. We walked the Via Dolorosa carrying a huge cross through the narrow, winding streets in the old part of the city. At first, I felt slightly disappointed by all the hubbub and congestion, by the shopkeepers hawking their wares, by the total irreverence for this holy path that Jesus had trod. It was like Times Square on New Year's Eve. But then I realized that it might have been that way in 33 A.D. That thought intensified my prayer. I prayed for my family and friends, and for all the prayer intentions that I kept in a special envelope that I brought with me. I also asked God for the grace to really surrender my problems—like Jesus did—in total trust for God's perfect will to be realized in my life.

One of our last stops before leaving the holy city was a visit to the Church of the Holy Sepulcher, the most sacred Christian site in Jerusalem. It is a vast complex, housing Golgotha (an Aramaic word meaning "the skull"), which was the site where Christ was crucified. (Originally it was outside the walls of Jerusalem.) Also in the Holy Sepulcher was Christ's tomb, the anointing stone where His body rested when He was taken down from the Cross, the Chapel of St. Helena and Jesus' tomb. All these places are divided among five communities: Roman Catholic, Greek Orthodox, Armenian, Coptic and Syrian Orthodox.

The Golgotha of today is accessible by steep steps that bring you to a level at the top of the rock on which Christ was crucified. There are two chapels standing side by side. One is Roman Catholic and one is Greek Orthodox. They are decorated in an ornate fashion with life-sized icons of Christ, the Blessed Mother and Saint John prominently displayed. On the Greek side there is an altar, under which is a round silver marker with a hole in it. If you reach down into the hole you can touch the top of the rocky outcrop where it is believed the Cross of Christ stood.

I had purchased a bunch of olive wood rosaries in the market, which I brought to Golgotha. When it was my turn to venerate this sacred spot, I knelt down and put the rosaries down the hole, hoping to touch them to the rock. What I didn't expect was the outburst of tears that came gushing out. I felt as if I was at the scene of the Crucifixion. My prayer came from the deepest part of my heart. There were no words. Only tears.

After a minute or two I got up and regained my composure. I drew comfort from my rosaries, which I held close, thanking the Lord for the extraordinary spiritual privilege of being at Calvary.

Several days later we renewed our marriage vows in the little mountain village of Cana (not far from Nazareth where Jesus was born and raised) where Jesus and His mother attended a wedding and where He changed water into wine. If there was ever a perfect place to pray for the healing of a marriage, it was here. Surrendering our relationship to God gave me peace and a deep sense that, in the words of the fourteenth century English mystic, Juliana of Norwich, "all will be well." We posed for a photo beside one of the huge stone water jugs that held between twenty and thirty gallons of water. The Jews used this water for their purification rituals. What was shocking was the sheer size of the jug. It must have taken the servants at the wedding feast at Cana a long time to fill these water pots. When we posed for the picture, the jug was almost as big as we were. The miracle was that Jesus miraculously turned the water in six of these jugs into the finest of wines.

We returned from the Holy Land totally renewed in spirit. If my faith was strong before the trip, it doubled during it. Walking in the footsteps of Christ made me want to be closer to Him and listen more for His direction. I had blind trust that Jesus was guiding and healing me.

The trips were also good for our relationship. We did have so much in common and enjoyed each other's company immensely.

Two months later, in May 1996, we flew to New York to attend Danny's graduation from Columbia University. It was a beautiful warm and sunny day and we basked in the joy of celebrating Danny's achievement with our youngest son Richard, who flew in from Santa Clara University in California, and with Katie and Tommy who flew in from Chicago. We had dinner in the dining room of the New York Athletic Club overlooking

Central Park, a place where my parents often took me to dinner as a child and where a group of us spent Saturday nights in high school drinking 7 & 7's and dancing to big band orchestras. I was extremely thankful to be able to enjoy the high points of the city where I was born and raised, with my family.

Back home in Chicago I plunged into a rigorous work routine starting two projects at once: compiling quotes for *My Daily Eucharist II* and researching the background for the video on the Eucharist in the Early Church. For weeks I tried to ignore recurring stomach cramps, until they began to wake me up in the middle of the night. I had always had a strong stomach and thought that if I just cut down on coffee, the pains would stop. But they didn't. It was two months before I could see a gastroenterologist and in the interim I tried Zantac and all manner of home remedies. They helped a little, but not really. Finally, an endoscopy showed that I had not one, but two, gastric ulcers.

Doctors were debunking the theory that ulcers are psychosomatic in origin, favoring a new line of thinking that says they are caused by the presence of Helicobacter pylori (H. pylori), bacteria in the mucous lining of the stomach. (The person who discovered the connection to bacteria was Barry Marshall who won a Nobel Prize for this finding in 2005[1].) Yet, in the endoscopies and biopsies of my stomach, doctors never found H. pylori bacteria. I *wanted* to believe that there was a physical cause for the ulcers, and wondered if the Clindamycin and Minocin antibiotics I took for scleroderma were eating away at my stomach.

But I also couldn't rule out a psychosomatic component, questioning if the ruptures in the intestinal wall were related to the emotional hole I fell into periodically. The ulcers were like a wake up call forcing me to try to reduce stress in my life. The tension of trying to behave as if everything was fine while I was often in a pit of hopelessness drained me. Perhaps my stomach took the brunt of the tension. It was no wonder I had ulcers. I was walking an emotional tightrope—and could fall on either side. On one side there was immense joy and love I received from my family, my faith and apostolate, special friendships, trips and events; on the other there was a pool of darkness stemming from the uncertainties surrounding illness as well as an ongoing struggle with my emotions. *How can I have so much and yet so little?* I was walking through a revolving door in my marriage, always coming out at the same painful place. Like two people, I acted one way on the outside but felt differently on the inside. *I want to be me and nobody else,* I wrote. *My deep depression drives me to hurt, to punish Tommy for all that he doesn't give me in our marriage. I do not want to hurt him, but I do not want to hurt myself either. Please, God, help me to stay focused on what I must do to stay loving. Please give me the strength and courage to walk this tightrope.*

This was one of the first times in my journal that I used the word "depression." Was this at the bottom of my pain? Was depression the dark cloud inside of me that burst periodically, flooding me with negative thoughts and feelings? Denial and projection were defense mechanisms that were so embedded in my personality that I was unable to see the problem in myself. I still saw "depression" as my mother's problem and was programmed to believe that the cause of my suffering was outside of me, namely in my husband. My mantra was: *If only he would change, I could be happy.*

In addition to dealing with the ulcers, my knees were hurting so badly I could hardly stand. An MRI showed a torn ligament in the right knee as well as disintegration and arthritis in both knees. The doctor prescribed a knee brace that I wore sometimes for support. I scheduled an appointment with another orthopedist at Evanston Hospital for a second opinion. It took enormous effort to walk the long halls to get to his office. I waited in the examining room for an hour, and when he didn't show up, I got dressed and left. I purposely didn't tell the desk that I was leaving. They would find out soon enough and make their own assumptions.

It seemed like illness was trying to overtake my body. Rheumatism was spreading to my left shoulder and lower back. An MRI showed two bulging discs. Compensating for the pain in my knees probably threw me off balance. The summer and ocean salt water brought some relief, as did losing a few pounds at Jenny Craig. By the fall the doctor's notes record that "most of the difficulty seems to be in her knees. Has difficulty walking, and after sitting for a prolonged period of time. Continues to have swelling of her hands. Pain and stiffness seems to be worsening."

By December, 1996, when my husband arrived home from visiting Richard who was studying in a semester abroad program in Ghana, West Africa (where I urged Tommy to go without me, out of fear of contracting a disease in a Third World country due to my weakened immune system) I was practically bedridden. The ulcers and a flare of scleroderma just about paralyzed me. Even lifting a hairbrush was painful. My body was pretty broken. But so was my soul. When Tommy came home, he brought me a beautiful beaded malachite necklace and a magnificent hand-carved ebony crucifix—in addition to the exquisitely carved jungle animals he bought for our grandsons and himself. He regaled me with stories about their adventures in such a childlike way that I should have felt only gratitude for this wonderful man. Instead, I found it difficult to be happy that he was home.

It was becoming evident to me that my physical sickness and emotional health were probably related. *Lord, if this is a depression, it is awful. In the mall today amidst the sights and sounds of Christmas I was fighting tears, tears of terrible sadness, loneliness, fear, guilt. I'm walking away from a thirty-year marriage by sleeping in another room. It feels so good yet I wonder if I'm doing the right thing. My heart is spliced in two. What is my/our problem? I'm crying on the inside twenty-four hours a day. My hands are swollen. I can hardly walk. Life is seeping out of me. Touch me Lord. Lead me through this and let me know You are with me.*

I was on a continual seesaw. One minute I thought that the pain I was feeling in my relationship with my husband was coming from inside of me, from repressed wounds that his behavior triggered. The next minute I would project my pain on him, thinking that if he were different or if I were married to someone else, I wouldn't have this suffering. Should I stay or go? And if I did opt for the latter, where would I go?

Feeling trapped with no way out was the essence of my pain. It was also the constant cry of my mother: "Joanie, I feel so trapped," she'd complain, then blame her unhappiness on my father. Her cry was like a broken record that never stopped. My dad's favorite saying was, "The apples don't fall far from the tree." I was repeating the behavior I detested in my mother. I was living it.

The stress was killing me. Literally.

9

Learning to Forgive

To forgive and to ask forgiveness are like summer lightning that announces the long-awaited rain.

—Fr. Emiliano Tardif, *Jesus Lives Today*

IN JANUARY 1997, I threw myself into healing the ulcers, worried that these intestinal sores would start bleeding. Whatever medical theories were in vogue—whether the ulcers were caused by bacteria or by stress—down deep I felt that the gastric pain was a signal that my inner house was out of order and I had better clean it up. With tips from health and nutrition books (drink *lots* of water), I tried to purify my diet. How I gave up coffee I'll never know, but I did, for almost a year. Along with that I sacrificed Diet Coke, red meat and chocolate—as best I could. Nutritionists recommended alkaline foods, so I ate lots of non-acidic fruits, steamed veggies and leafy green salads. Yogurt became a staple. Bananas were good and so was chamomile tea. I never liked licorice (an excellent medicine for peptic ulcers) so I took supplements for healing. The pains stayed with me for months. When I saw a photo of the ulcers I understood why.

The food choices paid dividends by increasing my energy. Exercise helped, which I did three times a week on the elliptical machine at the health club. Cutting out sugar and decreasing carbs helped me lose weight. Although my knees were a problem, I ignored them in favor of taking care of the rest of me.

I SIGNED UP FOR a retreat at the Hazelden Renewal Center in Minnesota. Alcoholics Anonymous' 12 Step work appealed to me ever since a good friend found sobriety by attending the treatment program in Center City, Minnesota. When I read the life story of A.A.'s founder, Bill Wilson, I realized that the Twelve Steps had a spiritual base and could benefit people who weren't alcoholics and who were just working on their lives. I saw the Steps as tools of transformation that I could integrate with Christian spirituality; I looked at them as a practical means of finding "emotional sobriety," hoping that they would help me "let go and let God."

At the Hazelden Renewal Center, an idyllic place in the woods perched on a lake with a great view and a cozy living room with a giant stone fireplace, I met a counselor who introduced me to the concept of "codependency." "When a codependent dies, whose life flashes before their eyes?" she asked our small group attending the five day retreat. The answer was, "their friend's." A codependent, she said, is someone who suffers from an addiction, not to drugs or alcohol, but to others, to *their* needs to the neglect of their own needs. They are preoccupied and extremely dependent on others, giving them power over them to the point where they might even lose their own identity.

She told a remarkable story about living with her alcoholic husband and how she became codependent in the process. Her behavior enabled his drinking and her own dysfunction led her to despair. She felt powerless to change him or herself and allowed his drinking to control her life. She loved plants and decided to macramé a hanging plant holder for her kitchen. She worked on this diligently every day, knowing that she was knitting it not for a plant, but to use as a noose to hang herself.

One day a neighbor invited her to attend an Al-Anon meeting. There, she broke through her denial and saw her own sickness. She decided then and there that she had to change her life and to stop giving her husband complete power over her. She set boundaries and started to take care of herself by attending to her needs. Her changed behavior influenced her husband who eventually sobered up and went to A.A. They saved their health and their marriage.

Her testimony inspired me. Although my husband wasn't an alcoholic, I realized that I was like this counselor, trying to control his behavior instead of my own. I was more invested in his life than I was in my own. I wrote in my journal: *It is time I took charge of my life and started really living it. The first step is to admit that I am powerless over others. I keep trying to tell Tommy how much I hurt. What I really need to do is become aware of how much pain I am in and start taking care of myself. I have been feeling trapped, locked in a victim role. Every happening in my life (not just in the marriage) seems like it is designed to do me in. I constantly give away my power and allow myself to be victimized. I'm also trying to control my pastor on the parish council—and I'm becoming a victim of his deficiencies in the process. I need to let go.*

Through the lectures at Hazelden I realized that I was powerless over my emotions and that if I could learn how to detach, it might end the pain. In other words I saw that I was responsible for stopping my pain, for setting boundaries, for making choices, saying no, and for creating a fulfilling life for myself. I was not a victim. Before leaving Hazelden, I wrote in my journal: *God, give me the power to let go completely, to become utterly detached, to stop trying to fix Tommy, to detach from his behaviors and focus on what I need to do to be me, to be happy, to be who I am, the person You created me to be. I give up.*

Learning to detach was a challenge that I welcomed because it promised relief from pain. I also saw it as a tool to help me surrender my life to the Lord. I had a chance to practice it—and failed—as soon as I got home when I attended a parish council meeting. I had been having problems restraining my anger at the monthly meetings. I felt blocked by our pastor, who wasn't listening to me—and didn't seem to care. At one meeting I had a bone to pick with him: I wanted to know why he didn't pass out the respect life literature that had come from the archdiocese. It was circulating in other parishes and I was upset because our parishioners were denied it. I told him that I thought the parish suffered as a result of his inaction. He was enraged. He was furious at me and let everyone know it. The parishioners on the council came to his defense.

I was boiling mad and when I got home, told Tommy what had happened. He agreed that the parish was suffering because of the pastor's inaction. I didn't know why I was so angry. It festered for days and I couldn't seem to shake it. I was frustrated because I couldn't control my pastor and therefore what was happening in the parish. "Detachment" wasn't working. I tried to pray it away.

In late January 1997, a brochure came in the mail advertising *The Good News Ministries,* an International Catholic School of Evangelization in Pensacola, Florida. It promised to teach the laity how to evangelize using the documents of Vatican II, the Nicene Creed and Scripture. Since we were becoming more involved in our Eucharistic apostolate, I felt the need to bone up on the teachings of the Church. My husband agreed so we signed up for the program. True to its literature, the school delivered on its promised teaching, but what we didn't expect was to be evangelized ourselves!

At 35 Charlie Osburn (who founded the school) was a successful businessman and a prominent politician but his alcoholism was driving his wife and his children away from him. With the help of a priest friend who urged him to "give it all to Jesus," Charlie reached out to God in desperation.

During the week, Charlie shared how Christ healed him and then how he was led to proclaim Christ's message of love and forgiveness to the world. But it was the forgiveness piece that really touched me. He told story after story of how the Lord called him to unconditionally love and forgive everyone, especially those who hurt him. He was to live a spirit of dying to self—constantly—particularly with his wife and children. God even asked him to forgive his neighbor for sexually abusing two of his children. Although it was extremely difficult, Charlie knocked on his neighbor's door one day saying, "I've come to ask your forgiveness for hating you."[1] When his wife Jeanne later met the neighbor in the supermarket, he shared that he had come back to the Church and given his life to Christ. Three weeks later he died.

This message resonated deeply with the both of us. It was in accord with everything we had been taught and believed and was probably an area where we both needed to grow. The message that I heard loud and clear was: live the truth. If we are not living the truth, what good does it do to worship the Truth? Or, in other words, faith that isn't put into practice is hypocrisy. If we forgive others, then our heavenly Father will forgive us.

In Pensacola we learned how to "walk the walk." On the flight home we shared with each other our issues around forgiveness. I knew what I had to do: to ask forgiveness from my pastor for trying to control him. While I still disagreed with him and would tell him so, I had no right to tell him how he should run the parish. My husband had his own issue over a lost box of our Witness books that the owner of our local postal facility was responsible for but refused to acknowledge. Tommy was so angry it kept him awake at night.

We arrived home on Sunday. On Monday morning after Mass I followed my pastor into the sacristy. With as much humility as I could muster, I asked for a meeting with him saying, "I have something I want to share." I figured I had better say that lest he not agree to meet with me. He made me wait a week to see him.

When we finally sat down face to face I said that I wanted to apologize for trying to shame him at the parish council meeting. I told him I was angry at the way he was dealing with the respect life issue, and I was trying to manipulate him into doing things my way. He was stunned. I continued. *You are the pastor,* I said, *and you have every right to lead the parish as you wish. I may disagree with you, but I have no right to tell you how you should behave. I am sorry for my behavior and I have come to ask for your forgiveness.*

Silence. His eyes teared up. Then he said that he was sorry for the ways he tried to block me. It was honest. He thanked me for reaching out and said that I shouldn't expect change to happen overnight; it would take time. We talked for a few minutes and before leaving I said, *One more thing. I'd like to thank you for showing up for daily Mass. Some days I don't even get there because I want to stay in bed. You don't have that option because you are faithful to the Lord—and to your parishioners. Thank you Father.*

I felt a hundred pounds lighter. My apology lanced the boil of resentment that was poisoning me and creating stress. I had studied enough psychology to know that whatever I was angry at in my pastor, probably originated in my own heart. My anger was gone. At daily Mass I no longer felt seething resentment towards him, only love and compassion. Soon after this I resigned from the parish council because I didn't feel in sync with the group.

And, I realized, I had just detached. To detach is really to forgive, to release the other person from the hold we have over them, to let them go. "Forgiveness" writes my good friend, Fr. Bob DeGrandis, "is love in action."[2] When we forgive from the heart in the same way that we have been forgiven, he writes, we will be healed and set free: "Something wonderful will happen as you surrender to this healing process. God is going to open your heart and empower you with new vitality, new energy and new health. As you repent and forgive, you are perhaps at that moment most completely united to Jesus. You enter into the miraculous realm of God's love. You are truly set free."[3]

Around this time I had a speaking engagement in Texas, and Father Bob invited me to Galveston to give a talk on the Eucharist to his parishioners. Sitting in his office one day, he walked me through my entire life, praying the Forgiveness Prayer for all the significant areas where I needed to ask forgiveness either of myself, others or groups that had hurt me. I cried a lot and felt deeply peaceful afterwards. The act of forgiveness *is* freeing, and healing.

Something wonderful did happen when I forgave my pastor. I was freed from the anger and rage that had such control over me. And that wasn't all. When I got home from the meeting with my pastor and walked into our Witness office with a cup of coffee, I realized that my right knee that had been hurting for so long felt fine. I couldn't believe it. I put weight on it, stretched it out in front of me, went up and down the stairs and didn't feel the slightest pain. It was astonishing considering the pain I had endured for months. At morning Mass later that week, I stopped in the sacristy to tell our assisting priest my story. Father Larry Hennessey was a personal mentor to me, as well as a consultant for my writing on the Eucharist. He was a Patristic scholar and a professor at the Chicago archdiocesan seminary where he was a much-in-demand teacher. Father Larry listened with interest about my anger, the workshop in Florida, my apology to our pastor and the disappearing pain. "What happened, Father, that I no longer have pain in my knee?" I remember his exact words: "When we remove the obstacles to God's grace, we make room for God's love that heals." The obstacle to His grace was the anger I felt for my pastor. When I let that go, I was set free—emotionally and physically.

A story that I read in one of my favorite books confirmed this. Fr. Emiliano Tardif, a French Canadian Missionary of the Sacred Heart who worked in the Dominican Republic for thirty years, wrote *Jesus Lives Today*[4] a book small in size but mighty in content. This holy priest was skeptical of miracles until he was healed of tuberculosis through the laying on of hands. The following is one of many testimonies he shares about healing as it relates to forgiveness:

> One day I felt that the Lord was asking me to forgive a person who had done me a lot of harm. As I didn't want to give up the chance of taking my revenge, I put up a lot of resistance, and justified myself by saying: "Lord, why do you want me to pray for him when you are so good that you will bless him anyway, even if I don't ask you to do it?" I clearly heard a voice within me that said, "Foolish man, don't you realize that, in praying for him, the first to be healed will be you?"[5]

I had been learning the same thing from different teachers, Charlie

Osburn, Fr. Larry Hennessey, Fr. Bob Degrandis and Father Peter McAll. They were all saying the same thing, that when the Lord heals a person, it is effective at every level because He unties the basic knot that causes all the other complications. He doesn't deal with symptoms, but heals the root of the problem; that is what sets a person free. Father Emiliano points out that on more than a dozen occasions in Scripture, the word "sozo" (which is usually translated "to save") is used to mean "to heal." This means that salvation includes the action of healing that includes the whole person. "Jesus didn't come just to save souls," Father Emiliano wrote, because "He is concerned with the total person, which means both the soul and the body."[6]

OVER DINNER ONE NIGHT with our good friends, Fathers Patrick and Steve with whom we had gone to the Holy Land in 1996, we planned to go on a two-week vacation with them to France in the spring of 1997. We were also interested in designing an itinerary for a possible future Eucharistic pilgrimage we would undertake for Witness Ministries.

Flying in and out of Paris, we literally circled the country by car with Tommy at the wheel. Our itinerary included stops at the Normandy beaches, Rouen, Lisieux, Mont Saint Michel, Solesmes, Chartres, Orleans, Nevers, Fontenay, Paray le Monial, Ars, Lyons, Avignon, Narbonne and Lourdes. Fathers Patrick and Steve were fun companions on a very ambitious road trip. They appreciated long leisurely dinners in those wonderful European outdoor cafes as much as we did. We never lacked for conversation and, best of all, laughter. Thankfully my knee no longer hurt, but walking was a problem due to the scleroderma. The climb to the top of Mont Saint Michel was difficult, but Father Patrick took my arm and with great patience, escorted me ever so slowly to the top.

We immersed ourselves in the lives and works of medieval French saints whose heroism and love of Our Lord and Our Lady lives on in the monasteries and monuments of faith that encourage and inspire us today. I fell in love with St. Joan of Arc, my patron saint, whose remarkable faith in her "voices" fueled her mission to recover her homeland from English domination and abuse. Seeing the exact spot in Rouen where this 19-year-old visionary was burned at the stake burrowed its way into my imagination, leaving an indelible scar in my heart. She was so young and so brave, and at the bitter end asked that a crucifix be raised to her eye level so she could die looking at the crucified Christ. She sacrificed herself to remain faithful to her convictions and her mission that she believed were inspired by the spirit of God.

It seemed like this young woman, who led the French army to several important victories and King Charles to his coronation, led us all over France, because we would see statues of her with plaques in almost every town where we stopped. This was obviously the route she followed. Father Patrick took a picture of me standing next to a life-sized bronze figure of her on Mont Saint Michel; he then talked me into buying a small statue of her tied to a stake. Today this six inch wooden statue of Joan of Arc tied to a stake stands in my office across from my desk (with all manner of statues collected from other trips) where I can hear her urging me on: *Stay true to yourself and listen to God's voice. He will lead you to victory.*

At home I was preparing for two speaking engagements, a retreat in Connecticut and a Eucharistic conference in Indianapolis, and was suffering from that old anxiety, feeling that God picked such a broken vessel to witness to His love. I was praying for direction because I wanted to speak from the heart and to speak the truth. Nothing was coming. In France I was lifted up into a rarified spiritual atmosphere, so to speak, immersing myself in the lives and mission of the French saints. At home, I came crashing back to reality. I wanted to grow in virtue like the saints, but my shadow side was robbing me of inner peace. I fought to keep a lid on negative emotions that would rise up unexpectedly from some murky depths and ruin my joy. Learning about detachment was one thing; practicing it was another. If I were to describe myself in terms of a house, most of the rooms would be welcoming and peaceful, but there were a few storerooms in the basement that harbored unhappy, disturbed entities. Somehow I had to get a handle on what was in those rooms—whatever was causing such unrest. How could I give inspiring talks when my house was in such disorder?

I asked God why He didn't heal me on the spot, like He did so often when He walked in Galilee and restored the blind man's sight or healed the woman with a hemorrhage. With just a word, He brought the dead back to life. I told Him that I have been asking for new life for years, to be set free of whatever is dragging me under and trying to drown me in despair. It didn't seem fair. I was journaling one day and sensed that He was telling me that I had much to learn yet about love—that if He were to heal me miraculously, I wouldn't grow in holiness, in wholeness. This was truth. There were lessons I had to learn and, said Robert Frost, "miles to go before I sleep."

I stopped in church quite often just to sit in the presence of Jesus in the Blessed Sacrament. The silence and darkness invited meditation. One day I drew a heart in my journal, and absent-mindedly filled in the bottom half in pencil so that it was completely shaded. I realized that it was the broken part of myself that was in darkness—closed off from myself and from God. It was the deepest part. I asked the Lord where this part came from. *It comes from your need to protect yourself from pain and abuse, from emotional abandonment, from hunger for love. You craved attention, care, and touch. Sometimes, love wasn't reflected to you; there was anger, insult, and lack of trust, negativity, and coldness. In sealing yourself off from that you sealed yourself in. Until you recognize it and give it to Me for healing, it lives in you and hurts you (and others) and sometimes controls you.*

When I asked the Lord what I should do, He said that I should bring this broken piece of my heart to Him every day at Mass and put it in the chalice with His Blood. He said He would seal up the cracks in my heart with His Blood. Then I asked Him if this will help my talks and He told me He wanted me to be a true reflection of Him, like a mirror through which I would reflect His love to the world. I prayed and asked Him to shine His light like a laser beam into the whole area of my heart, exposing the dark places to His healing rays of love.

One morning I felt inspired to search for a book that I had in my own library (one more book that I bought and shelved until I needed it). It was *The Healing Light*[7] by Agnes Sanford. Almost as a direct answer to my prayer, a teacher came into my life with a lesson I needed to learn. She herself was healed when Jesus walked back into her past and healed her of depression, which, like the years of the locust, kept her bound for seven years. I started reading and couldn't stop.

A woman of deep prayer and one of the preeminent spiritual healers of the twentieth century, Agnes Sanford wrote about the power of prayer, urging her readers to open themselves to a continuous inflow of God's power. "You are the light of the world," the Lord said to the crowds gathered on the mountainside (Mt 5:14); Agnes saw Christ's followers as "the electric light bulbs through which the light of God reaches the world."[8]

She offered many pearls of wisdom that came from her personal prayer life and experiences of healing, but there was one in particular that spoke deeply to me. One of the ways we diminish the light within us, Agnes wrote, is through negativity—which also impacts our health. Sanford compared the conscious mind that influences the unconscious to a captain on the bridge that signals the engineer in the bowels of a ship. God, she says, has ordered these control centers to preserve the body in His image and likeness of perfection. But we can sabotage this by sending conflicting orders to the engineer down below, which confuses the system and weakens the operation. For instance, the captain sends a message to the engineer: "Oh dear I'm catching a cold." The engineer (unconscious) picks up the suggestion and orders: "catch a cold." Our white corpuscles are our defense, but a negative thought sends a contrary order and confuses (and weakens) them.[9]

Sanford taught this in the earlier part of the twentieth century, when the phenomenon of mind-body psychology was popular. The connection between negativity and our health was central to her message—and the heart of my struggle. These negatives live in our subconscious and register at the cellular level of our being, Sanford said, weakening the life-giving forces of the body (the immune system) so that we fall prey to sickness, to infections, to pain and weakness, to nervousness and to a host of maladies. Through her eyes I saw the destructive power of negative thinking; I also saw how we have the ability to reprogram our minds with positive thought habits. When we focus on God's gifts and light instead of meditating on a headache, Sanford wrote, we will build into our consciousness a new thought habit of health and eventually the positives will outweigh the negatives.

If I wanted to find inner peace—and health—I would have to silence the negative voices that ran around in my brain trying to do damage. The Bible calls this "repentance," which comes from the Greek word *metanoia*, which means to "change your thinking." But it is deeper than that. It implies transformation. In Catholic theology, repentance means a change of mind from unbelief to faith, a change of heart from sin to the practice of virtue.

But it would take more than the flip of a switch. To erase the dark side of my heart—or rather to fill it with light—meant that I would have to acknowledge and embrace its contents, to replace hatred with love, injury with pardon, despair with hope, like Saint Francis did when he kissed the leper. Although he was repelled by the sight and smell of lepers, when Saint Francis came face to face with a leper during his travels, he jumped down from his horse and kissed the leper's hand. When the leper returned the kiss, Francis was filled with joy. The story goes that as he rode off, he turned around and saw that the leper had disappeared. He always looked upon it as a test from God that he had passed.

What I was learning was a challenge: to love the hidden, depressed part of myself into life. Change would mean seeing things in a new way. The Lord raised this kind of love to the level of a commandment when He replied to the scribe's question about which was the most important commandment. The first, He said, was to love God with all your heart and mind and strength, and the second was to "Love your neighbor as yourself " (Mk12:31).

It was not a matter of choice. It was our Christian mandate: to embrace the leper within, to see one's self as God sees us and so to be transformed into a new creation: "If anyone is in Christ, she/he is a new creation; the old has passed away, behold, the new has come. All this is from God" (2 Cor 5:17,18).

Christ was an intimate friend to this prayerful woman, close by, within her own heart, always at the ready to answer even the smallest of prayers. He was power, He was light, and His love was like sunshine that was everywhere and restored life. She likened His love to divine energy that filled every cell in our bodies. The image of a porous sponge described it best. We are like sponges, Agnes said, floating in the ocean. We are in God and He is in us.

I wanted Agnes Sanford's kind of faith.

JUST BEFORE CHRISTMAS OUR first grandchild was born to our eldest son, Tom Jr. and his wife, Sinead. When I first set eyes on Tommy McHugh III, I started to cry. He looked just like his father looked when he was born. He wasn't even twelve hours old and when I approached him he looked straight into my eyes as if he knew me. Sinead and Tom Jr. arrived at our house a few days before Christmas with newborn Tommy in the Moses basket that they placed right in front of the stone hearth. Katie, Danny and Rich came from near and far, and we so enjoyed being together and welcoming the newest McHugh into the family. On Christmas morning we lit the traditional white candle to celebrate the birth of the baby Jesus, and of our own baby Tommy. With instrumental Christmas music playing in the background, my husband said, "It doesn't get any better than this."

10

Cancer Diagnosis

> Depression is a partial surrender to death, and it seems that cancer is despair experienced at the cellular level.
> —Arnold A. Hutschnecker, M.D., *The Will to Live*

AFTER CHRISTMAS I WANTED to get away to spend some quiet time in prayer. I hoped to decide which of the creative spiritual projects swirling around in my head I should undertake. My main criterion was to find a place where I could come and go as I pleased, without a set routine.

As a child I enjoyed going off by myself—into the woods, on solo bike rides or on long walks on the beach. Then later, as a teenager and in college, I sought out places where I could be alone with God. When I was in college at Marymount in Tarrytown, New York, I went for a walk one day and discovered a lake bordered with trees and brush on three sides, hidden from view except for anyone like me who wandered down a path leading to nowhere. It was my secret refuge where I often went just to commune with God. This place meant a lot to me. In some unexplained way it nourished and healed me and always sent me away a little happier than when I arrived. At my twenty-fifth college reunion, I walked down the hill from campus in heels intent on finding my hidden refuge. My heart skipped a beat: there was my bench and the scene, just as I had remembered it. I felt as if I had come home—to myself and to my God who had been so good to me in the years since my graduation from Marymount.

In early January, 1998, I phoned a retreat house in Wisconsin to book a room for a short getaway. A single room that would have a bathtub—my only request—was available in vacant wing of the complex. There was a galley kitchen in the sub-basement and a chapel on the third floor. No meals would be served in the dining room in the main part of the basilica, so the sister taking my reservation suggested I bring some TV dinners to heat in the microwave. The bookstore would be open sporadically and there would be Confession and Mass every day at noon in the main chapel.

"You will be all by yourself in that wing," she cautioned. "Will that be a problem?" "No, sister, not in the least. I will enjoy the solitude."

On the day of my departure, a blinding snowstorm swept over the Chicago area. It didn't stop me from getting in the car, although it should have, because the weather was worse in Wisconsin. My car windows kept fogging up and I had to pull over constantly to clear them. A trip that should have taken an hour and a half took three hours. When I finally crawled into the parking lot, there were tons of snow on the ground and I had to force my car into a slot that was already a foot deep with snow.

I found the "wing" without any trouble. It was just as Sister had said, ancient looking and standing tall at the very end of a complex of buildings. After a hike up three or four flights of stairs, I found my room at the end of a long hall. It was eerily empty. No sound except the blizzard outside, nowhere to go except to the kitchen or chapel, and no one to talk to except my husband when I called him on my cellphone. *Why in the world did I come here?* I thought. *I must be crazy to go through all this to just be here alone in the middle of winter.* I already missed home (the Christmas tree was still up). *Oh well, make the best of it Joan. No one is forcing you to stay here. You can leave when you want.*

I searched out the kitchen and the chapel, two places other than my cell-like room where I would spend most of my time. I took the TV dinners down to the kitchen, descending about four flights of stairs to get there. They weren't kidding about a *sub-basement.* After storing some Healthy Choice dinners in the freezer and putting away a few groceries, I was getting ready to go upstairs to find the chapel when I heard a noise, like a door shutting. A chill ran through me. No one was supposed to be in the building. Was I imagining something? Was it the wind? Was Sister coming to welcome me? Maybe this place was ghost infested. I didn't move, waiting for the noise to continue. Seconds later I heard footsteps. Someone was coming down the stairs. I froze. Should I call out or hide?

I decided to be brave and just stand there. In walked a middle-aged man who was friendly and excused himself for bothering me. He said he came here sometimes to go to Confession and Mass (*Then why was he in this sub-basement kitchen?*), and he brought a sandwich to eat (*Why didn't Sister mention him to me?*). I was growing a little uneasy when he said, "My parents drop me off and pick me up."

My heart skipped a beat. "How nice of them," I said. "Don't you drive?"

"No. They took my license away some years ago because I have a psychological problem."

Then he said, "Do you remember reading a story in the newspapers some years back about a guy who led the police on a high-speed thirty-five mile chase from Deerfield, Illinois, to Wisconsin?" I remembered the story because we used to live in Deerfield, and it was all over the local news one night.

"Yes," I said, "I remember it."

"Then you recall that when they finally stopped him and he got out of the car he was stark naked?" he said.

I knew by the weird smile on his face that he was the guy.

How could this be happening to me? How did I end up in this sub-basement with a crazy loon, for all I know a serial killer, and if anything happened to me, it would be days before anyone knew? I looked around for a knife or a weapon. I had seen an old-fashioned rolling pin and thought about casually moving towards the cupboard. The cell phone that I *always* had with me was upstairs. *Dear God in heaven. Please help me.*

He liked to talk and seemed starved for company. So we talked for maybe two minutes. My confusion deepened. I couldn't figure out if he was totally insane or totally innocent. The tip off that he might be harmless was his parents. *Why would parents of an insane serial killer drop their son off at this revered basilica?* The conversation switched to faith and he told me that he was genuinely grateful to his parents for taking care of him. As soon as he said that, I relaxed. *God bless them*, I thought, and *God bless this man* who struggles through life with such a mental disability. I had come full circle from wanting to stab him to wanting to hug him. This honest man was blessed by his faith that gave him strength and purpose. I would pray for him.

When I went upstairs to my room I made the mistake of calling Tommy and telling him about my encounter. "What?" he shrieked, "you have

no business being there by yourself. It is not safe. You must come home!"
I reassured him that the danger had passed and not to worry because I
would be fine. While I believed this in my mind, my emotions didn't follow
suit. During my five days alone in that building, I was always on guard—
listening for noises. At night the howling wind caused strange creaking
sounds in the hallway. I had to keep reassuring myself that no one was
there and I was safe.

THE CHAPEL ON THE third floor was a spiritual haven. The red vigil light
beside the tabernacle indicated that Jesus was present. For me this was a
privileged place of encounter where I relished the thought of spending
five days sitting at the Master's feet like Mary did in the Gospels—where I
could commune with God.

On the first day at twilight as an ice storm pelted the windows of the
chapel, I felt safe and calm in this peaceful sanctuary. But my mental motor was racing as I considered my agenda: to discern which of the projects
I would undertake for our Eucharistic ministry. I wanted to do all of them
but that was unrealistic. I came away to seek guidance for which work to
do.

It seems like God had other plans. I spent the better part of the five
days in this chapel by myself where I filled a notebook with reflections,
only devoting one page to discerning the upcoming work for Witness.

My thoughts first turned to my new grandson, who I had recently held
and rocked as a newborn as if he were my own son. He resembled my first-
born son so much that I couldn't tell the difference between them. I started
to cry. My gratitude seemed to open doors of grace that just poured into
me as if through a faucet. In my desire to love my grandson, I was giving
love to myself, to my inner child who never received such affection. I must
have yearned for it and suffered because I don't think that my mother and
father were capable of giving me that kind of nurturing love. I think I was
a burden and they treated me like an object. For a few minutes I just let
this liquid love pour into me. It felt like a mother and father's love all at
once. It was the love I have craved all my life and have been trying to give
myself in so many ways and through so many people—especially through
my husband. I had been asking God to heal my heart, and it seemed like
He heard my prayers and was showering me with love to fill in all the dry
spots that were so parched for lack of love. This may have been the reason
why I felt called to get away and spend time in prayer.

Each day I trudged through the snow to attend noon Mass in the main chapel and then to spend a few minutes browsing and socializing in the bookstore. On the first day I went to Mass, the Gospel was on the healing of the man with the unclean spirit in the synagogue at Capernaum. When the spirit began speaking to the Lord, Jesus commanded the unclean spirit to leave the man saying, "Be silent, and come out of him" (Mk 1:21-28). Scripture says that they were all amazed.

When I went back to my cozy chapel, I was feeling a bit jealous and complained to God, telling Him that I had been asking for healing for years, and sometimes the pain seemed to increase rather than decrease. It had been eating me alive, so to speak, and I wondered if this was the source and origin of the scleroderma and ulcers.

I was running on empty a great deal of the time. Or, to use another analogy, my well often ran dry. I suffered periodically from feelings of desolation and repulsion that made it difficult for me to give and receive love—at a deep level. Instead, it sucked love from me. This problem had been with me my whole married life. As I wrote, the more I realized that this pain had been with me since childhood, perhaps even in the womb. I sensed that when I was born my heart was already old because it was filled with fear, anxiety, depression, the feeling of being a burden and worst of all, feeling unwanted. (I don't know how I know this, but I very deeply sense an intense state of anxiety around my birth.) When I was actually born, I felt alone and lonely and craved love and touch. Although I know that my parents loved me, I don't think I received this warm nurturing love from them and as a result I blocked off a part of my heart. It was almost as if that part of my heart atrophied; blood couldn't flow through it and I almost died from a lack of love. I think part of me did die. Or, to use another analogy, my heart was paralyzed or frozen which made it difficult for me to give and receive love.

Part of me broke off from depression and I built walls to protect myself from pain. The walls kept others out, but they also cut me off from myself. My feelings of abandonment, rejection and loneliness were always so intense because I buried that part of myself alive, so to speak. This split me in two. In place of the real me that was buried, I adopted a persona that tried to please others and behaved in certain ways in order to win love. I grew up trying to be somebody else, somebody that would be loved and accepted. I concealed my real self from everyone, especially my parents, because I was ashamed of myself and thought I wouldn't be loved. As I wrote, I realized the damage this did to me. I repressed shame, fear, hurt and sadness. I didn't know how to "be myself," to be loved for who I was and not for what I could accomplish. It was no wonder I was so driven. I didn't know who I was!

The Lord was answering my prayer for healing by showing me the barriers to love that surrounded my heart. I realized that it was the hidden, shadow part of myself that felt pain when someone or something triggered it, usually my husband. When we don't acknowledge our shadow side, "the enemy now appears in the guise of other people," wrote Jungian analyst John Sanford, "and the hostility that has its origin in ourselves takes the form of hostility to others."[1] For many years I worried that that if I got in touch with emotions that I had buried, they would overwhelm me. But I was beginning to realize that the exact opposite is true. When we ignore the repressed hidden parts of ourselves, we project them onto others. In this way we think we are dealing with our problems but in reality we force others to carry the burden of our own darkness. Then we cut off those on whom we project our feelings, thinking that they are causing our pain. John Sanford and other psychologists maintain that when we acknowledge our inner enemy, we diminish its power over us and are on the road to healing and wholeness.

Before going to bed one night, I asked the Lord to give me a dream that would reveal the root of the pain in my marriage. At 3 A.M. I woke up and went to the chapel where I said the Chaplet of Divine Mercy and a Rosary, praying for many people. When I went back to bed at 4:00 A.M. I had a powerful dream. The main message seemed to be that I was enraged at being left out. The rage was deep and was directed at my husband, whom I realized was not responsible for my pain. At the core of me I felt unwanted and resented others for not giving themselves to me, when really the problem was inside of me. This is what I wrote: *Being unwanted and left out is my core issue. Until I heal it, I will continue to leave others out. We perpetuate what has been done to us. Perhaps that is why I want to leave Tommy. I want to leave anyone or anything when I am not getting my needs met. Cut them off. Lord, I can feel the enormity of the pain underneath. It is like a tidal wave dammed up. Once the wall breaks, it will come crashing down with a fury and a force that is enormous.*

I knew that God was answering my cry for help. I wrote what I sensed He was saying to me: *"If you continue in my word, you are truly my disciples, and you will know the truth, and the truth will make you free" (Jn 8:31). I am the Truth and when you seek Me, you will uncover Love and Truth. You will find Me and you will recover your own self as well. I yearn to give My children their inheritance, a full measure of life and love, brimming over with joy. You are a child of the King. Everything in my kingdom belongs to you my daughter. You have only to ask.*

I left the retreat feeling deeply peaceful, grateful and hopeful. I was excited by my experience of sensing the nearness of the Lord who opened a window into my soul to show me my brokenness. Seeing it brought compassion—and hope—for myself, and for my marriage.

WHEN I GOT HOME from Wisconsin, the Lord confirmed the lessons about brokenness I had learned at the retreat in a book I was reading about inner healing. *Broken but Loved*,[2] was written by Fr. George Maloney, S.J., the founder of the John XXIII Institute for Eastern Christian Studies at Fordham University. This brilliant Jesuit is recognized worldwide for his works on prayer and Eastern Christian Spirituality. In a chapter titled "I Am Broken," he explains how deeply we human beings crave love and how unfree we really are to give and receive love. I couldn't believe what I was reading! It was my exact struggle. It all had to do with unfulfilled needs, he wrote, that cry out from our depths to be fulfilled.

He quoted from Dr. Arthur Janov, who originated "Primal Therapy" and is one of the world's leading psychologists, who claims that our unfulfilled early childhood needs are "the primal pains." These pains, Dr. Janov maintains, create a split between one's *real* self (the subject of such desired needs) and one's *unreal* self (created in defense to avoid greater pain). An excerpt from Janov's *The Primal Scream*, was so applicable to my experience that I include it here:

> The child is born into his parents' needs and begins struggling to fulfill them almost from the moment he is alive. He may be pushed to smile (to appear happy), to coo, to wave bye-bye, later to sit up and walk, still later to push himself so that his parents can have an advanced child. As the child develops, the requirements upon him become more complex. He will have to get A's, to be helpful and do his chores, to be quiet and understanding, not to talk too much, to say bright things, to be athletic. What he will not do is be himself . . . . Each time a child is not held when he needs to be, each time he is shushed, ridiculed, ignored, or pushed beyond his limits, more weight will be added to his pool of hurts . . . . As the assaults on the real system mount, they begin to crush the real person.[3]

Father Maloney spoke to the heart of my issue. As we grow our split widens, he said. We strive to live according to our unreal selves because it is less painful and we don't even know we've lost our spontaneity and our freedom. We think we are our real self and don't know we are postulating. But when someone temporarily unmasks our unreal self, he wrote, we can become fiercely aggressive. I felt like he wrote the following two sentences just for me: "We treat them who often truly love us as though they were our great enemies. This is seen often in the hate-love ambivalence found among married couples."[4]

"Ask and you shall receive" Jesus said (Jn 16:24). At the retreat the Lord showed me the inner fracture that resulted from the separation in myself. Was this the crack in the foundation that I saw in the basement of my "inner house" at Hazelden? I think so. At home I learned the psychological reasons for the pain. What the next step was I didn't know, but I felt grateful that I was getting a handle on my emotional problems.

ABOUT A WEEK AFTER my retreat in Wisconsin, I came home from doing errands one afternoon, took my coat off, and the phone was ringing. My gastroenterologist asked me to stop by the office "at my convenience" to discuss the results of a recent endoscopy. She was trying to sound nonchalant. *Why didn't the nurse call with the results like she usually did?* Something was up and it was not good. A few hours later Tommy and I sat across from Dr. Cynthia Wait in her office, expecting the worst.

She was one of my favorite doctors, with a sunshine personality. I had often thought I'd like to be her friend. "First, the good news" she said, "Your ulcers are gone." All I could think of was that my homespun remedies had worked. I was thrilled. "Now, I don't want to alarm you, but the biopsies I took of your stomach turned up a population of B-lymphocyte cells consistent with lymphoma." *Did she say "lymphoma?"* I couldn't believe my ears. The word "lymphoma" hung in the air like a poisonous tarantula. *No, no, no I silently screamed, this is impossible.*

In a rather upbeat tone of voice, she carefully explained that it was a type known as "MALT," fairly new in the world of medicine. It was discovered as recently as 1993 in studies conducted in Switzerland, Italy and Germany. They found that this type of lymphoma is usually associated with a bacteria called, "H. pylori." After aggressive antibiotic treatment, it usually regresses, though twenty percent of people don't respond. Then came the best part: "The research suggests that this is a very non-aggressive, slow growing lymphoma" the doctor said slowly and emphatically, "and it will let you live a long life." Perhaps the spider was not so deadly after all.

She recommended I make an appointment with an oncologist and gave me the name of one whom I still see today. *Oncologist? Lymphoma? This can't be happening!* I made an appointment as soon as I got home.

One week later I was sitting in the oncologist's office and trying to keep a lid on my anxiety, assuring myself that I didn't look like the cancer patients in the waiting room. Some looked pretty sick. A gentle and rather laid back, tall Lebanese female doctor calmed my fears, reassuring me that the type of cancer I had was so indolent that it was probably best to leave it alone and do nothing; just observe its behavior. On one hand that was reassuring; on the other hand, it was a bit unnerving. She recommended a bone marrow test for which I could schedule another appointment or I could do it now in the office. *Now,* I said, wondering what form of torture this would take. I wanted get it over with rather than go through the worry of waiting for it.

It would be the first of three or four of these gruesome tests. I prayed for courage and looked out the window during the procedure imagining Jesus being nailed to the Cross. If He could endure nails being hammered into His wrists and feet, then I could bear a little poke in the hip! But it was more than a poke; it was rather like boring a screw into the bone. Even with Novocain, it was deep, grinding pain. Offering it up for my family helped me endure it.

The bone marrow test was normal, thank God! But a subsequent CT scan showed three questionable areas: the thyroid, the right lung and a lymph node behind the sternum. A thyroid scan ruled out any imminent danger, but I would need to monitor it closely. The lung and lymph node involvements were small and just needed watching. No treatment was recommended—for the time being.

I was in my third year of receiving monthly intravenous clindamycin treatments for scleroderma that now was "controlled," according to the doctor. That was somewhat of a relief.

DEALING WITH THESE HEALTH issues distracted me from my work and from focusing on what writing project I would undertake next. This was one of the main reasons I had gone to Wisconsin in the first place, to decide which of the ideas on the table was worth pursuing. In reality I had been home from Wisconsin three weeks and hadn't thought about any of this—until one morning when I awakened at 5 A.M. with a brainstorm: *Why not turn the DVD on* The Real Presence *into a book?* I couldn't believe I hadn't thought of this before. I woke up Tommy to see what he thought of this idea. *Hmmmmnnnnn, interesting,* he said, *better than your other ideas,* then he went back to sleep. At least he didn't squelch it or say it was off the wall, which he often did with some of my brainstorms.

I couldn't go back to sleep.

That day happened to be the Feast of St. Thomas Aquinas, *the* theologian in the Church whose life centered in his belief in the Real Presence of Christ in the Eucharist. He was my husband's patron saint, to whom I had developed a strong devotion because of his love of the Eucharist. Was he was paying me back for the chapter I wrote about him in my first book, *Feast of Faith: Confessions of a Eucharistic Pilgrim?* At Mass I wondered if this inspiration to turn the DVD into a book came from him. It also occurred to me that this could be an answer to my prayer in Wisconsin.

My favorite story about St. Thomas Aquinas took place when he was teaching at the University of Paris and some of his fellow professors challenged him with a question about the mystical change in the elements of the Blessed Sacrament. He prayed for guidance, we are told, and then wrote a thesis that he placed at the foot of the crucifix on the altar. He left it lying there, as if awaiting judgment. According to the friars who witnessed it, he returned to his seat and seemed lost in prayer when the figure of Christ came down from the cross and stood on the scroll saying, "Thomas, thou hast written well concerning the Sacrament of My Body."[5] Then the saint was borne up miraculously in mid-air. He was 30 years old.

The reason why I love this story is because Our Lord manifested Himself physically to Saint Thomas in order to acknowledge His Real Presence in the Eucharist. Another reason is because it inspired me to place all my writing projects on the altar, if not actually, then intentionally.

At Mass I thanked St. Thomas Aquinas for the idea to turn the DVD into a book. I also asked for his guidance. While the DVD presented the highlights of Eucharistic revelation, this book would require *much* additional research. Then there was the matter of locating the art. I had no idea how one could possibly find all the art necessary for a book of this nature. The enormity of the task was worrisome. But not really; I would find a way. Besides, I was thankful to be back in the groove again, devoting my time to something I cared about so much. It took my mind off the new health threats and afforded me the luxury of filling my days with productive—and enjoyable—work.

I DON'T KNOW WHICH was more energizing: researching the theology of the Eucharist, or searching for appropriate art to accompany the essays. My husband and I were both amateur art connoisseurs. Wherever we traveled in the States or in Europe, we usually visited art galleries and occasionally purchased a treasure that we could afford.

I can pinpoint the time when I first began to appreciate art. It was in high school, junior year to be exact. Mother McCaffrey, R.S.C.J. (I never knew her first name) a plump and loving grandmother-type nun who taught the history of art, combined historical background with details that made paintings come to life. Her slight irreverence appealed to me as did her Irish wit. Mother McCaffrey liked me and often called on me. I usually had an answer and wasn't afraid to raise my hand. She made me feel good about myself, as if I had a brain.

In most classes we counted the minutes till the bell rang, but not in hers. I usually went up to her desk after class to chat about something. One day she asked me if anything was wrong. I didn't seem myself, she said, I looked tired, and she was concerned about me. I wanted to burst into tears. Instead, I slipped on my suit of armor that protected me from such outbursts. "Really," I lied, "I'm fine." My mother was in the psych ward at the Reese Pavilion in St. Vincent's Hospital. My father gave me taxi money every night so that I could visit her after school. Then I'd come home, cook dinner for my dad and do homework. I was physically and emotionally exhausted. Mother McCaffrey picked up on this and I regret to this day that I didn't have the courage to tell her the truth.

My denial was so deep it silenced me. I simply didn't have a voice. The words would not come out of my mouth. Repress and deny; that was my style. No one knew, not even my best friend, Kandy.

At Prize Day in June, pupils who had excelled in a subject that year received a certificate of recognition for their work. It was usually the top students in the class who received these awards year after year. In June, 1958, during graduation ceremonies, I heard my name called: "The History of Art Prize is awarded to Joan Carter." I was stunned. This was the first and only prize I received in all the twelve years I attended Sacred Heart. As I walked up to receive the honor, I felt like I had made it—as a person. Words can't describe my joy. I have loved art ever since.

How I would find all the art necessary to fill a coffee table book on the Eucharist was now consuming me day and night. I went to our local library and spent hours pouring through books of religious art. While leafing through a book illustrated with works of the Great Masters, I came across a painting of *The Madonna of the Grapes and the Child Jesus* that was so beautiful, I wondered if I would want to include it in my new book. An art museum in Boston owned the copyright. When I got home I phoned the museum. The young man who took my call not only answered my questions about copyright permission, he pointed me to some art libraries in New York that stored thousands of images on computers. I had no idea such places even existed and felt as if I had just stumbled upon the entrance to a gold mine. This one tip really jump-started the book. I phoned one of these art libraries and within minutes, they faxed me about twenty images of *The Last Supper*. (Email was in existence but I was not yet set up for it.) They were in black and white but I could imagine how magnificent they would look in color. *The Madonna of the Grapes* never made it into the book, but, in hindsight, I sense that Our Lady was behind this endeavor.

I was on the phone constantly asking these computer librarians to fax me images of Eucharistic themes such as *The Manna in the Desert, The Wedding Feast of Cana,* and of course of my good friend, *St. Thomas Aquinas.* Each one eventually made it into *Eucharist God Among Us.*[6]

I had a gut sense about the story-telling potential of art. I was not interested in being a commentator like the talented art historian, Sister Wendy; rather I wanted to use art as a visual aid to enrich the historical essays and to foster meditation. For people like myself who are visual, art would help place readers in a scene and personalize it for them. (*Eucharist God Among Us* has since found its way into chapels of Eucharistic Adoration all across the country where people use the art for meditation.)

Of the many religious paintings used to illustrate my books, two belonging to French master Nicolas Poussin are my favorites. He spent many years in Rome under the patronage of several Italian cardinals who commissioned him to paint works for Saint Peter's Basilica. When Louis XIII called him back to Paris in 1641, he painted *The Last Supper* for one of the royal chapels in Versailles. (It now hangs in the Louvre—and this image is also on the cover of my book on *The Mass.*) Poussin also painted another version of *The Last Supper* which hangs in The National Gallery of Art in Edinburgh, Scotland. I have framed photographic copies of both of them (treated to look like oil paintings) displayed on my office wall. In one of them, the Apostles are gathered around a table with Jesus in the center, and they are either sitting or laying on couches listening intently to Him. It is subtle, but Jesus is pointing to His heart at the same time that many of them are putting something (bread?) in their mouths. Poussin wants us to understand that Jesus is saying at that moment, "This is My Body." It is a stunning image, a study in color and realism.

For me these paintings not only lead to prayer, they *are* prayer!

11

Losses and Gains

The Bible is the story of God constantly calling His people out of something: out of chaos, out of Egypt, out of captivity, out of darkness, out of the depths, out of trouble. And so He calls us out of depression. But God does not just call us out of something, but into something else, something better. He calls from chaos to creation, from Egypt to the Promised Land, from darkness into His own wonderful light. Depression, then, can be the occasion for moving into a new stage of emotional and spiritual growth.

—Fr. Martin Padovani, *Healing Wounded Emotions*

IN THE SPRING OF 1998 we led a *Witness Ministries* pilgrimage to Italy. I was grateful to have enough stamina to even make the trip, let alone do a lot of sightseeing. The scleroderma that was now under control slowed me down, but really didn't hinder me from doing all the things we planned.

We were forty-four strangers (though several couples who were friends came on the trip) at the start, but it took no time for us to bond together through our shared faith. We looked at the towns we visited and the saints who made these cities famous through a Eucharistic lens, so to speak, because it was our love of the Eucharist that drew us together in the first place.

We literally walked in the footsteps of some of the Church's most beloved saints (Thomas Aquinas, Francis and Clare of Assisi, Rita of Cascia, Catherine of Siena, Benedict, Peter, Paul and Padre Pio) and visited their cities: Orvieto, Bolsena, Siena, Florence, Assisi, Cascia, Lanciano, San Giovanni Rotundo and Rome. I wrote extensively about many of these saints in my first memoir, *Feast of Faith: Confessions of a Eucharistic Pilgrim*, the trip Tommy and I took in 1992. For the cover of that book I used a stunning painting of St. Clare holding up the Blessed Sacrament to defend her community from the invading Saracens. During this pilgrimage we read from their biographies and spiritual writings. I dare to say that this trip, which really resembled a retreat, was a watershed moment in the life of each and every pilgrim!

We kept up a grueling schedule, thanks to the energy and spirit of the group, who never complained or let their fatigue show. An affable Dutch woman who was traveling by herself, Margaret from California, who enjoyed saying, "If you ain't Dutch you ain't much," tripped on a step in the hotel in Assisi and sprained her ankle. We brought her to the local hospital where they X-rayed her and taped her up. Margaret found out when she returned home to California that she had suffered a fracture. The hospital personnel in Assisi actually gave us a rickety old wheelchair that looked like a prop from the Victorian theater; the wheels were uneven and had a mind of their own to go to the left. At first we took turns pushing Margaret until a strong and very kind gentleman named Paul took it upon himself to be her chauffeur. He somehow rigged it to go straight.

Paul pushed Margaret's wheelchair for the remaining seven days of the trip. On our final day in Rome we had tickets for an outdoor Mass that Pope John Paul II was scheduled to celebrate on an altar in front of Saint Peter's. When one of the officials was seating our group, he saw the wheelchair and directed Margaret and Paul down an aisle of barricades. We thought they might end up with people in other wheelchairs, which they did, but to our great joy and utter amazement, we saw Paul wheeling Margaret onto the stage just feet from where the Holy Father would say Mass! It was a spectacular moment. We cheered and waved, rejoicing that our fellow travelers were rewarded for their struggles with such an honor. We were with them in spirit on that stage—forty-four strangers from all over the United States—bonded together by our faith and love of our Eucharistic Lord. We were, in the words of Saint Paul, one body, "one body in Christ" (Rom 12:5).

GOING ON A PILGRIMAGE is a little bit like flying. It lifts you up into a rarified atmosphere, above the din and chaos of everyday problems where you have space and time to appreciate the wonders of God's world. But I came crashing back down to earth rather quickly when we arrived home because I had to schedule a follow-up CT scan and an endoscopic ultrasound that my doctor had recommended. The latter was a more sophisticated—and scary—procedure that would monitor the extent of the lymphoma in my stomach. The thought of swallowing a camera was frightening. I had it done at the Medical College of Wisconsin in Milwaukee. It was tolerable only because of the twilight sleep they administer to make you unconscious.

A few days later the gastroenterologist reached me on my cell phone while I was driving home from an appointment with my scleroderma doctor. "You have persistent malignant lymphoma" he reported, "which shows deep involvement of the tissues." I pulled over.

He was a "bare bones" kind of doctor, which is to say he was brusque and in a hurry. I had the feeling that while he was talking to me he was looking at the next report on his desk before he called another patient. I made him stay on the phone. "Doctor, please tell me what this means?" "I don't know for sure" came the response, "but we should keep a close watch on it so that it doesn't penetrate the stomach wall," he said matter-of-factly. "But exactly how deep is the involvement, and what does that really mean?" I pressed. "I told you all I know" he said, "these are tumors that need watching. So far, they haven't penetrated the stomach wall." I wasn't satisfied. "How long will it take before they penetrate and can I do anything about them now?" I wanted to know. "No" he said without explaining why we shouldn't do anything. "Let's just keep a close watch, OK?" He was done and I was angry and upset. "OK doctor. Thanks." Click.

"Persistent malignant lymphoma." The thought of it was frightening. I kept repeating it to myself in disbelief, as if a judge had just sentenced me to death. I inwardly collapsed and cried all the way home.

On the heels of that news came more problems: a negative CT scan report and a flare-up of scleroderma. The CT scan showed that the lymph node behind the sternum was growing. It had gone from two to two and a half centimeters. What to do? Nothing, the doctor said, because it wasn't large enough—yet. The scleroderma flare came on suddenly and just about paralyzed me. It may have come from stress created by the new scares—the lymphoma diagnosis and the recent enlarged lymph node. When I walked I looked like someone a hundred years old. Fortunately I could drive and went for daily intravenous antibiotic treatments that slowly brought me out of the flare. It was a difficult time, full of anxiety and especially, fear of the unknown.

All of this set the stage for another ulcer. I was back on the Spartan diet, Prilosec and twelve glasses of water a day.

No sooner would I work through one problem than another would surface. I lost weight (a good thing!) but I was also losing my grip emotionally. As much as I tried to pray and surrender my life to the Lord—and I did every day at Mass—I took it back constantly, often feeling depressed. I cried at the drop of a hat and felt sorry for myself.

Then a new—but really old—worry surfaced. Had I brought this illness on through my own fault? Was God punishing me for my sins? I knew the answer. It was "no," but I think my own sense of guilt was making me anxious. Most afternoons I put my feet up in the Barcalounger to rest. While reading Scripture one day, I stumbled onto the answer to my question about sin in relation to illness. In the story about the man who was born blind, the disciples asked the Lord, "Rabbi, who sinned, this man or his parents, that he was born blind?" Jesus answered, "It was not that this man sinned, or his parents, but that the works of God might be made manifest in him" (Jn 9:2-3). There it was. Sin had nothing to do with this man's affliction. God had allowed it in order to manifest His glory. Jesus made clay with mud, put it on his eyes and told him to go and wash in the pool of Siloam.

We had visited this site during our Holy Land pilgrimage and it was nothing like what I had imagined. It is a narrow channel of water flowing out of a tunnel that was built in the days of King Hezekiah (715-687 B.C.) to supply Jerusalem with water in case of a siege. Tourists accessed the pool by climbing down a steep narrow set of stairs. Initially the scene looked very uninteresting until the priest read the passage from the Gospel in which Jesus directed the blind man to go and wash his eyes in the Pool of Siloam. I could visualize the blind man kneeling down and washing the mud off his eyes in the spot where we were standing. Scripture says that he went and washed and received his sight.

While listening to the Gospel I was trying to relate to the blind man. Although I am not physically blind, I thought about how I have been blind to my own denial, to the ways I have been dishonest with myself. The real prayer, it seemed to me, was not to beg God for this or that, but to ask to see with the eyes of faith. I think that the Lord was asking me the same question He asked the blind man: "Do you believe in the Son of Man?" (Jn 9:35). A "yes" answer was an invitation to God to manifest His glory—through me!

In late spring I went back to Hazelden for a 12 Step "tune up" at the

Renewal Center. I wanted to work on breaking my codependent patterns of behavior so that I could stop giving others power—especially Tommy—to ruin my peace and joy. (Initially, I thought that by understanding codependence, I would get over it. It was not that easy.) Tommy planned to join me at the end of the week for a couples retreat.

Soon after arriving I was making a cup of tea when two women asked me to join them. What I love most about Hazelden is that everyone there is working on their lives and trying to take responsibility for their problems, be they related to addictions or relationships or both. There is a refreshing air of openness and honesty among the retreatants, who are unafraid to cut to the quick and share their struggles. One of the women was struggling in her marriage. Her husband was a successful attorney and quite outgoing socially, she said, but at home he was depressed and withdrawn. She had been married for thirty-one years and was at the end of her rope. At the time he was undergoing a thirty-eight day in-house treatment for alcoholism, but was always on the phone to his office and wanted to bolt. She feared that the next step would be for her to move out. She wondered why she should have to move out. She recently had taken a three-month sabbatical and went to their home in Colorado where she painted and felt so free and happy.

I felt her pain. While my situation was quite different, I struggled with wanting to separate. I didn't believe in divorce ("In sickness and in health until death do us part") and felt that God willed our covenant relationship. Our life together had been blessed in so many ways, I simply couldn't imagine walking away from it. Yet I thought about it.

When I met with my former counselor we went over the same ground as before. I told her that I thought I was part of the problem, that I'm probably to blame for being very controlling, judgmental and critical. I didn't like the person I was becoming and wanted to figure out what I needed to do to change. I asked her how there could be so much success and gift in one area of my life, and so much pain and darkness in another. I had been riding this seesaw my whole life and wanted to get off.

She responded by asking me what I got out of our relationship; she said the bottom line is that my needs are not being met. She gave me an assignment: to write a letter to my husband expressing my needs. She said that I am a very giving person and its time to think about my needs being met in this marriage and to face the fact that maybe they won't be met. Then I will have another decision if Tommy doesn't want to meet these needs. But the monkey will be off my back. I will be putting the burden where it belongs. I told her that I couldn't carry it anymore; it was making me physically sick.

I wrote two letters. I tore up the first one because it was laced with anger. In the second, I wrote plainly and honestly about my need for emotional connection that would require openness and honesty on his part. I felt that he knew more about me than I did about him and I asked him to stop hiding behind humor. Initially I was attracted by his sense of humor. His timing was better than Bob Hope's (according to me) and he always made me laugh. But eventually I felt diminished by his sarcasm and put-downs, which sometimes reduced me to tears. Also I told him that I needed him to pay real attention to me, to listen with his heart, and not just give me lip service. I was tired of feeling alone and lonely in the relationship: I wrote: *I've been trapped in fear and a sense of hopelessness that no matter what, it won't work between us. When I'm away from you I realize what a gift you are to me. My goal is to realize that when I am with you!* I ended by telling him that I felt more hope and gratitude than I have in a long time for all that he has been to me, and that I wanted to recover our relationship and make it great—like it was when we started.

I think that writing the letter was a way of detaching, of letting go of trying to control and manipulate my husband into meeting my needs. This way I was up front and open, not hiding behind anger. After mulling over what I had learned in the lectures and from the counselors, I realized that my main relationships were damaged: first, my relationship with myself, second, my relationship with Tommy and third, my relationship with God. I wrote in my journal: *Today I realized why God brought me here. I'm seeing that I have to repair my spirituality by focusing on my negative spiritual issues: blaming, judging, criticizing, isolating, selfishness, control. It seems like I'm having a nervous breakdown. I'm like a raw wound, especially around my husband.*

When I asked to see a psychologist to be evaluated for depression, they assigned me to meet with a minister-turned-psychologist. After telling my story, I filled out a lengthy questionnaire. The result? He said that I suffer from a "moderately severe" depression. He emphasized that it is not a minor one.

This stunned me. Me? Depressed? It was difficult to wrap my brain around this because I still saw depression as my mother's problem. And I was certainly not like her. Or was I? He asked if I'd consider going on a drug. Yes, I said. One of my college roommates had pretty well convinced me how well the drug she took for depression was working for her. Looking back, I think that this psychologist did me a favor. He was the first professional person to name my problem. When I walked out of his office, I remember thinking, "This is serious. The jig is up. Now I will have to deal with this."

As always I felt grateful to be at Hazelden and thanked the Holy Spirit for inspiring me to go there. I kept a running commentary in my journal: *It is becoming apparent to me that this is true spirituality, getting in touch with what is true in me, sharing it, processing it and then integrating it with faith. To stress faith without getting in touch with ourselves is to live in an idealistic place. That is unreal.*

On the afternoon of the third day I took a walk and said the Joyful Mysteries of the Rosary. I enjoyed the warmth of the sun, but also felt a new inner glow. Here was my prayer: Annunciation: *Thank you God, for the Good News You have been announcing to me here at Hazeldon; for blowing a trumpet of truth through these lectures, these people who share so deeply of their struggles, their hearts, their hopes, their failures. Just to be here is an "annunciation."* Visitation: *Please Mary and Jesus be present when Tommy and I have our visitation with each other this coming weekend. Bring Your Holy Spirit into the middle of us so that we can give and receive truth and love.* Birth of Our Lord: *Jesus, new life is awakening in me. Thank you! New love. Please help me give birth to Your love in everyone I meet so that they can see You, know You, love You. I am such a poor example. All I can do is to love others, treat them with respect and sensitivity, and You will do the rest!* Presentation: *I pray in thanksgiving for what You have presented to me here, for the learning, the new awareness, and the new path You have shown me. Please help me integrate this psychology into my spirituality to share with others, and please help me present my letter to Tommy with love. Please be in the presentation.* Finding in the Temple: *Please, oh please, help me find peace, love, joy, and fulfillment in my relationship with Tommy, in the temple of our marriage, our sacrament, our lives and our children. Please continue to draw my children into Your perfect will for their lives. Amen.*

On the last morning before I met Tommy for the couples retreat, I felt peaceful. I was in a better place than when I arrived and felt as if I had a new handle on my life. *Gloria from Texas left today with her son Bill. She is a very special lady who inspired me by her loving example. She's had a lot to deal with but through it all (her husband was in the treatment center) she cares for people and brings out the best in everyone. I have a new love for people and yes, for myself. And of course for Tommy and my children. Thank you Jesus for sending me here. I phoned our family doctor to set up an appointment for next Tuesday so he can prescribe a drug for the depres-*

sion. I read today it is due to a breakdown in neuro-transmitters. I wonder if that will stabilize me so I won't always be in this pain. We'll see. I'm hopeful.

Tommy read my letter and appreciated my honesty; he said he felt the love that prompted it. He also said that he wanted to give me what I needed and that he would try. The timing of the couples retreat couldn't have been better. It was really an answer to my prayer for emotional connection. We learned some techniques of sharing such as making the following statements: I feel mad because…, I want …, and I feel …. We practiced "active listening" which brought us more laughter than anything else. We each took turns speaking for five minutes while our partners listened. Then our spouses had to feed back to us what we said. It was hysterical. It was apparent how poorly we really do listen to each other. This was the experience of the other couples as well. We practiced this for hours, and then went home where we assumed that our new listening skills would kick in automatically. They didn't.

ON THE WAY BACK to Chicago we spent an afternoon in Stillwater, Minnesota, browsing in the Loome bookstore, no doubt one of the largest used religious bookstores in the U.S. It was an old mission church converted into a store. I don't know which one of us loves a bookstore more, my husband or myself. We spent hours canvassing the stacks where we discovered not one, but two special artists whose paintings were a gift for our new book. We first came across a turn-of-the-century edition of *The Life of Our Lord Jesus Christ* illustrated by James Tissot. A popular French artist who painted provocative social scenes at the end of the nineteenth century, Tissot experienced a "divine revelation" while sketching in a church and spent the next ten years in the Holy Land retracing the footsteps of Christ. Tissot eventually gained international renown for his illustrations of the entire Old and New Testaments.

We also found a book illustrating the religious paintings of Carl Bloch, a Dane, who painted around the same time as Tissot. His historical paintings of the life of Jesus are known and valued all over the world. They, along with Tissot's images, would add a special warmth and vitality to *Eucharist God Among Us.* We chose Carl Bloch's representation of the Last Supper for the cover. I had never even heard of these artists and leaving the bookstore I was as happy as if I had just discovered gold.

AT HOME I SAW our family doctor to request medicine for depression.

I think deep down I didn't want to really take it. I listened to the pros and cons and then told him not to bother writing a prescription. My gut told me that I needed emotional root canals and once I did the inner work, I wouldn't be depressed.

Later that year, in October of 1999, Dr. Mercola noted that my scleroderma was in remission. It was a stunning triumph, considering the fact that it is a chronic, progressive and usually fatal disease for which there is no cure. In the United States 300,000 people suffer from this disease and of those, approximately thirty percent of them die within five years. Remission didn't mean that I was totally free of symptoms; I think my hands will always be slightly hard and swollen. But that is minor considering what the disease could have done to me. I discontinued the antibiotics, which was a relief. I had been on them for too long and had a sense that it was overkill, not knowing if they might have contributed to the recurrence of ulcers.

IN NOVEMBER MY ROOMMATE from Marymount, Ann Marie Lynch, called, asking if our coffee table book, *Eucharist God Among Us*, would be printed in time to exhibit it at the University Club book fair in Washington, D.C. in December. We rushed a color proof of the cover and the upfront pages to Washington to be reviewed by the selection committee. I was on pins and needles, hoping that a religious book would be an acceptable entry alongside mostly history and political submissions from the District. Not only did they approve it, Ann Marie said, but also they would be *honored* to include this magnificent book in their exhibit.

The book displayed beautifully and attracted many buyers. Our exhibit table was adjacent to that of author David Maraniss, who wrote a biography of the legendary football coach, Vince Lombardi. We had a lot to talk about with Maraniss as my dad had been a good friend of Lombardi's and Tommy and I had been to dinners in his honor in Teaneck, New Jersey. Other people who exhibited at the book fair were Catholic author George Weigel, popular writer Michael Farquhar, Michael Isikoff who wrote a book about President Clinton, NPR radio talk show host Diane Rehm, and White House reporter Helen Thomas. It seemed like all of Washington turned out for this event and we had a wonderful time meeting and greeting so many interesting people. Among them was a longtime friend of the McHugh family, Fr. Bill Byron, S.J., former president of The Catholic University of America and a prolific author himself, who stopped by our book table. He was so impressed with *Eucharist God Among Us* he said he would find a way to put the pages in a binder to use in the classroom. Score one for success!

My worries about including our book in this book fair were unfounded. *Eucharist God Among Us* ranked third highest in sales for the evening. If this small victory was any indication of how the book would sell in the open market, it was a sure sign of success. Just why it did so well in such a secular environment I'll probably never know.

TOWARDS THE END OF 1999 the Church was preparing for an event of great significance: the Great Jubilee Year 2000. The jubilee is mentioned in the Old Testament where it occurred every fifty years. It was a time during which slaves and prisoners were freed, debts forgiven and the mercies of God were manifested. Pope Bonifice VIII convoked a holy year for the first time in the Church in 1300. Since that time the Church has celebrated jubilees every 25 or 50 years.

It would begin when Pope John Paul II opened the Holy Door of Saint Peter's Basilica shortly before midnight Mass on December 24, 1999, and end when he closed it on January 6, 2001. Most of the time, the holy doors of the major basilicas were bricked shut. On the occasion of a jubilee year, the pope would open the door of Saint Peter's as a symbol of opening the doors of grace. Walking through it signified the passage from sin to grace, which all Christian are called to do. A pilgrim could gain the Jubilee indulgence by walking through the Holy Door provided he or she had fulfilled at least the main conditions: Confession, Communion, prayer for the Pope and renunciation of all attachment to sin.

And there were other ways to receive the indulgence: by going on pilgrimage to Rome or the Holy Land and visiting certain churches and basilicas, or one could stay at home and receive it at a church or cathedral designated by the bishop, as the Jubilee was extended to all dioceses of the world. And one could also obtain this special gift of grace by performing works of charity, fasting, or donating money to the poor.

After I received the Sacrament of Reconciliation from a Canadian bishop at an Association of Christian Therapists conference in Florida, the bishop asked the Lord to grant a Jubilee indulgence on my apostolate and my marriage. I didn't expect that and it gave me a feeling of hope—as if the Lord would honor his prayer.

We watched the "opening of the Holy Door" at the Vatican on TV that preceded midnight Mass on Christmas Eve. It was thrilling to listen to the prayers and hymns punctuated by the sounding of African elephant tusks. We watched the Holy Father, who was clad in a purple cope, push gently on the massive two-part bronze doors with his hands (as they were drawn open from the inside). He then fell to his knees on the threshold of the Basilica and prayed, clutching his silver papal crucifix. He and his entourage processed to the front of the altar where the Gospel book was enthroned, then the *schola* and the assembly intoned the *Gloria in excelsis Deo* to begin Mass. It resounded throughout the Basilica—and all the way into our living rooms.

It was a celebration of our Christian faith that formed around a Man from Galilee who attracted disciples wherever He went. The Church began with a group of people who followed "the Way" at the beginning. Their number grew rapidly and they, too, celebrated their belief in Jesus Christ with pomp and pageantry. On Palm Sunday when Jesus mounted the back of a donkey to go to Jerusalem for the Feast of Passover, the crowds lined His path with palm branches, waving them in praise and worship of the Son of God. As the procession slowly wove its way towards the city, the crowds sang and cried out, "Hosanna to the Son of David! Blessed is he who comes in the name of the Lord! Hosanna in the highest!" (Mt 21:9).

That was 2000 years ago. Today, we are still waving, singing and praising the Son of God, not on the dusty roads outside of Jerusalem, but in places of worship all over the world where people of "the Way" celebrate their faith in Christ. When Pope John Paul II entered Saint Peter's after opening the Holy Door, I felt a rush of joy and gratitude. I was never so proud and happy to belong to the Church as I was at that moment.

12

A Prayer and a Healing Dream

> Most of the time illness is not a premeditated act; all of the time
> there is some relationship between an illness and our thoughts. Noth-
> ing happens onto us; we are the happeners. The mind and body work
> together, with the body being the screen where the movie is shown.
> —Dr. Bernie S. Siegel, *Peace, Love & Healing*

IN THE NEW YEAR I was in a "wait and see" mode regarding the lymphoma and the curious lymph node that was growing behind my sternum.
The less I thought about these things the better. I had my hands full managing my emotional life, which was still in turmoil. I kept up an internal
running dialogue on whether I should take the medicine for depression
recommended by the psychologist at Hazelden. I was always on the fence
about it and never did take it.

In January 2000 I flew to New York to speak to the senior class at my
alma mater, the Convent of the Sacred Heart. These young women (wasn't
I just sitting in their place?) were polite, but seemed a bit disinterested in
my slide lecture on the Eucharist as seen through the art of the Great
Masters. It was the same presentation that had adult listeners fascinated
and engaged, and I wondered why these girls seemed bored. When the
slides ended they wanted to know if I thought women should be priests.
They were dissatisfied with my orthodox answer: "No, I don't think that
women should be priests." I gave them my best educated reasoning why
not, saying that according to the Gospels, Jesus chose a male-only priesthood, a belief that was accepted without question by the early Christians
and has remained an unbroken Tradition within the Church to this day.

It had nothing to do with His opinion about women, as if He considered them inferior. He loved and revered women, especially His mother and His many women friends whom He held in highest esteem.

I suggested that Jesus was very deliberate in everything He did and behaved in ways that opposed popular customs such as eating with "sinners" or healing people on the Sabbath. With that in mind, it would have been easy for Him to include women when He ordained the Twelve. But He didn't.

The girls disagreed with my answer. I couldn't help but think how different they were from my generation who tended blindly to accept everything we were taught. I felt proud that these young women thought for themselves, but saddened at their seeming lack of interest—or was it faith—in the Eucharist, the Sacred Mystery that is the core of our Catholic faith.

I LOVED BEING BACK IN New York. It brought back so many memories, mostly happy, and thoughts of people who were a part of the fabric of my life. I missed them—my mom and dad, Gertrude, my close friends with whom I had gone through twelve years of school, and even some old boyfriends. I thought of Mike, whom I dated on and off and who wanted to marry me, he said, and would follow me to the ends of the earth. Our hangout was the Stork Club, a swank New York nightclub where the owner, Sherman Billingsly, knew us by name and where we danced for hours on a postage stamp-sized dance floor. Afterward we would walk for blocks and Mike would sing, "They say that falling in love is wonderful" at the top of his lungs. I've lost track of him and wouldn't mind bumping into him someday just to give him a high five and say, "Remember all the fun we had?"

In New York I spent long leisurely mornings writing in my journal. The tension of my inner conflict came out in my journals: *There is more darkness in me than ever and I am powerless over it when it attacks. The heart of the ache is in my marriage relationship. One day I am at peace and count my blessings, especially for a husband who loves me and supports me in every way imaginable, and the next I want to leave and have my own life. The battle rages almost daily. An incident will trigger an emotional reaction in me that sets off alarms that blares in my ears: leave, leave, leave and you won't have this struggle anymore.*

I knew I couldn't leave because I would never be able to survive that wrenching emotional pain or the hurt it would cause our children, not to mention the both of us. In the Gospels, Jesus asked His Father to "sanctify them in the truth" (Jn 17:17). I prayed for that: *I need truth; I need to own it and live it. Please Lord, show me where the root of this pain is. I need a root canal because the nerve is exposed and it robs me of my peace and joy. Lord, I give You this pain. Consecrate me as Your child of truth and light.*

MY INTUITIVE SON RICH picked up my hidden struggle at dinner one evening, saying, "You don't seem like yourself, Mom." He said it twice during dinner, with utmost compassion. He sensed my inner struggle but I honestly didn't know how even to begin sharing my issues with him, so I didn't. I also wanted to be careful not to say anything negative about his dad, which I knew Rich wouldn't appreciate. So I kept quiet. Then he proceeded to share his problems with me, whether to follow his heart and pursue a writing career or to stay with an unfulfilling job. It would be risky to branch off by himself, and lonely, he said. My heart went out to him. I urged him to entrust his life to the Lord and risk following his heart. Ironically, we both had similar struggles. I cried myself to sleep that night, feeling more alone than ever.

The next day I walked to Saint Patrick's Cathedral for noon Mass where I used to spend lunch hours before I was married, while working for NBC-TV across the street at 30 Rockefeller Plaza. The priest talked about how God the Father speaks to us. I felt close to God the Father and asked Him to lead me down a road to light and peace. Of course I couldn't help but think of my father, whom I loved almost more in his absence than I did when he was alive. But here in New York City, my home, I missed him so much and the tears flowed freely—and embarrassingly—down my cheeks.

The priest said that God speaks to us through prophets, and they can be friends or experiences in our daily life. Do we listen to them? We don't listen, he said, and this is the problem. Prophets see problems as stepping-stones to growth. They invite us to hear a lesson for life. He suggested that we review the prophets in our lives and experiences—and God will speak through them saying, "Today when you hear His voice, do not harden your hearts" (Heb 3:7). The truth was I *had* heard God speak to me through doctors, friends, authors, counselors, my husband and my own children. I trusted that He was using these people to guide me—every step of the way.

I made one last stop before leaving Saint Patrick's, at a side altar dedicated to St. John Baptiste de la Salle that my grandfather, Domenico Borgia, built. I only learned that he was the artist about ten years ago through a second cousin who searched me out through Witness, the quarterly magazine we once published. Mary Ann La Cava was my great aunt's daughter who lived in Connecticut and knew a great deal about our family history. She told me about the work my grandfather had done in Saint Patrick's (and also about the altar he designed at a Catholic Church in Binghamton, New York that we subsequently visited). In Saint Patrick's he also may have designed the main altar rail, Mary Ann said, but we have never been able to verify that. Stopping at the St. John Baptist de la Salle altar where I light candles for my children is now a ritual whenever I go to New York. Then I deliberately look for my grandfather's name, "D. Borgia," carved in the lower right hand corner of the base. I never knew him but this gives me a connection to him.

AFTER MASS I MET Richard at Barnes & Noble. I was overjoyed to find a lone copy of *Anatomy of an Illness* by Norman Cousins that a friend had urged me to read. Richard bought some books on writing, and then we sat in overstuffed chairs in Starbucks to read them while we sipped our coffee. It was a joy to share a common interest in writing and reading with Richard. He is such a talented writer—and editor—with an innate sense of style. Richard is a best-selling author in the making.

I knew very little about Norman Cousins, the once-popular editor of the *New York Evening Post* and later, the *Saturday Review,* who was in his prime when I was in college in the 1960s. Cousins told a gripping personal story about his battle with disease and the role he played in his own healing. He was a pioneer in the emerging world of mind/body theory of health. Scientific research had recently ascertained the debilitating effects of negative emotions on body chemistry. Cousins was influenced by the work of Hans Selye's classic book, *The Stress of Life,* which detailed how adrenal exhaustion could be caused by emotional tension, such as frustration or suppressed rage. Selye showed the negative effects of the negative emotions on body chemistry. So Cousins used himself as a guinea pig to see if positive emotions could produce positive chemical changes in his body. Disregarding conventional medicine, he took matters into his own hands when he was hospitalized for a rare and painful autoimmune disease, *ankylosing spondylitis,* in which the connective tissue of the spine disintegrates because of a breakdown of collagen, the fibrous tissue that binds the body's cells together. (In my case, I have the exact opposite problem: scleroderma results from an over-production of collagen, causing "scarring" and hardening of the organs and tissues of the body.)

Cousins became convinced that mental processes had an effect on physiological processes. In his research he found studies proving that emotional states affected the secretion of certain hormones called endorphins, which were similar to morphine and heroin in their ability to relieve pain. With the approval of his doctor, he checked himself out of the hospital and into a hotel room, so that he would not be awakened all night long and where he found "delicious" serenity. Cousins then watched reruns of *Candid Camera* and the Marx Brothers. This, he said, led him to the joyous discovery that "ten minutes of genuine belly laughter had an anesthetic effect and would give me at least two hours of pain-free sleep."[1]

But one story he told did more for me than the rest of the book. Cousins described the six months he spent in a tuberculosis sanitarium, when he was 10 years old, as a watershed moment in his life. He remembers that the patients divided themselves into two groups: those who were confident that they would beat back the disease and be able to resume normal lives and those who resigned themselves to a prolonged and even fatal illness. Cousins recalled that the boys in his group had a far higher percentage of "discharged as cured" outcomes than the kids in the other group. Even at 10, he wrote, he was being philosophically conditioned; he became aware of the power of the mind in overcoming disease.

This story still persuades me. It reinforced my own experience when I was hospitalized with polio so long ago, when I saw that I had a different attitude than most of the kids who were whiners and crybabies. I had a different outlook. I refused to dwell on the downside, and put my energy into doing anything that would get me out of the hospital faster.

I think this message is powerful: healing and faith are inseparable. They go together. To me, becoming well is a mandate embedded in our faith. I look upon faith as a healing life force within us, bestowed by our Divine Physician, who heals through us. When Cousins visited the famous theologian and physician Dr. Albert Schweitzer in Africa he asked him to comment on his approach to healing. The Third World doctor explained that healing is a secret that doctors have carried inside of them since Hippocrates. "Each patient carries his own doctor inside him," he said. "We are at our best when we give the doctor who resides within each patient a chance to go to work."[2] Amen to that.

WHEN I RETURNED TO Chicago I phoned Fr. Bob Sears S.J., the priest whom I had seen occasionally in the past for spiritual direction. Father Bob was a member of the Association of Christian Therapists and also taught at Loyola University in Chicago. He had many areas of expertise: theology, family systems, healing, adult faith formation and Ignatian spirituality.

He is also trained in TheoPhostic prayer counseling which claims that our present situation is rarely the true cause of our ongoing emotional pain. (I was intrigued with this and attended a weekend intensive to learn about it). Our pain, according to this theory, is due to an original wound in which a lie is embedded. (For instance if I suffered a beating as a child, and told myself that I was a bad girl, the wound is in the lie.) The lie is the heart of the pain. When God speaks a truth into the reality of the memory and releases a person from the lie, healing happens. The memory will still be there, but the lie will be gone along with its painful emotion.

I looked forward to working with Father Bob. If anyone would know how to help me, he would. I brought him up to date on my illnesses and he reiterated what he told me before: disease is the body's effort to get healed. He said I should thank my illness for bringing me to spiritual direction. My symptoms, he said, physical, emotional and spiritual, were showing me that I need to attend to some unresolved issues and that once I make the necessary changes in my life, I won't need the disease anymore and it will go away. I trusted Father Bob and his insights, which held out such hope.

We spent the hour going into my past, namely the relationship between my mother and father that was so hurtful to me. I felt like a broken record; the pain of their disconnect was still raw inside of me—even many years later. I idolized my father and when he came home at night, I sat beside him in the living room and asked him how his day went. My mom and dad had long before divorced each other emotionally and probably physically. So I filled in the breach, feeling a bit sorry for my dad because he had no one to talk to when he came home. I played "wife," which is to say I played up to him, being the good, dutiful and loving daughter.

Father Bob asked me why I tried so hard to please my father, to take care of his needs. I told him that I must have been afraid that if I didn't, he would abandon me. I wanted home to be a happy place and I made it my responsibility to create happiness. Then he asked me how I felt about my father's abandonment of my mother. The way my dad treated my mother had really upset me. I was in a bind. He was our provider, giving us everything, and for me, anything my heart desired. So that was my payoff.

I could have anything (almost literally) if I took care of him emotionally and behaved as the loving, caring daughter who made him proud. I don't think this was literally true. In reality, my dad's love for me had nothing to do with me taking care of him. I was acting irrationally out of a deep-seated fear.

I told Father Bob that I was angry at myself for swallowing so much pain and never once telling my dad how I felt about his treatment of my mother. I did the opposite of what I was feeling. Even though deep down I was troubled by his behavior, I behaved as if he was the greatest father on earth. I didn't have the courage to confront him, to express what I was really feeling and thinking, to tell him off. I hated myself for being so spineless, for not speaking the truth. I was caught in a trap of my own making.

I thought that it was my responsibility to take care of my mother and my father. If I didn't do it, I feared that my world would fall apart and I would be abandoned. I believed that if I could just make them happy, all would be well and we could be a normal, happy family. Nothing that I did brought them closer together or made us a happier family. I just got deeper into my own rage. I was trying to win love, to merit love, to deserve love, to become loveable by showing how well I could take care of situations. My real needs never entered into my mind. The only needs that mattered were my parents, and I took it upon myself to give them what they didn't give to each other.

God, I am sure, put Gertrude and the nuns in my life to give me the love and attention I craved. There was a huge void inside of me, a part of me that wanted to be cherished and loved. But I behaved in ways so as not to admit that, or I pretended to be was fine when in reality I was often depressed.

Even today, I struggle with these issues. Father Bob suggested that what would help me now would be to learn to speak the truth, to stop hiding from the truth. In many ways I'm continuing the patterns of denial and hiding that I grew up with. I don't tell Tommy what I'm really feeling because if I did, I think he might abandon me. Or, if I really got in touch with the depth of my feelings, I might abandon him. So underneath is fear.

The historical reality is a fact, and I can't change that. There was pain and abuse, even cruelty. By swallowing it, I owned it, so to speak. I took it into myself where it had a life of its own. The lie that I lived as a result of this was: I thought I was responsible to repair their relationship, to fix the problems so that we could be happy. Underneath I guess I may have thought it was my fault that things were this way.

After meeting with Father Bob the truth slowly began to dawn on me. I was not responsible for my parents' relationship. It was not up to me to fix them or to make them happy. Their relationship was their responsibility. I am responsible for myself, to care for myself, to love myself by being truthful, open and honest. I must own up to my feelings and share them. This is what love is. Jesus said "The truth will set you free" (Jn 8:33). When I can love myself, then I will be able to love others.

Through Father Bob I began to see that I couldn't fix anything—that all the trouble I went to when I was growing up didn't do a thing for my parents' relationship. It only hurt me. And all the effort I've put into my marriage to fix my husband and our relationship hadn't done a thing either. Father Bob was confirming—and reinforcing—everything I learned during my retreats at Hazelden, encouraging me to admit my powerlessness over Tommy and the marriage and to surrender them to the Lord. What I heard from Father Bob and the counselors at Hazeldon was that I needed to love myself in the true sense of the word. When I can love and care for myself, they said, I can love Tommy. I cannot give him what I don't have; and if I don't give him truth, then I don't really love him. I realized that by not being truthful, I was compromising myself just like I did growing up, hiding in order to keep things stable or protecting him out of fear that if I really shared what I was feeling, the marriage would end.

Even though I was gaining in understanding all this, I was going through an emotional revolving door. One minute I was happy and full of life, and the next, my mood matched the bleak February weather. One grey, rainy, cold winter morning I wrote in my journal: *God, Jesus, Holy Spirit, this is the Great Jubilee Year in which You have promised to free us from bondage. I pray for this freedom with all my heart. It will take a miracle. I feel bad, like a hypocrite. One day I am giving talks in churches on the Eucharist and the next I am in the pit of hell flailing about in the darkness, desperate for a way out.*

Jesus, You are the Light of the world. I beg You to throw me a beam of light to guide me to the next step. I even question Witness and the amount of work I am taking on. Is it for me or for You? Why am I killing myself with work—trips, talks, new books, retreats—the calendar is full and I am empty. I have never felt so alone in my life. This is a bottom that I've hit so hard. I wish I were dead. God, if you want me to live, then please show me how. Touch me Jesus, put a spark of love in my dead heart and bring me back to life. Please reveal Yourself to me.

That night I had a powerful dream that seemed to be a direct and immediate answer to my prayer.

BEFORE SHARING THE DREAM, I want to explain my understanding of how I came to believe that dreams can be a communication from God. I first became interested in them when my children were growing up because I had so many dreams that seemed to relate to problems in my daily life. I began reading books and going to workshops in order to decipher their meaning. One dream in particular that I had years ago awakened me to the possibility that dreams might be a form of divine inspiration.

During that time in my life I was praying about an important decision I had to make. As each day went by, I leaned on friends asking them for their input and also to pray for God's guidance for my decision. Then one night I had a dream: I saw myself as a fat sheep straddled over a fence. I was stuck and couldn't move one way or the other. I was calling out to the other sheep to help me but no one seemed to be able to help. Then I saw the Shepherd. He was walking toward me and with great love told me that only He could get me off the fence. When I need something, He said I must call Him and He will come to my rescue.

Ever since then I have believed that dreams are the voice of Divine Wisdom that comes to give us insight and direction. Dreams abound in the Bible, in both the Old and New Testaments (as well as in the major religions of the world), and these "visions of the night," as the Early Church Fathers called them, were viewed by the Church as one of the most important ways in which God revealed His will to His people. Suffice it to say that understanding dreams forms an essential part of our Christian heritage.[3]

If there is one example that makes a case for dreams being gifts from the Spirit, it is a dream that Saint Monica had that was instrumental in the conversion of her wayward son, Augustine. Before he converted, Augustine steeped himself in the heresy of Manichaeism that was rampant in the latter half of the third century. Monica gave her son a swift dose of tough love and threw him out of the house. One night she had a dream in which she saw herself standing on a wooden ruler. A handsome man was coming toward her. He was smiling and joyful, but Monica was sad and filled with grief. The young man asked her why she was crying. She said that she was grieved over the lost soul of her son. The young man replied telling her to rest secure, because if she looked, she would see that "where she was, there was I also."[4] Then Monica looked and saw her son Augustine standing beside her on the same ruler.

Augustine tried to distort the interpretation, telling her that her dream meant that she would abandon Catholicism to become a Manichee. Monica replied without any hesitation saying, "No! It was not said to me, 'Where he is, there also are you,' but 'Where you are, there also is he.'"[5] Saint Augustine later confessed that he was more disturbed by what he felt was the Lord's answer to him through his mother (and the fact that she was not bothered by the falsity of his interpretation) than by the dream itself. (It would take nine long years for Augustine to see the error of his ways and change his life.)

The rest is history.

NOW TO MY DREAM. It was of the most numinous I have ever had. In the dream I was going to a wake. There was a nun in a casket and as I approached I realized that the nun was me and she really wasn't dead; she opened an eye and looked at me. In the next scene we were downstairs and someone was taking her temperature rectally. The thermometer registered 32 degrees.

The dream bothered me. It seemed sinister and I wondered what dark message it was sending. But I knew better. Most dreams come to gift us in some way either by asking us a question or revealing an issue or by opening us to new possibilities for our lives. I thought about the dream constantly and wanted to understand it. If God sent me this dream to teach me something, then I needed to know what that was.

At an Intensive Journal Workshop founded by the renowned psychologist, Dr. Ira Progoff, I had learned the technique of dialogue to explore the meaning of dreams. By extending the dream consciously, they taught us that we can gain information and insights from the unconscious that we didn't know we knew, if we can silence our egos. It is also similar to the process of contemplation that Saint Ignatius taught in his *Spiritual Exercises*. Basically it involves using one's imagination to dialogue with biblical figures, an exercise that allows one to personalize the scene and enter into prayer. Apparently Saint Thomas Aquinas entered into a dialogue with Saints Peter and Paul during a dream, which helped him clarify a difficult theological question.[6]

So I had a dialogue with the nun in the casket. I gave her a name:

"Sister Joan" because she looked like me. I asked her who she was. From that moment on, the conversation flowed freely.

Sister Joan: I am the part of you who is full of love and faith and life! The whole purpose of my being is to give glory to God through my life. I am grounded in faith, my goal is to become holy, to be a perfect disciple of my Lord and Savior, Jesus. I live to bring Jesus' life to others, to give them hope, to give them His love. I am at peace and usually full of joy which uplifts everyone around me. I am full of enthusiasm and have many talents and gifts to share with others. I like to inspire people to greater faith, to learn to love themselves, and to be good to themselves. I am authentic. What you see is what you get. Honest to a fault, and generous. My charism is "goodness" which comes from a very big heart that wants to embrace the whole world. I will go out of my way to help people. I have humility because I know all my gifts and strengths are from God and have been given to me for others. I have my feet on the ground and my head in the clouds.

The conversation took on a life of its own.

Joan: You sound too good to be true! Anyway, you are lying in a coffin in a funeral parlor but you are not really dead. Are you pretending to be dead?

Sister Joan: Yes, you see part of me has given up any hope of living my life authentically. I have had to keep repressing my enthusiasm, squelching my inspirations, tabling my ideas and hopes, ignoring my dreams, stifling my emotions. Over a period of years, these "deaths" have taken their toll. They have taken the wind out of my sails, the joy out of my life; the fun and laughter have all but disappeared. I have decided at some deep level that I cannot be myself within my marriage so I gave myself up—my real self—to appease the marriage. All the dreams and hopes and enthusiasm are still alive and that's why my eyes are open. A part of me is laying low in the coffin pretending to be dead but is really still alive. I have "given up" because I think that really to be true to myself would destroy the marriage.

Joan: So you are "hiding" in a coffin and your marriage is still not very good?

Sister Joan: Right! We are just existing and working side by side, functioning together. Task-oriented with very little life flowing between us. I don't know what to do to bring life to the marriage. Sometimes I wish I would die and end the pain.

Joan: So what is keeping you alive?

Sister Joan: I guess I still have some hope that I could be myself and have a fulfilling marriage at the same time. I have always looked to my husband to bring life to the relationship. When he doesn't do that, I feel abandoned and hopeless and I hide in pain.

Joan: It seems like you are using the coffin as a way to cover up your pain. People don't know how much pain you are in, because they think you're dead. You hide your pain from them by appearing to be dead. You disguise yourself by playing dead.

Sister Joan: Right. That way I don't have to deal with anything or struggle with anything. I can numb out.

Joan: So why did you come to me in a dream?

Sister Joan: To tell you that I'm still alive and that I have so much hidden from you that would bring life to you—and to your marriage. I put myself in the coffin little by little. As I allowed each hurt to kill part of me, to squelch me, to abuse me, I started giving up hope that I could be myself in the marriage.

Joan: So really then you put yourself in the coffin?

Sister Joan: Yes. I guess I did it to hide and protect myself, to escape pain, to find refuge, to seek relief.

Joan: Do you want to come out of the coffin?

Sister Joan: Yes, I do. I don't belong in there. Besides, I'm living as an escapist. I'm taking the easy way out and I hate people who do that. I want to come out now and begin to love myself by being myself. Maybe my illnesses, scleroderma and lymphoma, are a direct result of giving up on myself.

Joan: You have so much life in you. I'll bet if you begin to really love yourself and embrace life, you will overcome your sickness. You swallowed too much negative stuff and took it in until it became part of you. It literally started eating you up.

Sister Joan: Yes, that's right. Now I have to regurgitate all the negative stuff and fill myself with truth, love and joy so there will be no room for sickness.

This dialogue broke the wall of denial that I had been building since my childhood. It clearly showed me where my pain originated: in myself.

It was a confirmation of all that I had worked through with Father Bob. The dialogue enabled me to see how I had sabotaged myself, how the authentic, spontaneous and carefree part of me began hiding when I felt hurt, abandoned or ashamed. For so long I blamed the pain on others, especially my husband, and felt trapped because it seemed hopeless that he could give me what I really needed. Because I "knew" I couldn't have what I wanted, I decided to go underground, in a coffin, so as not to hurt. By denying myself, or numbing myself, I thought it would numb the pain. Instead, the pain increased.

The dream also showed me that I was behaving just like my mother who put herself and her life on hold because of my father. She became mentally ill. She "gave up," saying, "What's the use?" My suffering mother lived as a victim and wallowed in resentment and anger that she directed to my father. She blamed him for her misery and unhappiness, saying if only he'd leave her, she could be happy. Negativity was always brewing inside of her. As much as I disliked her behavior, I had to admit that there was a part of me that was just like her.

The dream was a direct and immediate answer to my prayer, a gift from God revealing the crux of the problem: myself. I saw how I put my inner self in a coffin to hide and to protect myself from pain. I thought Tommy was responsible for my unhappiness but I was in a bind: I felt powerless to change him or to leave the marriage. I was a complete victim, which left me no choice but ostensibly to "die," so that life could continue.

"Sister Joan" helped open my eyes and my heart to see the love I denied myself—let alone Tommy.

13

Waking up "Sister Joan"

When the Prodigal Son finally came to himself out in the "far country," he suddenly saw himself in a larger context, and he came home. He was free. He had released his greater potential. The father received him with open arms and cried out, "Rejoice . . . for my son who was dead is now alive again." This was a very real resurrection. It didn't involve dying and returning from the grave, but it did involve waking up to the awareness of his true being.
—Eric Butterworth, *Discover the Power Within You*

DURING THE JUBILEE YEAR 2000 I was in a different city, state or country every month except for the final two, November and December, when I had surgery. There has never been another year like it—before or after. First Tommy and I made a swing through Florida and New England in the winter making multiple stops at parishes and retreat centers where I gave presentations on the Eucharist and the Mass. We went to Rome for Easter, after which we went on another trip to the Holy Land and finally we led a pilgrimage to France for Witness Ministries in the fall. That I had the energy to keep up such a hectic travel schedule and be on my feet for talks and retreats was astounding. I was grateful for the work—and the trips—because they were enjoyable and very spiritually nourishing.

IN THE SPRING OF 2000 I saw an advertisement for a Thomas Merton Retreat on Contemplative Prayer led by Jim Finley, a Merton scholar and retreat master who had lived with Merton at Gethsemane in Kentucky for a number of years. It was scheduled for the third week of Lent at Our Lady of Guadalupe Abbey in Pecos, New Mexico. Everything about it appealed to me: Thomas Merton, Jim Finley, Pecos and Lent. So I made a reservation.

I became a fan of Thomas Merton in senior year of high school when I read *Seeds of Contemplation*, a spiritual gem of a book that appealed to the mystical side of me. Back then I thought I wanted to enter the convent. While reading *Seeds of Contemplation*, I copied a paragraph from the book in red ink on parchment paper, perhaps to frame. I still have the page that I keep in a box of things that I can never throw out. It reads: *I who am without love, cannot become love unless Love identifies me with Himself. But if He sends His own Love, Himself, to act and love in me and in all that I do, then I shall be transformed. I shall discover who I am, and shall possess my true identity, by losing myself in Him. This is sanctity.*[1] The message meant a lot to me then, and when I came across it recently I figured out why: it is my mission statement, the *raison d'etre* of my life.

One morning at Pecos I awakened very early and went to the chapel to pray. It was 5 A.M. and still dark save for the vigil light beside the tabernacle and a fluttering of votives near the door. Jim Finley suggested a very simple form of contemplative prayer: to breathe out "I love you" to God then breathe in, "I love you" from God. I did this for a while in the silent darkness of the chapel. I began to feel God's closeness; it was as if I had made a phone call to heaven and God was on the line. He wasn't saying anything, but I knew He was there! The dream about the nun in the casket was very much on my mind and I asked Jesus and Mary to help me to resurrect the dead part of myself. I felt that the nun came to me in my dream to make me aware of my real self, hoping that I would help her come back to life. (Which is to say deep down I wanted to come back to life.) I prayed: Lord, *please bring me back to life and forgive me for hiding, for denying, for burying my true self. If sin is alienation then I have been living in sin. Part of me has been frozen, unable to give and receive love, unable to reach out to give others and my husband the love they deserve. I have lived in a barren desert within myself. Thank you for bringing me here, thank you for loving me and please help me to come to life. There has been so much suffering.*

During Mass on the fourth Sunday of Lent, the celebrant wore a rose colored vestment to denote joy and a reprieve in the midst of the penitential season. I felt as if the abbot wrote the homily for me. He said not to fear suffering but to rejoice in the Cross of Christ because Jesus has borne it for us—for our glory. He wants us to share His glory, the abbot said, and He wants us to trust Him with our pain. When I went back to my room I wrote down what he had said: "He will redeem our pain. He will answer us, and He will resurrect us." This leader of the community of Benedictine monks spoke words that were so nourishing I drank them in like a baby sucking milk from the breast. United to Him, the abbot continued, our pain can turn to joy. The point of it all, he said, is that "Jesus wants us to celebrate Easter with Him. We are His elect, His beloved. He loves us no matter how we've sinned and turned away from Him and longs for us to unite our brokenness to His death so that He can heal us and make us new and whole in His love."

The retreat confirmed that I was heading in the right direction on my spiritual journey. When I left Pecos later that afternoon, I was grateful for my faith that continued to steer me on the right path and which brought me hope—always when I needed it.

WE HEADED TO THE Jersey Shore in July for an extended vacation. It felt like I was going home because I spent most of my childhood summers at the Shore where I reveled in the freedom and fun that life at the beach afforded. We often took our kids there during the summer so that they could learn to appreciate the ocean. During our stay I had several memorable encounters with people, one of whom was my brother with whom I had a long, leisurely lunch one day.

Howie was eleven years older than me. After his birth and before I was born, my mother miscarried four babies. Then I came along. I barely knew my brother because of our age difference. When I was in first or second grade, Howie was finishing high school and then went off to Dartmouth College. I adored my brother even if I often felt jealous of the praise my dad heaped on him. Daddy would often brag about him it seemed, for my benefit, saying, "Howie won nine varsity letters at Fordham Prep. Can you imagine? Nine!" I was always striving to measure up to his success.

Howie was blessed with the heart of my mother and the brains of my father. I saved some of the letters he wrote to me from Dartmouth when I was in grammar school. They were tender notes that showed his gentle, loving spirit, qualities that I love in him. One spring break when he came home from college he unzipped a small duffle bag and out jumped a white bunny rabbit, an Easter gift he couldn't wait to give me.

When I was growing up, Howie often advised me not to get in the middle of my parents' relationship. He knew the dysfunctional patterns all too well and wanted to spare me some of the pain he had endured. He reminded me about his homecoming from the Army. When he returned from a two-year tour of duty that he served in Fontainebleau, France, just outside of Paris, he was excited to share his travel adventures with his family. We were sitting at the dinner table and he couldn't get a word in because my dad was pontificating about anything and everything that interested him. It was after that when Howie moved out to live on his own.

That day when I met Howie for lunch the talk turned to our parents. His memory of our mother was so positive. He said that she was always thinking of him and had his best interests at heart. His friends, he said, thought she was wonderful. I loved hearing this. My memory of her was so different. Howie recalled with great affection that the mom he knew was vivacious, outgoing, warm and friendly. He stressed that she was *very* caring. But there was another side, he said. A shadow crossed his face when he remembered that their home life was depressing. He described our mom as "anguished." Apparently she was always asking him, "What can I do?" "How can I get out of this?" saying, "I have nowhere to go." This was more in keeping with my painful memories. Howie described my parents' marriage as "loveless," saying that my mother had love but that my father did not.

I appreciated the loving picture he painted of my mom. I think that deep down I knew she must have been like he described her, but it was a side of her that I rarely—if ever—saw. I knew about her suffering because I felt her pain for so many years. As for my dad, Howie verbalized what I already knew, that everything revolved around J. Howard: his stories and his memories—it was all about him. His children were like his satellites reflecting his light.

We ended the discussion on a cautionary note. Howie warned of the possible harm that could result from dredging up all this stuff. He suggested that it might be better to let sleeping dogs lie. He said he saw no redeeming value in dealing with any of this. I told him that as long as all these negative memories didn't bother him, then he probably shouldn't force them to the surface. Perhaps his wounds weren't as deep as mine. But I suspect that he swallowed pain too, and when he left the apartment that night long ago, the anguish went with him. In my experience, the past was a prologue to the future. I told him that the wounds and pains of childhood and adolescence grew up right alongside of me and they acted like monsters in the basement rattling around, screaming to be set free. Because they ruined my peace, I had to deal with them.

Before leaving the Shore I spent a few days at the Stella Maris Retreat Center in Elberon, New Jersey. Sitting on the porch overlooking the ocean I had a cup of tea with Sister Madeleine, a spiritual director who was crippled with multiple sclerosis but whose joy was contagious. We were talking about something when she said, "Joan, the whole bottom line is for us to know how much God loves us and gifts us. The spiritual life is about recognizing our gifts, the love that is in us, and spreading that love to others." She was a prophet, speaking words that stirred my soul. I wrote in my journal: *Lord, help me to appreciate the gifts and the love You have given me. If I don't recognize my own goodness then how will I see good in others?*

IN SEPTEMBER TOMMY AND I returned to France to lead a Witness Ministries pilgrimage to the sites we had visited three years before with our priest friends, Fathers Patrick and Steve. This time, we took thirty-eight people with us!

We needed a spiritual director for the trip and found one unexpectedly at our former parish where we went for Mass one Sunday. Father Jerry Boland happened to be the celebrant that day and gave a homily on the Eucharist that was so exceptional it earned him a round of applause. We invited him to lunch the following week. Father Jerry was head of the priest's placement board in the Chicago Archdiocese and he also had a following of parishioners who adored him. When he realized that we were asking him to be the spiritual director on a trip to France, he was beside himself with joy. He told us that he had wanted to be able to make a pilgrimage during the Jubilee Year, and that our invitation was an answer to his prayer.

Beginning in Paris, we visited Lisieux, Mont St. Michel, Chartres, Orleans, Nevers, Paray-le-Monial, Ars, Lyon, La Salette, Avignon, Carcassonne and Lourdes. After Lourdes we took the TGV train back to Paris and then home.

Of all the unforgettable experiences we had on that pilgrimage, there is one memory that I will treasure forever: Lourdes. Although we had visited Lourdes once before, this was the first time I went into the baths. Just before they lowered me into the water, two women attendants gave me a few moments to pray. My eyes focused on a tiny statue of Our Lady at the foot of the bath about eight feet away, and I tearfully poured out my heart to her begging her intercession for all the prayer intentions I carried with me. I put my physical and emotional health in her hands, imploring her to ask her Son to bring "Sister Joan" back to life. Whey they lowered me into the water, I didn't even feel the cold. I felt as if Our Lady wrapped me in a warm blanket of love.

I FOUND MYSELF PRAYING to Our Lady more often, asking her to intervene with her Son when I needed help. I think my love for her was growing largely because of my study and research of the Eucharist. By growing closer to Jesus, it was not surprising that I was drawn closer to the Mother who bore His body.

Sometimes I felt like Our Lady was pursuing me. One evening when I was working late in our home office I received a phone call from a woman who tearfully recounted an amazing story. She knew about our Eucharistic ministry and simply wanted to share a spiritual experience involving the Eucharist.

One day she received a desperate phone call from her daughter, Ellen, who had been suffering from multiple sclerosis. The side effects from the medicine combined with a lack of sleep and overwhelming feelings of loneliness brought on a depression in which she felt like she couldn't go on. In her early 30s, Ellen felt physically and mentally unhealthy and didn't know how she'd get the strength to raise her children.

It was her mother, Jane, who called me to tell me that she felt inspired to drive Ellen out to Marytown, about an hour from their home. Ellen sat for a long time in front of the Eucharist. She kept staring at the monstrance while begging God to help her. She prayed asking God to love her more (she had once heard a priest say if you want more faith ask Jesus to love you more).

After about an hour, she heard someone open the doors to the side chapel, known as the Sorrowful Mother Chapel. She slowly turned her head and above the altar caught sight of the most beautiful mosaic of the Pieta. At that moment, she heard Jesus say to her, "You will be all right; my Mother will take care of you." Ellen knew that she was going to get well.

Ellen continued to heal—physically, emotionally and spiritually. Her right side, which had become numb, went back to normal, and she found new hope in God. Even though she had attended Catholic schools, she thought the Eucharist was a symbol. For the first time in her life, Ellen realized that Christ is really and truly present in the Blessed Sacrament.

AFTER OUR TRIP TO FRANCE I was at Mass one morning when I felt a nudge to return to the Renewal Center at Hazelden. Online I found a retreat called "Cleaning House" a few weeks out that would fit my timetable perfectly. I made a reservation.

In order to help us figure out what needed cleaning in our inner house and how to put it in order, a counselor led us in a guided imagery session, asking us to imagine what our "house" looked like. I enjoy doing imagery and saw a home that was welcoming with fires ablaze in winter and screen doors flapping open and shut in the summer wind. But downstairs was an old dirty basement that was dark and unfamiliar with rooms that made me fearful because they held secrets that were foreboding. The place was in a state of disorder and there were cobwebs everywhere. Part of the foundation of the house was exposed. I saw a large crevice, indicating a major fault in the structure of the house. It made the house unbalanced; it wasn't set in perfect alignment. A hurricane-force wind might even cause it to collapse.

It was clear that my inner basement (unconscious) was a problem. It was a place of pain and darkness. I was embarrassed at the sight of it and I wanted to clean it out and get rid of whatever was polluting the air and causing sickness so that I could live in my house and be happy. The pollutants were the negative emotions that trapped me in depression. In every room there was anger and fear that had been there for years. It was really rage. There was no hope down there, and no light or warmth. I didn't know where all the emotions originated, or why, but they were like poison spilling over into the upstairs. They polluted the environment of my clean and beautiful home with their noxious fumes.

I wasn't sure what the fault in the foundation was. I suspect it had to do with a disconnect within myself, between the outer and inner me. Perhaps I was born with it. I asked God to teach me how to repair my house, to reconstruct myself according to the original blueprint He designed. *Lord, show me how to eliminate the toxic fumes of anger, fear and all the rest that are stored in the basement. Sometimes Tommy unwittingly opens one of these doors through a remark or a behavior of his, and then my house fills with fumes of dark smoke. It is poisonous to me and to others, especially to him! Is that what is in my lungs? My oncologist called them "infiltrates," tiny specks that don't belong there. Lord I give You permission to do a thorough housecleaning in me. Please send your Holy Spirit to wash every inch of me with Your love and healing.*

During the retreat a counselor shared her personal story of growing up in a home with alcoholic parents. She set out to save them both. She became extremely responsible, a people-pleaser, controlling and compliant. She practiced these behaviors in order to belong. As a young adult she realized that these dysfunctional behaviors weren't working and were causing her a lot of pain and depression. There was a part of her that wanted to be dead. She had what she called "emotional blackouts."

She did some Gestalt work in order to let out her rage—at herself. (Gestalt is a type of psychological therapy that involves putting yourself in a chair and talking to yourself.) We split off from ourselves, she said, we banish the shadow we don't want to the basement, and the rage we don't deal with comes out on everyone else. She had verbal dialogues with her shadow side. She told "herself" off, then that self spoke back, asking "Who do you think got you through your traumas?" She had hope for the first time because she realized that she was not all bad. The part of herself that she banished actually was trying to help her. It was then that she realized that ongoing healing was possible through the mercy she had toward herself.

My story was so similar to hers. I learned from her: the way to healing is not to banish the shadow side of ourselves, but to love it. This resonated with what a priest had recently said to me in confession when I told him that there was a raging madwoman inside of me whom I hated. He said that Jesus loves me—all of me—even the unhealed part. I started to cry, imagining Jesus loving the "ugly" me.

Then the counselor used the metaphor of a garbage can to describe the toxic waste that comes from stuffing everything about us that is not okay into a place inside of us. We think that the lid covers it over, but in reality it leaks out in judgments, criticisms, anger and resentments. When we work the Third and Fourth Steps (a decision to turn our wills and our lives over to the care of God as we understand Him and make a searching and fearless moral inventory of ourselves) we surrender ourselves and take the lid off the garbage can.

This was one of the most important lessons this counselor taught me: that taking the lid off the garbage can and going through the trash is the only way to get to the bottom—the real self—who is the *Imago Dei*, the source of our being. Like a compost heap, the garbage acts as fertilizer and helps our garden grow. It is not about getting rid of it, she said, it is about transforming it. As it gets transformed, the bottom part (real self) emerges as we become filled with light.

One day I worked the Fourth Step (taking a moral inventory) by listing people and/or institutions that I had rejected through resentment, anger, fear or shame. It was sobering to see my character defects. (It was similar to the Sacrament of Reconciliation that always brought me healing.) It was also obvious how I had been projecting my shadow onto my husband. Actually, it was a clever technique; see something I don't like in him, then make him see it so that he will change and then I can be happy. This allowed me to avoid looking within and dealing with my own issues.

After one of the lectures we broke up into small groups. There was an older couple sitting next to me who had a son in the treatment center in an adjacent building. This was his fifth attempt at getting sober and his parents were at the end of their rope. They were understandably frustrated, but instead of dealing with their own issues and trying to acknowledge their part in the family problem, they were stuck in blame, lashing out at their son for putting them through this ordeal. They projected all their frustration and anxiety onto him, saying things like, "He is making our life miserable," "He is draining us and we are sick and tired of it." I couldn't help but see myself in them. This couple didn't know it, but they showed me what denial looked like, and it wasn't attractive. It was ego-driven. They were trapped in a prison of their own making. Through them I saw how the walls that I built to protect myself actually caused my pain. Once again I saw how I was trapped, not by my husband or the marriage—but by my own denial and delusion.

I wrote in my journal: *Lord, please help me clean house. Show me the root of the problem that puts me in such bondage, that tries to kill me, that traps me and makes me feel hopeless and despairing and gives me the urge to run away. I give You permission to purify me of these toxic emotions. I beg you, Jesus, to free me from the bondage of that self so as to make room for my real self. Please, Lord, resurrect her from the basement and set her free.*

At Hazelden I began to let go of a lot of garbage—resentments, angers, hurts, memories—that blocked me from giving and receiving love, from being myself. Owning up to all the "dirt" in my house and humbly admitting my faults was cleansing as well as life-giving. I felt like it was a first step in reaching out to "Sister Joan" in the casket, coaxing her to wake up.

In November I made an appointment with a new doctor, a thoracic surgeon, who wanted to check out what was going on in and around my lungs. A recent CT scan and a gallium X-ray showed "infiltrates" in my right lung and two enlarged lymph nodes behind my breastbone, next to the windpipe. So I checked into the hospital for a thoracoscopy and a bronchoscopy, somewhat invasive procedures that allowed him to examine the tissues. The surgeon created "ports" so that he could videotape the area around the chest. If these turned out to be cancerous, I saw the possibility of being really sick. On a conscious level I felt rather calm although I needed sleeping pills at night. On an unconscious level I think I was terrified at the prospect of only having a year or two to live.

Yet a gentle joy bubbled up inside me. I felt new gratitude for the beauty of life itself, for colors, sounds, sights and people. When we flew into New York for a short visit to watch Rich run the New York marathon, as we approached LaGuardia Airport I looked at the skyline and began to cry. They were tears of joy. I was overwhelmed with love and thankfulness for my life, which was so rich, so full of gifts, so blessed by wonderful experiences and people to love and be loved by. I didn't feel sick in the least. My energy was at a high point.

At Mass the next morning I offered my life, body and soul, to Jesus during the Consecration, asking Him to consecrate me to Him through this cross of uncertainty. On a spiritual level, I was trying to surrender my life, and on a physical level I vowed to do everything possible to keep living. I asked Jesus to fill me with the gifts of His Spirit so that I could live in accordance with His perfect will for my life. I thought about slowing down and spending more time in meditation and in adoration of the Blessed Sacrament. And I wanted to do more healing imagery. I had just read a book written by a woman who survived three different bouts of cancer. She imagined swans eating the bad cells. She developed a routine of doing this so that even when she wasn't conscious of meditating, she felt the swans were at work in her body, eating the bad cells. The idea excited me, although I didn't have a feeling for swans. I was thinking of asking either angels or saints to be my infantry, to go after the cancer cells and replace them with perfect, healthy cells.

I still harbored the concern that my physical problems were the result of the "cancer" of sin in my life, so to speak. I wanted to seek forgiveness for the people I had hurt through my selfishness, anger and judgments, especially my husband. I wrote in my journal: *Has the darkness in me been eating away at me? Has my denial and repression come out from under cover in the form of lymphoma? I don't know for sure but I still have a strong feeling that there is a connection between the spiritual and physical/emotional. I keep wondering if my spiritual sickness has led to my physical sickness. I want to pray about this and ask the Holy Spirit for discernment and wisdom.*

Although I never did ask "Why me?," I was extremely curious to figure out how disease relates to our emotional/spiritual life. My search led me to a book by Dr. Carl Simonton, M.D., that has become a classic in the field of mind/body psychology. Dr. Simonton founded a cancer counseling and research center where, to this day, he motivates his patients by helping them understand how they can participate in their health or illness. He published the fruit of his study, research and the effect his theories have on his patients, in *Getting Well Again*. Simonton explains that while carcinogenic substances, genetic dispositions, radiation or even diet are the basic causes of cancer, none of those theories can stand alone to explain its origin. For cancer to occur, he says the immune system must be inhibited in some way.

To find out what lapse in the body's defenses allows the abnormal cells that are present in everybody's body to reproduce into a life-threatening tumor, oncologist Simonton and his psychologist wife point us to the emotional and mental factors in health and illness. They were the first Western practitioners to use imaging techniques against cancer with the goal of helping patients mobilize their own resources to actively participate in their recovery. They were working with a group of patients who suffered from malignancies that were deemed medically incurable, people who were not expected to live more than a year. Of the 159 patients they treated, fourteen had gotten rid of their cancer completely, while the tumors of twelve patients were regressing.[2] Those who did succumb to the disease doubled their survival time. That was back in 1978. Today, I imagine, their statistics have improved.

Simonton cites three clues that show us why one patient may live and another die with the same diagnosis and treatment. My own bare bones analysis of his explanation of this is as follows: first, Simonton maintains there is a strong link between stress and illness. Second, he claims that the incidence of cancer in laboratory animals is greatly increased when they are placed under stress and, third, there are substantially different incidence rates for cancer among patients with different kinds of mental and emotional problems. These clues, he says, point to significant connections between emotional states and illness.[3]

A doctor who agrees with him and who actually learned from him is Dr. Bernie Siegel, M.D., a physician and the best selling author of *Love, Medicine and Miracles,* a book that has literally been a lifesaver for thousands of people. In it he also explains how stress contributes to immune deficiency, adding that if we keep our stress response "on" all the time, the hormones released by the adrenal glands lower our resistance to disease, and even wither away the lymph nodes. Siegel claims that there is now experimental evidence that "passive emotions," such as grief, feelings of failure and suppression of anger, produce over-secretion of these same hormones, which suppress the immune system. Although science does not yet understand all the ways in which brain chemicals are related to emotions and thought, he concludes that our state of mind has an immediate and direct effect on our state of body. "We can change the body by dealing with how we feel," he says. "If we ignore despair, the body receives a die message. If we deal with our pain and seek help, then the message is 'Living is difficult but desirable,' and the immune system works to keep us alive."[4]

These doctors were convincing me that disease is related to our mental and emotional states. Dr. Siegel's theory that despair sends the body a "die" message interested me the most. Relating it to depression, he cites Arnold Hutschnecker, who wrote, "Depression is a partial surrender to death, and it seems that cancer is despair experienced at the cellular level."[5] This made great sense to me. Siegel also said that about fifteen to twenty percent of all patients unconsciously—or even consciously—wish to die. But if you ask them how they are, they say, "Fine." That would be me. These cutting edge doctor-therapists were opening my eyes to see how "Sister Joan" was enacting an unconscious death wish by putting herself in a casket. This, I believe, was certainly a factor that compromised my immune system and opened the door for illness to enter my life.

THE RESULTS OF THE BATTERY of tests I took during my hospital stay showed a mass or a type of an epithelial tumor, a potential thymoma or even a "non-small cell carcinoma" in my chest. A thymoma, the thoracic surgeon explained, is a tumor of the thymus gland. It can be benign (non-cancerous) or malignant (cancerous). I felt somewhat relieved when he said that he saw no evidence of lymphoma in the mass.

I did some research to learn more about the thymus gland. It is part of the immune system, which is the body's defense against infection. It works by activating special cells called T. lymphocytes (white blood cells that fight infection). With all my other medical problems, I didn't see how I could live without a thymus gland, one of the main organs that fight infection. Then I found out that the thymus gland is at its largest and most active around puberty, after which it becomes less active and begins to shrink in size. Apparently adults don't need it.

The doctor urged us to schedule surgery as soon as possible. *Surgery? As soon as possible? A tumor? More cancer?* "No, this can't be, I'm too busy," I protested, "I have too many commitments scheduled. I can't take time off for this. No way." The young doctor gave me a blank stare. He was probably used to his patients throwing anger fits—which was what I was doing—at the thought of surgery. He wondered what I was involved in that was so important. I knew it was useless but I told him anyway. "Well, I have presentations scheduled in parishes. I would prefer not to cancel because it is difficult to change dates once things are set in motion." It seemed weak considering the news he had just dropped in my lap. I was cornered and knew that I'd have to put everything on hold and schedule the surgery.

I asked more questions but really don't recall the answers. The one thing I do remember is that he said he would have to saw through my breastbone in order to reach the mass. The thymus gland is in the center of the chest behind the breastbone, so he would have to pull back the rib cage just like they do in open-heart surgery. I wish he hadn't told me that. I couldn't get the image of the saw out of my mind—and I couldn't sleep. We scheduled surgery three weeks out, during the first week of December. I was terrified.

ONE MORNING AFTER MEETING with the doctor I was sitting at my desk when the idea to call Father Peter Rookey popped into my mind. He was a "Man of Miracles" according to the title of a book about him. He has a worldwide healing ministry, and when people ask him about his gift he says simply, "It is God's work, not mine. He does all the healing, I just pray." I had actually met this humble priest at several conferences on the Eucharist. Each time I gave him one of my books, and each time he was so grateful and promised to pray for me. Now I would *implore* his prayers.

I phoned his office, never expecting to get Father Rookey on the line. He took the call and when I explained my upcoming operation, he prayed for me. Then he uttered what sounded like a prophecy: "Be at peace daughter. Your faith has made you well." Overjoyed with what seemed to be a word of knowledge from the Lord, I felt as if God was telling me through Father Rookey that He was watching over me and that I would be well.

It was consoling, but it didn't diminish my anxiety over the surgery. Now I couldn't sleep—or pray.

14

Thymectomy

The pain you suffer now is meant to put you in touch with the place where you most need healing, your very heart. The person who was able to touch that place has revealed to you your pearl of great price.
—Henri Nouwen, *The Inner Voice of Love*

MY NERVES WERE ON edge before the surgery. Two days prior to the thymectomy my friend Kandy phoned. Once again her timing was perfect. When I first contracted scleroderma, Kandy phoned and recommended the book by Dr. Thomas Brown, M.D., that changed my life. When I told her about my upcoming surgery she knew exactly what to do: phone Peggy Huddleston, a Harvard Divinity School graduate who wrote a guide about mind-body techniques to help people facing surgery to participate in their own healing.[1]

It was Sunday but I tried calling Peggy nonetheless. Thankfully, she answered, and after a long conversation on the benefits of deep relaxation to calm fears and reduce pain and anxiety, Peggy told me where I could pick up a copy of her book and an audiotape in Chicago. I dropped everything and drove 45 minutes into the city to get them. Before dinner I read half of her book and practiced deep relaxation by following the steps on her tape. Immediately, I knew it would help me.

Peggy claims that deep relaxation reduces anxiety, soothes the nervous system and stimulates the immune system. If we reduce stress through relaxation, she writes, insomnia will disappear, we will experience less pain after surgery, use less pain medicine and recover faster. She explains that when we are fearful or threatened, our bodies go into a fight-or-flight mode to protect us, releasing hormones into our system that are counterproductive when stretched over a long period of time. We become exhausted and our immune systems are compromised. It is only deep relaxation, she believes, that stops this process and creates hormones that relax the muscles and reduce our heart rate.

Her claim that focused thoughts, images and emotions are powerful medicine was similar to the theories of Norman Cousins, the author who participated in his own healing of *ankylosing spondylitis,* and who lived to write eleven books on health and healing. When he broke his arm, Huddleston said, he used visual imagery to speed his healing. At least several times a day for a number of weeks, he envisioned and felt the warmth of increased blood flow to his arm, bringing nutrients to his knitting bone. The x-rays showed that his bone had healed several weeks ahead of schedule.

I put on the earphones and practiced twenty minutes of deep relaxation exercises about several times on Monday, the day before surgery. That night, I slept like a baby—for the first time in weeks.

On the morning of the surgery, my daughter Katie arrived at the hospital and found me stretched out on the bed in the pre-op room listening to the relaxation tape. I had already scotch-taped a big white sheet of paper to the front of my hospital gown, listing statements I wanted the surgical team to repeat to me while I was going under the anesthesia. One of them was, "Following this operation, you will feel comfortable and you will heal very well." I asked them to place the earphones on me so I could listen to the relaxation tape during surgery, after which they would say multiple times, "Your operation has gone very well." Katie thought that this was some sort of a joke and that I was kidding, Assuring her that I was serious, she rolled her eyes in complete disbelief as if to say, *Why do I have to have such a crazy mom?*

My young handsome doctor wheeled me into the operating room. The big smile on his face matched my mood. The fear I had lived with for weeks was gone. I felt peaceful, grateful and optimistic, even euphoric. At the eleventh hour I found Peggy Huddleston, thanks to Kandy, both of whom intervened and handed me a gift: tools enabling me *really* to surrender: physically, emotionally and spiritually. I was in the surgeon's—and God's—hands.

The doctor performed a thymectomy, removing a tumor the size of an egg. It had originated in the thymus gland so the doctor removed the entire thymus gland too.

The operation he performed, according to his medical records, was this: "Median sternotomy with thymectomy and wedge resection of right upper lobe adherent to thymus." Thymoma is a rare disease that usually affects people who have something called *myasthenia gravis,* a neuromuscular disorder. But thymoma also shows up in a third of the population who have autoimmune disorders. That would be me. Notes from the Operation Record read: "A median sternotomy incision was made in the standard fashion with the oscillating saw." (There's that saw!) After several paragraphs about clearing the nerves and wedge resections involving the lobes of the lungs, the report went on: "Clearly the tumor only involved the right lobe but a total thymectomy was performed." Fortunately the tumor was completely contained (it was 6 x 4 cm.) and left no residue so there was no need for chemotherapy or radiation. Thankfully, it was not related to the stomach lymphoma. The surgeon placed wires in my sternum that, as far as I know, will always be there. A drainage tube protruded from my chest until the morning I was released to go home when they pulled it out.

That evening after the operation I was lying on my back in the hospital bed, so grateful that it was over and that the tumor hadn't metastasized. (I would have to learn to sleep on my back for the first time in my life.) There was a long scar down my chest with lots of staples. The attending nurse wanted to give me a bath. I was still groggy but remember trying to persuade her to just let me rest. I couldn't understand why she needed to give me a bath. The reasons she gave were lost on me. What I'll never forget is our contest of wills and her insistence that the bath was necessary. She won. This intractable nurse wanted to turn me over and I was thinking about my breastbone and how she might dislodge everything. She was so insistent that I had to agree. Just then I remembered *the tape!* I closed my eyes and walked myself through the relaxation steps. The whole time she was giving me a bath, I was in another place, feeling deep peace.

All the relaxation and imagery preparations paid off. The pain was very manageable and I was released from the hospital in four days—record time. According to the doctor, I tolerated the procedure very well. Several of the nurses remarked on my speedy recovery. I healed quickly from surgery and was able to enjoy Christmas as usual with my family and to resume a full work schedule about six weeks later, giving presentations on the Eucharist in local parishes and even a few in other states. It was a relief to have the thymectomy behind me and not to have to endure radiation or chemotherapy.

I CONTINUED SEEING FATHER BOB for spiritual direction. We were discussing a recent incident when I had become unglued over a silly misunderstanding with my husband in which my reaction was out of proportion to the actual happening. I thought he deliberately misled me about something, perhaps even lied to me. My overreactions to the simplest of disagreements were becoming a pattern. Although I rarely acknowledged any hurt or pain, I felt it deeply. Whatever the situation was never seemed to justify the intensity of my emotional meltdowns.

When Father Bob asked me to look into my past for an experience when I felt deceived, I remembered a time in high school when my mother told me that my father was unfaithful to her. I didn't believe her and told her that she was crazy to think that. Then one night I picked up the extension phone in my bedroom and heard my dad say, "I love you very much" to a woman not my mother. I knew who she was because my mom had identified her. She was my godmother. I hung up the phone and I never said a word, not to my mother or my dad or anyone. The pain was great. In a twisted sort of a way, I wanted to spare my mother the pain of knowing the truth, so I didn't tell her. In reality I think I could have validated her and been a friend to her by telling her what she already knew.

I treated my dad as if nothing happened. In doing so I lied, I hid from the truth. I told Father Bob that I felt like I had dissolved. He said that my husband triggered an issue that was foundational in my life: deception. The deception I experienced so long ago was one of the monsters rattling around in my inner basement. It had the ability to incite rage in me. I needed to address the buried hurt. Father Bob prayed asking the Lord to free me from my own self-rejection for not speaking the truth and to free me to stand in the truth.

What I'm really angry at is myself, my own deception, he said.

I wondered if this was the nun in the casket who buried her young self in order to do away with the hurt. She grew up, but was not fully alive; she pretended to be dead. Why did I go into hiding when I learned of the infidelity? I think I was afraid that the truth would devastate my world. Yet if I told my mom, she probably would have felt loved (by me) and comforted that I shared her pain. And if I had really been able to expose my hurt instead of burying it, it might have influenced my father. I think he would have been shocked to realize how much his behavior hurt me.

In that meeting with Father Bob I shed fifty-year-old tears of grief, sorrow and disappointment. I "lost" my father at that age, Father Bob said, and I will continue looking for him until I forgive him. I thought I had already done that. I guess there are levels of forgiveness.

Father Bob led me in a prayer of forgiveness, in which I asked the Lord to forgive me for my deception, and for not helping my mother and my father. I also forgave my father. Father Bob prayed: May Our Lord Jesus forgive you, and by His authority and the authority of the Church I absolve you from all your sins in the name of the Father, the Son and the Holy Spirit. We ask you to free little Joan from carrying that self-reproach all those years and Lord, we ask that the lie be purified even now after death so that Joan's father and mother can be reunited in You. (They took that lie to the grave.) Father Bob then extended that absolution to my mother and my father to the extent they received it, and prayed for healing back through all the generations, asking that any lies be lifted and that we be freed from them.

Father Bob reminded me that I should feel grateful for my husband who triggers these things. Husbands and wives are the best triggers for each other, he said. Because they have the deepest relationship, they trigger wounds in the deepest part of us. He suggested that I married my husband to have a father. That was truth. When I forgive my father, then I will be able to love him—and my husband—with my whole being. It will release me to love each of them for who they are and free me from expecting Tommy to be my father. At home I apologized to Tommy and told him that the incident around deception had nothing to do with him. It was my issue for which I took full responsibility. As always, he was quick to forgive and felt relieved, like a burden had been lifted from his shoulders.

We flew to Mexico City to spend Easter with Rich who was on assignment writing a travel book. It was a joy to be a part of his world and adventures. Rich was our tour guide, and a good one, having already put 12,000 kilometers on his rental car. He knew his way around this huge capital city, not to mention the rest of the country. On Easter Sunday morning Rich drove us to the Basilica of Our Lady of Guadalupe for Mass.

I was eager to see the famous image of Our Lady that hung over the main altar in the basilica. It is the original one that miraculously imprinted itself on the cloak of St. Juan Diego, a 57-year-old poor Indian convert to

Catholicism who was walking into the city one early morning in December 1531 when he saw a vision of a young girl of 14 to 16 years old, surrounded by light. She was the Blessed Virgin Mary who appeared on the Hill of Tepeyac and asked for a church to be built at that site in her honor. Juan Diego dutifully went to the bishop, who wanted a sign to prove his claim. As the story goes, the next day Our Lady asked Juan Diego to gather some flowers at the top of the hill, even though it was winter, when no flowers bloomed. There he found Castillian roses, which he gathered in his arms and then Mary herself rearranged them in his tilma. When Juan Diego presented the roses to the bishop, the image of the Virgin of Guadalupe miraculously appeared imprinted on the cloth of Juan Diego's tilma.

According to Church histories and documents, Our Lady came as the Virgin Mary and Mother of the true God with a message of love and compassion. She said that she knew the people's sorrows and saw their tears and came with a Mother's heart to console them. Beneath her folded hands in the image is a belt that many students of Aztec culture say represents pregnancy: Our Lady of Guadalupe was carrying the Child Jesus. When Pope John Paul II visited the U.S. and Mexico in 1999, he named Our Lady of Guadalupe Patroness of the Americas and declared December 12th as her feast day. In 2002 he canonized Juan Diego a saint before a crowd of twelve million and set his feast day for December 9th of each year.

After Mass we boarded the moving walkway in front of the original image on Juan Diego's tilma, set high above the main altar. The walkway moved a bit more slowly than they do in airports, allowing us enough time to get a good glimpse of this sacred artifact and a chance to pray in front of it. Holding an envelope filled with prayer requests from friends, I went around four times to be sure I prayed for everyone, myself included. As always, I asked for healing. This poor quality cactus-cloth that should have eventually deteriorated shows no sign of decay almost 500 years later, and still defies all scientific explanations of its origin. Apparently there is even a reflection in Our Lady's eyes of everything and everyone in her line of vision at the moment when Juan Diego unfolded his tilma in front of the bishop in 1531.

After spending the afternoon in and around the basilica, Rich drove us to San Miguel de Allende, a resort about three hours from Mexico City, for a few days of relaxation. It is an artists' colony and an oasis of beauty, not to mention a shopper's paradise. We went on several sightseeing expeditions and enjoyed long leisurely gourmet dinners with our youngest son.

My emotional troubles followed me to Mexico. During one of our dinners at an outdoor café, I was upset about an earlier disagreement I had with Tommy. Once again it was a minor matter that blew up like a balloon inside of me, causing a lot of pain. On one level I could carry on a conversation and act quite normally, but on another level I felt desolate and trapped and wanted to escape. Reading my body language (which I didn't think was so obvious), my intuitive son once again said, "Mom, what's wrong?" just as he had done in New York. Trying to keep a lid on my anger, I denied that anything was wrong, to which he responded, "It's like you're having a meltdown inside yourself." He was right on; I was on mute. When these incidents happen, I lose my voice.

AT HOME I SOUGHT Father Bob's help. I told him how I've pretended that "nothing is wrong" for so many years I don't even realize I'm doing it. I've swallowed, stuffed, denied, ignored and repressed negative feelings from day one, thinking that it was a sign of weakness to show vulnerability, to admit pain. We went over the same old ground about how I always ended up feeling emotionally disconnected or alienated from friends, but especially from my husband. At the bottom I didn't feel loveable or worthwhile. The painful wound is the place of healing, Father Bob said, because the wound and the pain is the guide to the lie. The lie is that I'm not worthwhile or loveable. I tend to believe the lie, that I'm not connected, not wanted, and not worthwhile, he said. That's probably when I experience an inner meltdown that renders me powerless.

Father Bob commented that instead of staying with desolation, I project it onto my husband. Then I feel trapped and want to end the marriage. "That's where the lie takes you," he said. I could see that. He continued: "The first part of the lie is that I should avoid the pain of desolation at all costs, when desolation is the key to healing." So, he said, "Stay in touch with desolation. That's the smoke that will take you to the campfire." My job was to search for the memory that takes me back to the source and origin of the desolation.

I closed my eyes to let a memory surface. I saw my mother and felt her inability to hear me. She was not really "there" because her unhappiness consumed her. She was usually in a bad mood that took up all her energy. It was as if she had a toothache from an exposed nerve; she could think of nothing else. I know that my parents cared about me, but as a child I had very little emotional connection with either of them. That led me to think, "I'm bad," and "I don't matter." I felt stuck. Father Bob prayed a deliverance prayer to bind the blocking spirit, after which I got in touch with the feeling that I wasn't emotionally reciprocated. Because of that, I felt that I didn't matter.

Father Bob suggested praying this way: "Lord, I'm wounded. Will you teach me how to find my true self that can stand there in the wound and bring healing rather than continual wounding?" He also recommended a story in the Gospel of Luke in which Jesus is a role model of forthrightness, clarity and honesty in speaking what's on His mind. When Jesus dined at the home of the Pharisee, a "sinful woman of the city" (Lk 7:37) showed great love to Him by kissing and anointing His feet with precious ointment. The Pharisee was inwardly mocking this gesture. Reading his judgmental thoughts, Jesus nailed the ridicule head on by saying, "Simon, I have something to say to you" (Lk 7:40). Jesus used the occasion to teach about forgiveness, and then He calmly and clearly contrasted the Pharisee's behavior with that of the woman's, pointing out all the ways the Pharisee failed to show love to Jesus. It showed how clearly and directly Jesus stood up for Himself and dealt with the problem.

This fired my resolve to try to acknowledge—and voice—my pain.

WE FLEW TO NEW YORK over Labor Day weekend for Danny's rehearsal dinner and wedding. Everything about the wedding was special: the church, Pippa, his bride-to-be, and the close friends and family who gathered from near and far.

When they decided to get married at St. Jean Baptiste I couldn't believe it. Little did they know how special that church was to me, beginning in high school when I went there one Sunday afternoon, along with representatives from every high school in the city, to attend a Catholic Youth Organization rally. There was a golden monstrance high above the main altar that held the large white Host which was Jesus in the Blessed Sacrament. It was the focal point of the church. A thunderous chorus of teenage voices proclaimed their faith in song. Amazingly, I still remember the chorus: *An army of youth, flying the standards of truth, we're fighting for Christ, the Lord. Heads lifted high, Catholic action our cry, and the Cross our only sword.* I wept in the joyfulness of that moment.

The church belonged to the Congregation of the Blessed Sacrament, an order founded by St. Peter Julian Eymard, a French priest who spent his life spreading devotion to the Eucharist. During our pilgrimage to France last year, we stopped in his hometown, La Mure, to see the parish church where his young faith blossomed. According to his sister, Peter Julian climbed a ladder behind the altar to reach the tabernacle. When questioned about this, he responded, "I'm near Jesus, I'm listening to him." He was 4 or 5 years old. I included this touching story in *Eucharist God Among Us, Essays and Images of the Eucharist in Sacred History.*

After the initial meeting with the pastor to book their wedding at Saint Jean's, there had been one possible obstacle: the pastor said in a kind but firm way that he didn't really know them, because they had literally walked in off the street, so he asked them to return for an interview. Pippa and Danny were understandably nervous and wondered what kind of grilling they would have to undergo.

On the evening of their meeting we were on pins and needles. When Danny finally phoned I could tell by his voice that he had good news. Before their interview, Danny said he was absent-mindedly looking at the books in the pastor's library, when he saw a large book that looked familiar. He pulled *Eucharist God Among Us* off the shelf and showed it to the pastor who was a bit taken back by the author's name "McHugh" on the cover. The pastor asked Danny if he knew her. "She's my mother," he said, at which point the pastor smiled broadly and said, "Oh, I don't think there will be any problem about you being married in Saint Jean's." They had a beautiful wedding in that magnificent church.

On the morning of September 11, 2001, I was in the orthopedist's office having an exam for possible arthroscopic surgery on my knee. We witnessed the replay of the horrific terrorist attack on TV. The only thing that the nurses, doctors and patients wanted to do in the office that morning was watch TV, myself included. I scheduled surgery a few weeks out, then went home to agonize over the TV coverage and to pray for the victims.

This tragically evil event shook the country to its foundation and brought people to their knees. Our own Francis Cardinal George of Chicago, writing in his weekly column in the *Catholic New World*, said that while our emotional reactions to the attack on our country range from shock to anger to fear, it is our faith that should give us hope and confidence. That confidence, he said, is not based only on our country's ability to recover and protect itself, but on God's ability to bring good out of evil. Our Cardinal has a gift for nailing the truth with his words.

A week later we were at a Conference on Divine Mercy led by Father John Corapi, a powerful speaker who testifies that Christ rescued him from a life of drug addiction and homelessness to become a Catholic priest and spread the Gospel. Questions about 9/11 were on everyone's minds. "How can a God of love could bring good out of such horrendous evil?" someone asked. There was a life-size crucifix on the wall behind Father Corapi. He turned around, pointed to Jesus on the Cross and shouted, *That is how*. "The crucifixion is the greatest evil in the world: deicide. Our God of love came into the world but we killed Him. Out of that evil came the greatest good, the salvation of all people." This placed everything in proper perspective.

IT TOOK EVERY OUNCE of courage I had to get on a plane a month after 9/11 and fly to New York in October. I wanted to attend Mother Mary Ranney's 90th birthday celebration at Sacred Heart, my alma mater. She taught me in first and second grade and I always felt a bond with her, I think because I knew that she loved me.

I'll never forget a lesson she taught me in second grade when I stole a beautiful doll that was sitting on the shelf in our classroom. Mother Ranney somehow found out that I had taken the doll and called my mother. When I returned the doll the next morning, she stood me up in front of the class. While holding the doll, she lovingly but firmly explained that taking something that is not ours is never permissible. It is our duty as children of God to always tell the truth even if it hurts. I loved Mother Ranney and didn't mind that she used me for this object lesson. Instead of shaming me, she described the goodness of telling the truth in a way that motivated me never to tell lies. She was only five feet tall, but she was a spiritual giant brimming over with wisdom and love. Mother Ranney hard-wired honesty into my brain.

When we gathered for Mass in our convent chapel to celebrate Mother Ranney's birthday, it overflowed with adoring alumnae. We sang "Oui, Je La Crois" ("Yes, I believe"), a song we sang throughout grade school. It reduced me to tears. My whole childhood flashed in front of my eyes and I mourned its loss.

At the reception afterwards, Mother Ranney took the microphone and encouraged us to look around and thank God for who we were, blessed children of His Sacred Heart who have been given a great power: to spread the light of love and faith into a world darkened with the evil of terrorism. She said she knew we were women of prayer and asked us to pray as we never have prayed before. She asked us especially to pray for the children of the world, that they would know love and truth and goodness, that they would know God's love for them. Mother Ranney encouraged us to entrust everything to the Divine Heart of Jesus, promising that He would not refuse us.

We also celebrated our 35th wedding anniversary with Rich and the newlyweds in New York. One day we took a taxi to Ground Zero and were only able to get within a block and a half of the actual site. Smoke still billowed from the wreckage. It was a sad and amazing scene, reminiscent of the bombed-out buildings and disaster areas in old war movies. We had hosted Danny and Pippa's rehearsal dinner over Labor Day Weekend—ten days before 9/11—at City Hall, a restaurant two blocks from the World Trade Center. We didn't receive an invoice for the dinner for eight months.

We concluded our visit to the East Coast by attending an honors convocation at Marymount College in Tarrytown, New York, where I received the Alumnae Achievement Award. It was wonderful to be back on that beautiful campus set high above the Hudson River where I used to sit at dusk and enjoy the magnificent view of the lights flickering on the Tappan Zee Bridge. It was also a joy to connect with friends I literally hadn't seen since I graduated. The Provost presented me with a gold "M" pendant and a citation praising Witness Ministries for our work in spreading devotion to the Mass and the Eucharist. It read in part: *You and your husband, Tom, founded Witness Ministries in 1992 in order to proclaim the Real Presence of Christ in word and art. Through your national speaking and publishing apostolate, you have responded to a growing need to restore faith in the Paschal Mystery. You show us how, in the Eucharistic Liturgy, Jesus renews and transforms us—and the world—in His life and love.* It was a distinguished honor that humbled and gratified me. My husband and Richard were in the audience.

The president of the Alumnae Board of Directors gave me a little gift. When I got home I retrieved the box from my suitcase and unwrapped it to find a chubby little white angel with golden wings dancing on a star, holding a message: "Believe in Miracles." This heavenly sign hangs on the bookshelf beside my desk where it offers me encouragement and hope whenever I need it.

These are my favorite photos of my mom, Sabina Borgia, and my dad, J. Howard Carter, taken when they were out to dinner in New York, in the late 1950s.

My brother Howie and I gave our dad a surprise 85th birthday party at the Spring Lake, New Jersey, Golf Club in October 1989. We surprised the guests with a copy of "Street Smart," an autobiography that my dad dictated and I edited. Daddy died two years later.

A picture of joy—and health! Tommy and I at our son Tom Jr.'s wedding in May 1994. Three months later I developed the first symptoms of scleroderma.

Posing with my mom and dad in front of our house in Spring Lake, New Jersey, circa 1944. I was 3 years old. Notice my body language!

I received my First Holy Communion in May 1948, in the chapel of the Convent of the Sacred Heart, in New York City. I practiced for it by solemnly administering graham cracker squares to myself after school.

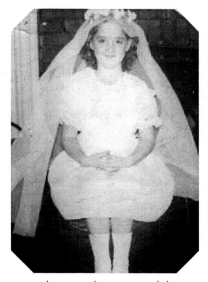

A newspaper photographer snapped this outside the local candy store in Spring Lake, New Jersey. Left to right I'm with my best friends, Johnny and Roger, who lived across the street. Two summers later, Roger and I were hospitalized with polio in the epidemic of 1947. I was released after a month, without any apparent side effects. Roger was in an iron lung, but recovered.

I was jubilant when I won the 18 & Under tennis championship in Spring Lake, New Jersey, on Labor Day Weekend 1959. Standing in the middle is my coach, Doris Hart, who won multiple Wimbledon, Australian, French and U.S. championships. At one point she ranked the world's number one female tennis player. Doris sharpened my mediocre tennis skills.

My dad took up flying when he was 57 and often invited me to be his co-pilot. We are standing in front of "2-0-Mike," his beloved Cessna that I soloed. Here we are about to "take a quick spin," as he used to say, in the 1950s.

October 22, 1966, my wedding day. Gertrude is giving me her familiar words of encouragement before we leave the apartment for the church. She was, and will always be (next to my husband), the best friend I've ever had.

Graduation from the Convent of the Sacred Heart, June, 1959.

"Jesus be our King and Leader,
Grant us in Thy toils a part,
Are we not Thy chosen soldiers,
Children of Thy Sacred Heart."

Best friends, Kandy Shuman and I, on the day we graduated from the Convent of the Sacred Heart (91st Street), in June 1959. Behind us is the statue of the Sacred Heart that greets everyone who enters the school.

At our 50th reunion from Sacred Heart, we are *still* best of friends. Left to right are Roni Dengel Rolf, Kandy Shuman Stroud and me.

I owe so much to the Religious of the Sacred Heart who taught me for twelve years. The late Mary Ranney, R.S.C.J. (above left), taught me in first grade and became a lifelong friend. Below left are some good friends from the class of 1959, and two very special nuns, Beatrice Brennan R.S.C.J., and Mary Brady R.S.C.J. (bottom right).

The first signs of illness appeared during a Marian pilgrimage to Caracas, Venezuela, in August 1994. Here I am having dinner with Fr. Joe Whalen, our good friend who became a La Salette Missionary at age 68. He was the spiritual director of the pilgrimage. Four months later I was diagnosed with scleroderma, a chronic and progressive autoimmune disease.

In February, 1995, I went on a retreat in St. Croix, hoping that the ocean water would reduce the inflammation and swelling and heal me. The scleroderma was overtaking me. My hands were twice their normal size.

Sitting in a church in St. Croix with Frs. Peter McCall, OFM Cap., and Bob McGuire, S.J., in the front row, and me between them. They prayed over my swollen hands every day. Father Peter was the first to teach me that emotional blocks could cause illness.

In April 1995, Tommy and I spent a few days with our youngest son, Rich, at Pebble Beach in California during his Easter break from Santa Clara University. I had been suffering from scleroderma for eight months and it was paralyzing me. I could hardly walk.

In May 1995, we went to the Shrine of the North American Martyrs in Auriesville, New York, to see the visionary from South America, Maria Esperanza, who was giving a keynote address at a Marian Eucharistic Conference. I was very swollen with scleroderma and had difficulty getting around. Next to me is Tommy's cousin, Hugh Humphries, who joined us at the Shrine.

At the Auriesville Shrine, someone introduced me to Maria Esperanza. (Maria is on the left, I am on the right, and the interpreter is in the middle. Tommy is behind Maria's left shoulder.) I asked for her prayers and she read my soul, giving me an insight into the cause of my illness, and telling me that I "would be completely healed through a wonderful doctor."

In November 1995, we were invited to attend Mass in the Holy Father's private chapel in the Vatican. Afterwards, Pope John Paul II greeted his guests, giving each person a rosary. He was warm, cordial and often humorous. Notice how swollen my hand is from scleroderma.

In February 1996, we went to the Holy Land with a group from Marytown, the National Shrine of St. Maximilian Kolbe in Libertyville, Illinois. Tommy and I took a turn carrying a cross through the Via Dolorosa. It was a year and a half since the onset of scleroderma, which really slowed me down. I had to buy a cane because my knee went out in the airport.

Tommy and I renewed our marriage vows in the small town of Cana, near Nazareth in Galilee. It is where Jesus attended the wedding feast and changed water into wine. Behind us is a replica of one of the water pots used in the miracle. It held between 20 and 30 gallons of water.

In the spring of 1997, we vacationed in France, mapping our itinerary for a future Witness Ministries pilgrimage. It seemed like St. Joan of Arc accompanied us everywhere we went. On Mont St. Michel I posed next to a statue of her. I could almost hear her saying to me: *Stay true to yourself and listen to God's voice. He will lead you to victory.*

May 1998. Tommy and I led a Witness Ministries pilgrimage to Italy. I had been diagnosed with MALT lymphoma and we were in a "wait and see" mode regarding the illness. Tommy (front row second from right) and some men from the pilgrimage gather in front of the Basilica of Santa Croce in Florence. Back row at the end on the left is Fr. Ted Keating, who called our office so often to order *My Daily Eucharist* books for his parishioners, that we invited him to be the spiritual director of the pilgrimage.

At a retreat on contemplative prayer given by Mother Nadine Brown (standing next to the Abbot), founder of the Intercessors of the Lamb in Omaha, Nebraska. The retreat was held at the Benedictine Abbey of Our Lady of Guadalupe, in Pecos, New Mexico.

Mother Angelica of EWTN and I greeted one another at a Call to Holiness Conference in Sterling Heights, Michigan in November 1998. EWTN ran our DVD on *The Real Presence* for several years.

This was taken in the 1990s at Marytown, the Kolbe Shrine, where I often lectured and gave days of renewal on the Eucharist. At the height of my illness, I always managed to have the stamina needed to give talks and retreats. Marytown is a spiritual oasis where I like to spend time in its magnificent chapel of perpetual adoration. It is modeled on the Basilica of St. Paul's Outside the Walls, in Rome.

Our good friend, Fr. Robert DeGrandis, a member of the Society of St. Joseph, stopped by our exhibit booth at the Eucharistic Congress in Washington, D.C., in May 1999. An author of more than forty books, Father Bob taught me about the healing power of forgiveness. He is a dynamic preacher who has supported our work from the start of our ministry.

In December 1999 we exhibited *Eucharist God Among Us* at the University Club Book Fair, in Washington, D.C. I had just learned that the scleroderma was in remission (after five years), but now I was dealing with MALT lymphoma in my stomach. Above, the late Robert Lynch, husband of my college roommate Ann Marie (left) who ran the Book Fair, tells me that he is drumming up business for our table.

In January 2002 Katie and I went to Lourdes, two weeks after my lumpectomy for breast cancer and two weeks before her wedding. It was the most wonderful mother-daughter vacation ever! We are standing beside the candles we had just lit for everyone for whom we promised to pray.

Anne Richards Tschanz, who manages our Witness office, and I are signing our books at the Religious Booksellers Trade Exhibit in Pheasant Run, St. Charles, Illinois in May 2003. I was signing my first memoir, *Feast of Faith, Confessions of a Eucharistic Pilgrim,* and Anne was signing her new book, *A Spiritual Pilgrimage to France.*

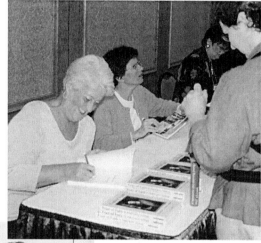

Bill Tomes, Velma Murphy and Anne Tschanz are the spiritual backbone of Witness Ministries! "Brother Bill" is a close friend who intercedes with the gangs in Chicago, bringing peace to many. Velma helps in the Witness office that Anne manages. Here we meet to pray the Rosary.

In November 2005 we met Francis Cardinal George at a reception at his residence in Chicago. He congratulated us on our newly released book, *The Mass, Its Rituals, Roots, and Relevance in Our Lives,* telling us that it was "a great gift to the Church." The Cardinal has always been supportive of our work.

These are my mentors, gifted counselors who guided my steps on the spiritual journey. Fr. Bob Sears, S.J. (left), specializes in spiritual growth and healing, especially healing family systems.

Sr. Irma Gendreau (right) belongs to the Little Franciscans of Mary. She gives spiritual direction and workshops on the PRH method of human development. Peggy Huddleston (lower right) is a psychotherapist who teaches people who are ill and facing surgery how to participate in their own healing. Brigham and Women's Hospital in Boston uses her book and relaxation CD for their lumpectomy and mastectomy patients.

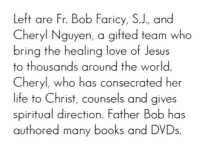

Left are Fr. Bob Faricy, S.J., and Cheryl Nguyen, a gifted team who bring the healing love of Jesus to thousands around the world. Cheryl, who has consecrated her life to Christ, counsels and gives spiritual direction. Father Bob has authored many books and DVDs.

Visiting a summer camp run by the Missionaries of Charity in the Bronx, in July 2009. Sr. Mary Marta M.C., (above facing picture on my right), invited me to speak to the children at St. Rita's Parish. On the left, my friend Colleen Ambrose, chats with Father Ramon who shared the story of his vocation to the priesthood.

These are my statues! The Sacred Heart of Jesus towers over the smaller statues that I've collected here and abroad. When my grand-daughters come over, they like to make up stories and rearrange the statues accordingly. I try to slip in some facts with the fantasy.

This is a professional photo we had taken of our kids, the summer before Tom Jr. went off to college. Left to right are Danny, Tom Jr., Rich and Katie.

Above are "my boys," doing what they love to do most: playing golf. Left to right are: Danny, Tom Jr., Tom Sr., and Rich. On the left Katie and I attend a bridal luncheon the day before her wedding.

Above, Rich and "Danie D" Mc Hugh
Left, Tom Jr. and Sinead with (l to r) Eva
Aidan, Gavin, Ryan and Tommy III.

Grandma and Grandpa
basking in glory! Our
eight grandchildren are
(l to r) top row: Aidan,
Oscar (on Joan's lap),
Tom Sr. and Ryan. Mid-
dle: Tommy McHugh III.
Bottom row (l to r): Erin
& Ellie Ranke, Eva and
Gavin McHugh.

Pippa, Danny and
Oscar McHugh.

Erin, Katie, Ellie, and Greg, Ranke.

15

Breast Cancer

As a psychoanalyst, I believe that every cancer has some form of internal conflict going on, whether it's on a conscious level or the unconscious level. When the body gets sick, it is giving a message that it is out of balance, it's out of alignment physically, spiritually, and emotionally. When my patients contract catastrophic disease, it's like the old Chinese saying, "There's always opportunity in crisis." You must find the good. You must find the lesson and then you will heal.

—Dr. Stephen Sinatra, M.D.
Excerpted from *Knockout: Interviews with Doctors Who are Curing Cancer*
By Suzanne Somers

ALONG WITH THE FIRST snows of winter came some serious new health challenges. In early November 2001, Tommy drove me to Northwestern Hospital in Chicago for an endoscopic ultrasound to determine the growth of the maltoma cells in my stomach. The same test a few years ago showed a slight thickening of the stomach wall, which my oncologist decided was microscopic and too minor to treat at the time.

I was still groggy from the sedative when the doctor handed me a picture of my stomach wall. It looked like some weird kind of modern art. He said that the "maltoma cells are a mucuosal association of lymphoid tissue"—and that there was "a proliferation of lymphocytes," which meant they were forming a tumor, but at a microscopic level. The bottom line: the maltoma cells had grown and I needed to see my oncologist who would decide on a course of treatment, probably six months to a year of either chemotherapy or radiation. When I asked him if I really had a chance of overcoming this, he said "absolutely," because I had a low-grade lymphoma that responds very well to treatment.

As we were walking out, Tommy put his arm around me and, with tender compassion, said, "we will beat this thing." His words had a calming, reassuring effect on me.

A few weeks later when my oncologist suggested that I take another bone marrow test, I jokingly refused because I had been down that road before and didn't care to repeat it. But I knew I was cornered and would have to take the test. Once again I focused on the crucifixion, but this time I could picture the nails because I had actually seen one (supposedly an original) in the Basilica of the Holy Cross of Jerusalem in Rome. The nail was about four inches long, horribly thick with a squared tip so it would inflict more pain. We know Jesus didn't have any Novocain and I couldn't imagine how He endured such excruciating torture. My little procedure was nothing by comparison. Nevertheless I offered the pain to Him and asked Him to bless my family, especially my children. I left her office not knowing the results—which I wouldn't know for a few days.

Then came more bad news. One of my doctors phoned with a negative report on a recent mammogram. He suggested that I redo it because he wanted to check on a suspicious finding. I felt myself sinking emotionally. A follow up mammogram showed a tiny shadow in my breast that needed to be biopsied. The prospect made me cringe. I wondered if the lymphoma was spreading, or perhaps it was something else? More stress. And now I had to find a surgical oncologist.

I phoned my four kids to share all the latest news. They wanted to be kept in the loop, and got upset with me if I forgot to tell them about something. I hated to add to the stress of their lives with more worries about their mom, but I needed to tell them about the negative breast report. I had called them too often with bad news: first scleroderma, then ulcers that led to the discovery of MALT lymphoma in my stomach, followed by the need to remove my thymus gland, and then the two latest findings: the maltoma cells in my stomach were growing and forming tumors and now breast cancer. It was all so much and they had a hard time keeping track of everything. I could feel their concern over the phone and reassured them—at least about the stomach— that this type of cancer "responds well to treatment."

I was trying to believe it myself.

In the midst of these storm clouds raining down problems in my life, several positive things happened to change my focus. The first was a request from my son Tom Jr. asking if his three boys could stay with us for twenty-four hours. Tommy, Ryan and Aidan were 4 years, 2 years and 6-months old respectively. After responding with an enthusiastic "Yes, of course," I had second thoughts that it would be too physically tiring.

Their visit actually had the opposite effect as this journal entry shows: *I become young when I am with them and so totally happy. They bring out the best in me and I think I do the same for them. They love my "soldier sandwiches" and "soldier cookies." We make everything a game and they are so open and vulnerable, willing to learn, unaffectedly being who they are at any given moment. I love them deeply and tell them so all the time. They smile at their silly nana. Tommy enjoys them just as much and actually plays the games with them. It is such fun to see him so childlike. We laugh with them a lot. On the way to the park there was a funny cassette tape that we played in the car. Their giggles set me off and I couldn't stop laughing.*

When it was time to drive them home the next day, 4-year-old Tommy invited me down to his playroom to see his toys and to share his world with him. The invitation was so sweet I could have cried.

The next surprise was a phone call from the Development Office of the Archdiocese of Chicago. They had selected *Eucharist God Among Us* to send as a Christmas gift to their generous donors: two hundred and twenty of them! For several days our Witness office was a cyclone of activity as our small staff—Tommy, Anne Tschanz, Velma Murphy and myself—carefully packaged 220 hardcover coffee table-size books for mailing. We enclosed a letter from Cardinal Francis George praising the book and its contents. This was a powerful endorsement of our work from the Cardinal and—I felt—from the Lord.

Another project that I had undertaken brought me immense joy. I wanted to make a CD of some of the favorite piano pieces played by my mother to give to our family. My children were young when my mom died and never heard her perform. Using a program from one of her piano recitals as a model, I went to Barnes & Noble where I scanned unopened CDs under a light to listen to the selections. The pieces were the work of other composers, but they were nevertheless "her" songs, the compositions she played. When I liked a certain rendition, I bought that CD to copy the song onto my master. The familiar melodies resounded through the earphones and flooded me with memories.

I could see her sitting by the window in our New York apartment practicing the piece over and over again. The windows spanned the width of the living room and, for many years, offered a great view of the Triborough Bridge (recently renamed the Robert F. Kennedy Bridge) that connected Manhattan with the Bronx and with Queens on Long Island—until a highrise went up and ruined the great view. My mom would sit at the piano for hours, wearing one of her many flowered "house" dresses that she ordered constantly from newspaper ads, and she would practice difficult sections of pieces until she mastered them. She was disciplined and determined but what struck me the most was her passion. She played with her heart, with an intensity of emotion that made the pieces talk. One of the most intricate and complex of the compositions was my favorite that I always asked her to play if a friend came over or if ever we had company. It was Chopin's Fantasie-Impromptu in C Sharp minor, Op. 66. (I called it "I'm always chasing rainbows.") To this day when I hear a pianist play that song, it sounds flat, or too fast, or too slow. No one plays those pieces like my mother did, because she put her heart and soul into each composition. Her touch was so sensitive and delicate it came from a place deep within her being, as if she was fulfilling her life's mission.

THANKSGIVING AND MY 60TH birthday fell a day apart this year, so we celebrated them together. I offered to cook and stuff two turkeys (because I love doing it!), one to bring to my niece Caroline's home for Thanksgiving and one to have at home for leftovers. All our children were there except for Danny and Pippa, the newlyweds in New York. Caroline, who can outdo Martha Stewart, set the most beautiful table with her Herringbone china and Waterford crystal. I love being with Caroline because she is so open and honest with her feelings. The way she shares whatever is on her mind is refreshing. My brother Howie and his son Philip were visiting from the East coast. In the wake of the terrorism of 9/11, the destruction wrought by al-Qaeda and the terrible war in Afghanistan, the grace that we said before dinner was a heartfelt thank you to God for the gifts of life and freedom and especially family. I was especially grateful to be feeling as well as I did, considering the precarious state of my health.

After dinner Caroline placed a gold crown on my head and piled gifts on my lap. The birthday cards from my children made me cry—as they always do—and my husband outdid himself, surprising me with tickets to *The Three Tenors*, *La Boheme*, and to a whole day of beauty treatments at Elizabeth Arden. After dinner we played the board game Balderdash and laughed ourselves silly.

AFTER THANKSGIVING I NOW HAD to deal with the problems resulting from the recent CT scan and bone marrow tests. They showed some tiny lymph nodes in my stomach that weren't there two years ago as well as traces of lymphocytes in the bone marrow. This meant that the disease was growing. The oncologist I had been seeing for several years reiterated that this lymphoma responds very well to treatment, although it does have a tendency to come back. I worried that it was spreading.

Now I needed to find a surgical oncologist. My son Rich intervened at the eleventh hour and called his friend Sean, whose father was a well-known surgical oncologist at St. Francis Hospital in Evanston. I was on the phone with Dr. Cunningham that evening, who listened to my health history with sensitivity and compassion. He said, "You have an old-fashioned disease with a new name: MALT lymphoma." He said it was very treatable and he was happy to meet with me next week. I felt encouraged.

The next week Dr. Cunningham spent an hour with us pouring over a thick stack of my records. He considered me "family" he said, because his son referred me to him. I felt so comfortable—and hopeful—in his presence. He had done some research and told me that Sloan Kettering in New York reported having seventeen cases of this rare lymphoma in the last five years, and they boasted a one hundred percent success rate in treating those cases with radiation. This was incredible news. Dr. Cunningham asked for permission to bring my case before a board of oncologists and pathologists at St. Francis Hospital the next day. Permission indeed! What an enormous gift.

Apparently the doctors discussed my case in depth. He phoned to give me their conclusions: I probably would need radiation for the stomach but not until I have three more tests: a biopsy of the breast, the stomach and another bone marrow test. He scheduled those for the following week as an outpatient at the hospital. He spared me knowing all that they discussed. (He told me long after the fact that several doctors wanted to remove my stomach!) I didn't sleep much in anticipation of the upcoming procedures—but I trusted this kindly and wise doctor and felt the hand of God guiding me in the dark.

At Mass the next week there was a reading from Isaiah that felt like another signpost offering direction: "Thus says the Lord, your Redeemer, the Holy One of Israel: I am the Lord your God, who teaches you to profit, who leads you in the way you should go" (Is 48:17-19). At home I wrote in my journal: *I believe God is leading me on the way I should go! This week has been proof that I am being carried on wings of grace, cared for by a wonderful doctor, caring nurses and a husband who suffers more than I do over my condition. I passed the three tests with flying colors (biopsies of breast, stomach and bone marrow), hiding my fears as best I could. I feel grateful actually to have something to give to God. I can offer Him physical suffering, the uncertainly, the fear, the anxiety—and hardest of all, the unknown. I enjoy the ability to offer God something—anything—however little it is.*

Perhaps it was not so little. When Dr. Cunningham phoned with the latest report, he said that the breast biopsy showed a small cancer that would need to be removed. He said not to worry, it is perfectly curable, but he was surprised—and sorry—to find it. He suggested that I schedule surgery for early January at which time he would also remove some of the surrounding lymph nodes. The bone marrow test was still inconclusive which meant they might have to do another one when I go in for the breast surgery. He said there was "a small population of lymphocytes" in the bone marrow but not enough evidence to suggest lymphoma. But there was no question about the stomach: the entire lower half contained MALT lymphoma. So we were still in a holding pattern regarding treatment until the bone marrow issue got settled.

Dr. Cunningham was extremely knowledgeable, so I shared my frustration and asked him how it is that I've had so many cancers: stomach, breast, thymus (removed last December but it was benign) and now possibly bone marrow. He said that I somehow inherited a faulty immune system that resulted in scleroderma, and it all could have something to do with abnormal genes. I understood the faulty immune system but I had never thought of or heard about abnormal genes. It made sense and satisfied me, at least for the moment.

One afternoon I drove out to Marytown, my place of refuge in troubled times. No sooner was I there than I ran into several friends who were concerned about my health. Brother David, the manager of the gift shop, asked me if I had thought of going to Lourdes. (I hadn't.) Minutes later, another friend said the same thing. Was the Lord speaking to me through these people? If a trip to Lourdes was in God's plan, then I trusted that a way would open for me to go. I would pray about it.

A FEW DAYS LATER we went to my grandson Tommy's 4th birthday party at North Beach, an indoor playground in Chicago. It was five days before Christmas. When we arrived, Tommy and twenty of his pre-school friends were jumping inside a huge moonwalk. As soon as he saw me he stuck his head through the netting and shouted, "Nana, I have a crown!" He was referring to the crown they had given me at my 60th birthday party. I felt the love in his big heart and wished I could hug him on the spot.

While my daughter Katie and I were watching the kids bounce up and down in the moonwalk, I was telling her about the latest diagnosis of breast cancer and sort of thinking out loud about going to Lourdes, saying that I'd love to take her with me—to which she instantly responded, "I'd love to go!" I was stunned by her response because her wedding was scheduled for February 9th—less than six weeks away. "Really, you would?" I said, incredulously. But before getting too excited about it, I would have to discuss the upcoming breast surgery with Dr. Cunningham as well as a treatment plan for the stomach lymphoma.

Driving home from the birthday party, I listened to a lengthy voice mail on my cell phone from Dr. Cunningham. He said that he and a team of pathologists concluded that there was not enough evidence to suggest that I have lymphoma of the bone marrow—and I wouldn't need to do another bone marrow test for six months. A giant wave of relief swept over the both of us. Tommy reached over and took my hand saying how happy he was. What a great Christmas present.

On Monday morning I phoned Dr. Cunningham to thank him for the good report. We scheduled breast surgery for January 8th, a month before Katie's wedding. Then on the Monday after her wedding, I would begin a 38-day radiation program for my stomach. That left a window of about a month—after the breast surgery on January 8th and before the wedding on February 9th—to go to Lourdes. I said a silent prayer and asked Dr. Cunningham if I could squeeze in a trip to Lourdes after surgery and before radiation. After a longer than usual pause, he said, "Yes, of course you can." I called Katie immediately and we *both* became emotional.

I GAVE MYSELF AN early Christmas present and bought *The Gift of Peace* by Joseph Cardinal Bernardin, Archbishop of Chicago. Fr. Don O'Connor, a Divine Word missionary from Techny, Illinois, who had spent most of his life in Papua New Guinea, mentioned the book in his Christmas card. He said that he read it before his cancer surgery and received the gift of peace while reading the book.

This Cardinal, whom I had met on several occasions and who always called me by name, told the story of the last three years of his life that included false accusations of sexual misconduct, a diagnosis of pancreatic cancer and the return of the cancer after being in remission for fifteen months.

He related his trials by fire to the suffering of Jesus, which, he said, is life giving and redemptive. "The essential mystery of the Cross is that it gives rise to a certain kind of loneliness, an inability to see clearly how things are unfolding, an inability to see that, ultimately, all things will work for our good, and that we are, indeed, not alone."[1] He explained that we are not alone because, as disciples of Christ, we suffer in communion with Him, but that doesn't extinguish the loneliness or sense of abandonment, which even Jesus experienced. I totally related.

Cardinal Bernardin said that his decision to share his cancer treatment publicly was mandated by a simple message: that faith really matters. He was able to accept his illness and his impending death because of his faith he said; it grounded him in the Lord and opened him to God's will. He re-iterated his belief in the redemptive value of pain and suffering. Although he prayed that, "this cup pass me by," this holy man concluded his life by embracing the pain. By looking into it and beyond it, the Cardinal said that he came to see God's presence—even in the worst situations.

The Cardinal's message gave me a sense of God's nearness and a desire to trust Him completely.

GOD'S PRESENCE WAS SURELY with us on Christmas. We were all together this year and the highlight was having my four grown children, two spouses and one fiancé stay with us—and our grandsons. Having the children meant that Santa would be coming to our house for the first time in many years. Tommy and I looked forward to Santa's arrival as much, if not more, than we did when we were young parents.

On the afternoon of Christmas Eve I ran to the grocery store for some extra shrimp for hors d'oeuvres. The line at the fish counter was so long I couldn't believe it. Where did all these people come from? No sooner did I get in line than a friend I hadn't seen in awhile came rushing over. She had heard rumors about my illness and wanted to know how I was doing. While I tried quietly to bring her up to date on my lymphoma and breast cancer, I had the uneasy feeling that I was broadcasting my personal health problems to a line full of strangers. After she left, the man in front of me turned around and said, "You know, I had lymphoma eleven years ago. I had it in my spleen and lung. They gave me radiation and today, I am cancer free." We chatted a bit longer then he put his hand on my shoulder and gave me a little kiss on the cheek saying, "Don't worry, you are going to be fine." Once again, I felt God's providential care through a total stranger whom I just happened to stand next to in line at the fish counter. I felt like it was a Christmas present from Jesus. I couldn't wait to share the news with my family. I went home with a song in my heart.

We decorated a birthday cake for the baby Jesus that Tommy and Ryan adorned with colored sprinkles, jellybeans and lots of candles. They embraced this project with unabashed joy and wonder. It was precious to observe their spirit of celebration and even more wonderful to witness their pride and delight when it came time after dinner to light the candles and sing "Happy Birthday" to Jesus.

On Christmas morning after we'd opened all the presents, Pippa, my new daughter-in-law, put her arms around me. She was full of joy and gratitude, "not just for the presents" she said, "but for all the love in this family." I don't ever remember a Christmas when I felt so blessed. Illness gave me a new perspective on life. I valued everything so much more, especially my family and friends. I was overwhelmed with gratitude and a deeper awareness of even the smallest signs of God's presence and love.

There was one gift left to give: the CD of my mother's music. Everyone opened the CD at the same time, sharing a sense of wonder—and gratitude. They simply couldn't believe their grandmother was such an artist, that she had the talent to play those songs. We sat there for the rest of the morning listening to the beautiful music.

Then Katie came over and put her arms around me. I couldn't stop crying. The music bridged the years—and the divide—between my mother and me, uniting me to her as never before. And it also drew me closer to my beautiful daughter whom I loved so much but probably hadn't told her so in years.

16

Lumpectomy

Illness is an invitation to love oneself into becoming the person God intended.

—Fr. Bob Sears, S.J.

IT WAS THE BEGINNING of the New Year, 2002, and as word of my breast cancer spread, I received an outpouring of support from friends and extended family. Fr. Joe Whalen, our friend with whom we had gone to South America, offered Masses for me on the first three days of 2002. Our new daughter in-law's parents, Helen and Nigel Bark, had a Mass offered for me on January 1, the Feast of Mary the Mother of God, at Our Lady Queen of Peace Chapel in Orangeburg, New York. And two close friends gifted me by having a year of Masses said for me at Holy Hill, Wisconsin, and at the Blue Army Shrine of the Immaculate Heart of Mary in New Jersey. Tommy's brother, Dick, a Jesuit priest in India, emailed promising to celebrate Masses for me saying, "Amazing how you take all this. In the words of Sacred Scripture 'Your faith has made you whole.'" This was the second time in a year that someone had repeated this Scripture verse to me.

Then after Mass one Sunday our friend, Fr. Larry Hennessey, asked if I'd like to receive the Anointing of the Sick. I hesitated because I thought I should save it for a time when I showed more signs of sickness—as if breast cancer wasn't enough! Yet I deeply appreciated receiving one of the seven Sacraments of the Church. The Catechism describes them as instruments

172

of grace that enable us to participate in the divine nature of God. I like to picture them as spiritual sap—the spirit of Christ—that gives life to our souls.

The tradition of laying hands on people dates back to the time of Jesus when the elders in the Christian communities anointed the sick and blessed them with holy oil in the name of the Lord. They were imitating Jesus, whose compassion was so great that when He touched people, "power came forth from Him and healed them all" (Lk 6:19). The early Christians believed that this prayer of faith would "save the sick" (Jas 4:15), meaning that it would heal their souls as well as their bodies—and forgive their sins.

When Father Larry blessed my forehead and hands with holy oil, he said some comforting prayers. I closed my eyes and pretended Jesus was standing in front of me. While I heard Father Larry's voice mouthing the prayers, I *believed* it was Christ touching and healing me through the Sacrament.

We had to get up at 4:30 A.M. on the day of my lumpectomy in order to be at St. Francis Hospital in Evanston by 6:00. A lumpectomy is a surgical procedure to remove breast tissue that is cancerous. It is also called an excisional biopsy or a partial mastectomy. We were admitted to a pre-op room, and then left alone for what felt like hours. But it was probably less than an hour. Tommy wasn't feeling well so he lay down on the hospital bed while I sat back in the recliner and practiced my relaxation. He started to snore, and when the nurse came in she wasn't happy to see him in the bed. In fact she was quite annoyed. I felt her vibes and quickly assured her that I didn't mind because it seemed like he had the flu and needed the sleep.

In the operating room I asked Dr. Kim, the anesthesiologist, if he would talk to me as I was going under the anesthesia and say, "Following this operation, you will feel comfortable and you will heal very well," just as I had done a year before during the surgery to remove my thymus gland. I had followed Peggy Huddleston's techniques to the letter for that surgery, and they worked. I was released from the hospital in record time, had minimal pain and felt really well through it all. I believed in Peggy's approach, which was to teach the people how to cooperate with the medical team in the healing process.

Dr. Kim said he would be happy to make the encouraging statements to me during the surgery, and he also offered to pray for me. I was thrilled. Before they put me to sleep, he told me that he had earned a master's degree in theology and that his father had been a Protestant minister. I wanted to keep the conversation going but by then he had inserted the I.V. into my hand (on the first try—a major accomplishment) and I was out.

The two-hour surgery went very well and was a great success. Even though the cancerous part was tiny, Dr. Cunningham said he removed more tissue than he had planned because they would not be able to administer any post-operative radiation due to my scleroderma. He also took out two lymph nodes that were benign—for which I was so relieved. The scar was a bit scary looking, I think because of the stitches that were black. It looked like the crescent of the moon—curved and about two inches long. I don't remember how many stitches there were or if it hurt. But if I had to guess, I would say there were ten. He decided not to send me home with a drain, saying that he would drain it during office visits. I felt somewhat relieved. My only worry was that I'd be disfigured. In reality, one breast ended up being slightly smaller than the other, but it has never bothered me in the least.

Amazingly, Dr. Cunningham allowed us to go home later that same afternoon. I collapsed on the couch to sleep off the effects of the morphine, and Tommy took a nap and some Aleve tablets for the flu. My post-op orders included no driving for two weeks.

That night Tommy began bleeding and couldn't stop. (A few days before my lumpectomy he had a routine colonoscopy during which the doctor removed a large benign polyp.) Early the next morning I had no choice but to get in the car and drive him to the doctor, who attempted another colonoscopy to stop the bleeding, but there was too much blood and he had to be rushed to the emergency room in an ambulance.

A very experienced but busy South African gastroenterologist, who treated him in the emergency room, told us several times that his condition was life threatening. I think he was aggravated by my husband's humor. When asked how much wine he drank, Tommy said with a straight face, "only one or two bottles a night." The doctor didn't crack a smile but the nurses and I laughed out loud. The doctors working on him had a difficult time stopping the bleeding. They were finally able to cauterize the area, but he lost almost half of his blood in the process.

Tommy spent the next four days in intensive care where they replaced his blood and stabilized him. Despite the bravado, I had never seen my husband in such a weakened state and my heart went out to him. Tom Jr. and Katie drove out to visit, and we were constantly on the phone to Danny and Rich in New York giving them updates on his condition. It was a tense time, but he finally pulled through it and we were relieved and grateful when he could go home.

I think his courage and my concern for him helped me forget about my own weakened condition from the breast surgery, and my healing progressed rapidly.

A WEEK OR SO LATER we drove downtown to Chicago's Second City for a matinee at the popular improv theater. On the way we stopped at St. Francis Hospital to have the stitches from the lumpectomy removed. Dr. Cunningham was very pleased with the success of the surgery and the way the scar was healing. While he was preparing an injection to drain fluid from the breast, I cringed at the sight of the needle. Before I had a chance to react, he stuck it into my breast, and I was relieved to have hardly felt it. I suppose it didn't hurt because it was like sticking a needle into cotton. There was no muscle to plow through. After that I never worried about the drainings.

After seeing Dr. Cunningham, we took the elevator to the basement for a consultation with the radiation oncologist, the doctor would administer radiation to my stomach beginning two days after Katie's wedding in February—now less than a month away.

When we walked into the waiting room, a woman was throwing up in the waste paper basket. Not a good beginning! A wave of fear engulfed me. *Is this going to be me in a month?* I liked this doctor immediately. He was calm, matter-of-fact and had an aura of confidence. He told me that I was famous at St. Francis Hospital, due to the fact that my case had been presented before two tumor boards at the hospital. Then he recited my health—or rather un-health—history to me, which all sounded quite grim. He only knew me on paper, through all the CT scans and lab reports, and I think he expected to see a really sick person. I enjoyed his obvious surprise—almost confusion—at how well I looked. It showed through comments like, "You look quite healthy to me," and, "You don't look like someone who is dealing with so many health issues." (It probably helped that I was dressed up that day with makeup on because we were going to the theater.) In a follow up letter he sent to Dr. Cunningham, he described me as "a very pleasant 60-year-old female with a very complicated history." He wrote that my "Physical exam shows a surprisingly healthy-appearing female in no acute distress." I would take this description any day over the remark the Wisconsin doctor made back in December, 1994, when he diagnosed my scleroderma saying, "she is certainly an interesting problem."

He wanted me to have radiation for four weeks. The radiation itself would last about a minute, he said. The possible side effects were nausea and tiredness. I was eager to get going with it and hopeful that a special vitamin and nutritional program a nutritionist gave me would decrease the negative effects of the radiation.

I PHONED MY FRIEND Grace Gibson with whom I had roomed in St. Croix, to bring her up to date on my latest health problems. I also shared my continuing struggle with depression. Grace was a spiritual director who felt that the pain was coming out in my body. She said it was "screaming for healing." She suggested that we pray together. I asked for the guidance of the Holy Spirit. While Grace was praying, I saw an image of myself as a small child, maybe 2 or 3, at the bottom of a well. When I looked up I could see light, but I was trapped and alone at the bottom of this deep well. There was that child again, the part that is often in darkness and feels desolate.

In my next meeting with Father Bob, I brought up the image of the child in the well. He suggested that I invite Jesus to be with me in that dark place. A pattern was emerging. First there was the nun in the casket, then the child, both of whom felt trapped, alone and despairing. They were obviously the same person, the part of me that gave up on life because she had no hope of ever being free.

Once again we discussed my habit of blaming the desolation on Tommy. When I begin to feel that I am in that wasteland, Father Bob said I project the pain onto him, thinking that if I were free from this marriage I could be totally happy. Father Bob said, "Why don't you say, '*if I were free in this marriage*'?" Part of me was imprisoning myself and, he said, the marriage was a projection of my prison, with my husband holding the key.

This was true. Classic codependency. Even though I knew better and tried to let go and detach, I still gave him power over me. In many ways I was living his life, not my life.

I worried about the toll this tension took on my body as this journal entry shows: *I wonder if the hopelessness and despair of the child in the well is what is causing my cancer. Our deepest beliefs have a huge effect on our emotional health. A core part of me believes she deserves to be in this well. This place of hopelessness is exactly what feeds cancer. It is no wonder I have it. Is the Lord leading me ever so gently to the source of the problem, giving me the chance to learn and grow from this experience? I really think that my illnesses are related to this depression and despair, and pray that God will heal my inner child—and my cancer.*

Father Bob explained that disease is a gift in disguise. He saw it as an invitation to love oneself into becoming the person God intended. When I asked him to elaborate, he explained that "disease" shows you that something is wrong, not just in general, but in a particular way. He shared an example from his own struggle with tongue cancer. He couldn't understand why he contracted it because he never smoked or abused his tongue in any physical way. After praying and meditating about this, Father Bob said it dawned on him that he wasn't speaking out his pain. His relationships got skewed because he wasn't speaking the truth. He realized that in trying to please others, he was not being true to himself. He also said that just dealing with the physical cancer wouldn't have helped if he hadn't dealt with the underlying cause.

"And what was the cause?"

"Deep repressed pain. Feeling that I wasn't welcomed in conception."

I understood—and related. The root of psychological illness, Father Bob said, is that we don't believe we're loved. We are all crippled by original sin, which at its root is a disbelief in God's love for us. When we can open ourselves to forgiveness, he concluded, and let the truth of God's love into our hearts, then we can heal and begin to celebrate our existence.

Two weeks after my surgery, Katie and I boarded an Air France jet to Paris en route to Lourdes where we landed almost twenty-four hours from the time we left Chicago. I felt like Dorothy who went to sleep and woke up in an unfamiliar location far from home. We arrived in a land of Our Lady, a place of mystical beauty, where the Gothic spires of one of the five basilicas in Lourdes greets pilgrims who come to this tiny city at the foot of the Pyrenees from all over the world to find hope—and healing.

We arrived exhausted and promptly took a three-hour nap, then trekked up a steep hill past the Hotel de la Grotte to the only restaurant open in town, an Italian pizzeria where we had dinner. We were the sole Americans in the place and each time we came back for lunch or dinner, the waitresses welcomed us with friendly smiles and nods. The food was delicious and we never ran out of things to talk about.

The next morning after one of those elaborate European buffet break-fasts, we headed for the Grotto for 10 A.M. Mass.

The Grotto is the site of one of the most famous of all of Our Lady's apparitions. It was in a place known as Massabielle, which locals referred to as the Old Rock, a cold, damp area by the river where pigs took shelter. On February 11, 1858, a young peasant girl named Bernadette Soubrious went out with two friends to collect firewood. They passed the cave of Massabielle, and when Bernadette sat down to remove her socks and shoes to cross the stream, she heard a noise like a gust of wind. When she looked up, she saw a Lady standing in a small cleft of the rock. The Lady smiled at Bernadette and beckoned her to approach. She had a rosary hanging from her arm. They prayed the Rosary together and Our Lady didn't say the Hail Marys, but she joined in for the Glory Be at the end of each decade.

As word of this event spread, crowds gathered at the site and Berna-dette's mother, who had at first refused to let her go back to the Grotto, gave her permission to return. Our Lady asked Bernadette to come for fifteen days and, during each apparition, she spoke to her. Others could not see the Lady when she appeared, but they could tell by Bernadette's radiance and joy that something very special was happening.

Our Lady asked Bernadette to tell people to pray for the conversion of sinners and to do "Penance, penance, penance!" Our Lady also wanted Bernadette to tell the priests to have people come there in a procession, and to have a chapel built at the site.

One day Our Lady pointed to a muddy area on the ground and told Bernadette to drink from it. People were appalled to see the child digging in the mud and putting it to her mouth. But a new spring of water began to flow from the spot, and when Bernadette's friend plunged her dislocated arm into the water, it healed before their amazed eyes. More cures began immediately, beginning with a stone-carver who had lost his eyesight but who miraculously was able to see after bathing his eye with water from the Grotto. The tradition of blessing people with holy water and bathing in the water at Lourdes originated as a result of these happenings. Today, faithful people from all over the world continue to believe in the power of Lourdes holy water to bring healing to body and soul. To date, there have been sixty-seven medically certifiable miraculous cures. (The archives of the Medical Office of Lourdes go back to 1873 and contain documents re-lating to more than 6,000 cases of healing. But the criteria for establishing a bona fide "miracle" are so strict, that the process eliminates all but those deemed "inexplicable.")

When Our Lady asked for a chapel to be built at the Grotto, Bernadette told the parish priest who didn't believe her. He wanted to know the name of the Lady. Bernadette kept asking Our Lady for her name, and one day she received a response: "I am the Immaculate Conception." Four years earlier in 1854, Pope Pius IX solemnly proclaimed as the dogma of the Immaculate Conception, that the Virgin Mary was conceived without any stain of original sin. Bernadette was a poor and uneducated girl, unable to read or write, and she had no idea what the words meant. But this message helped convince the local parish priest that the events taking place at the Grotto were of supernatural origin.

During one apparition Bernadette lit a candle at the Grotto, a tradition that continues to this day with millions of candles burned each year. Lourdes has become one of the most popular Christian pilgrimage sites in the world, with an estimated 6,000,000 people visiting the town annually.

Katie and I had a front row seat for Mass at the Grotto. There might have been twenty-five people there, compared to a thousand or more during the peak seasons. Being at the site of Our Lady's apparitions was very moving to me. The visuals alone inspired prayer: the tall, conical stand containing votive candles which burned constantly beside the altar, the cleft in the rock where Our Lady appeared, and which now holds a beautiful statue of Our Lady of Lourdes, abandoned crutches hanging high up in the cave, and one can even hear the sound of the water flowing within the Grotto, protected by a glass screen and lit from below.

I clutched an envelope filled with prayer petitions that friends and family had given me. Katie also had names of people for whom to pray. In a sense I felt like they were all on the pilgrimage with us. If ever I was grateful to have the gift of faith, and especially to have a devotion to Our Lady, it was here, in "her" land, where I believed she would take special notice of us.

I had grown a great deal in my understanding about Our Lady since my days at Sacred Heart when I wasn't invited into the sodality. In the early 1990s I was a guest on *Mother Angelica Live!* on the Eternal Word Television Network in Birmingham, Alabama. I was still publishing *Witness Magazine* and sharing my faith story as well as some of the powerful testimonies of healing and conversion that we printed in the magazine. At some point during the half-hour interview, Mother asked, "And where does the Blessed

Mother fit in your story?" I thought for a minute then remembered an insight I had recently learned about Mary from a speaker at a conference on the Eucharist. "When children in a family really want something," I said, "they go to their mother instead of their father." "Why is that?" Mother Angelica asked. "Well," I said, "the father is likely to say no. But they know that their mother will intercede with their father who will usually say yes to her." Mother Angelica was delighted with my answer. I continued to make my point, saying that Our Lady's role has always been to intercede with Her Son on our behalf, beginning with the time when they ran out of wine at the wedding at Cana, and Mary asked Jesus to do something about it. She said to the servants, "Do whatever He tells you," (Jn 2:5). It was there that Jesus performed His first miracle, changing six jugs of water into wine, today the equivalent of forty cases.

Some of these memories ran through my mind on that first morning at the Grotto, when I put my life in Our Lady's hands. It was a form of spirituality I first learned from the Sacred Heart nuns, then later from Pope John Paul II, whose papal motto was "Totus tuus," or "Everything for you," meaning, all for Jesus through Mary. It gave me real hope to surrender my life—especially my health and all the other problems that seemed to pursue me—to Mary's motherly heart. I trusted that she would have a word with her Son on my behalf.

After Mass, Katie and I headed over to the Baths in a small building not far from the Grotto. There were no lines and the dressing room was empty. That, in itself, was unbelievable. In fact, we were the only people in the Baths! The water for the Baths was provided by the spring at the Grotto, about which Our Lady had said, "Go drink of the spring and wash yourself there."

It was warm in the dressing area where there were lockers and large towels that provided utmost privacy. When I undressed an attendant then led me into the pool area, which looked like a long modern rectangular bathtub. There were a few steps down and it was quite shallow. I stood on the bottom step and two women attendants suggested I recollect myself and pray to Our Lady. There was a tiny statue of Our Lady at the foot of the bath about eight feet away. Then I silently—and tearfully—poured out my heart to her, begging her intercession for all the intentions I carried with me. Whey they lowered me into the water, I didn't even feel the cold. I literally felt as if I were wrapped in a warm blanket of love.

Altogether I went in the Baths three times, twice on the first day and once the next. I had read stories of people being healed after their third trip to the Baths. I really wanted to avail myself of this opportunity and while Katie contemplated going multiple times, we decided that one bath was enough for her because she was getting a cold.

On our second and final day I took my third bath. I was in the dressing cubicle with two children. One was a baby about six or seven months old, and the other was a pretty little girl about 3 or 4. Even though they didn't look sick, I thought they must have something really wrong with them to be in the Baths at such a young age, so I began praying for them. The little baby was lying on a stretcher—all smiles—until they immersed her in the water. She began crying and didn't stop for a long time. While praying for them I also asked Our Lady to heal my inner child. In fact I begged her to rescue me from that deep well of desolation once and for all.

Katie and I had Lourdes all to ourselves. Most of the shops were closed, save for a few near the Grotto, and we both appreciated the lack of crowds. The January air was brisk but the sun was warm. With only two days to spend, we did everything we could possibly do in Lourdes, including watch a movie about Bernadette in which we were the only people in the theater. The story was gripping and inspiring. After the movie we went to the Sacrament of Reconciliation, and then spent some time in the Upper Basilica praying quietly in the presence of the Blessed Sacrament. Katie was curious about the meaning of adoration, so I shared with her, as best I could, what it meant to me. Basically, I said that it is like being in the presence of someone you love. No words are necessary, as it is not an intellectual exercise. It is an act of love between you and the Redeemer of the world. And I once heard a priest say that praying the Rosary was the highest form of contemplative prayer, because when you pray all the mysteries, you meditate on the entire life of Christ, from His birth to His death and Resurrection. We each said the Rosary on our own, and then Katie went for an afternoon run while I sat in the sun.

We designated some time on our last afternoon for the "Lighting of the Candles," a gesture symbolizing the prayers we offered for everyone. We put enough money in the slot for over fifty candles, then bundled them in our arms and carried them to the place reserved for burning. Some dropped, and the whole thing got out of control. We couldn't stop laughing. Two men standing nearby were getting a real kick out of our antics and asked us if we wanted a match. We brought our candles over to the designated area and set them in a bay all by themselves—as if God would somehow take special notice of our friends and family gathered together in one place!

Then Katie reminded me that we would have to go through a similar process for the holy water. Our laughter was a gift of joy. Although Katie gets her sense of humor from her father, if he had been with us now, he would have been shushing us, telling us to quiet down because we were making a scene. We could not have cared less, and rather enjoyed the fact that people were staring. Mom and daughter brought out the child in each other. It was an act of unabashed enjoyment, with or without an audience.

On our last night in Lourdes we were walking back to our hotel from the restaurant when I noticed that the door to the Poor Clare Monastery was open. It was very cold and damp out so Katie went back to the hotel while I went in to make a visit. My heart was so full. The nuns were chanting their evening prayers in French and I joined them in spirit, thanking God for the gift of this trip, and for the many blessings of my life, especially my husband and children. I once entertained the idea of becoming a nun and now felt strangely comfortable praying with this community. I also thought of the people I loved who have died—my parents, Aunt Helen, Gertrude, and Father Anselm—who reflected God's unconditional love to me. I missed them deeply and sensed their presence.

On the way back to the hotel I thought of two more people I wanted to light candles for, so I walked back down to the Grotto. It was a very cold and dark but starry night, and there wasn't a person in sight. Fear almost prevented me from going, but a peace settled over me when I approached the Grotto. The candles glowed beneath the statue of Our Lady where some people were quietly praying. The whole scene brought a tear to my eye.

LESS THAN TWO WEEKS after we returned home from Lourdes, Tommy walked Katie down the aisle at Assumption Catholic Church in Chicago, once the parish church of Mother Cabrini (now Saint Frances Xavier Cabrini). Our good friend, Father Bill Byron, S.J., the former president of The Catholic University of America and the University of Scranton, was the celebrant of the Nuptial Mass. Father Bill gave an inspiring homily on the promise of love, challenging Katie and Greg to let the security of their wedded life rest on the great principle of self-sacrifice. While most or our guests appreciated his words, a few young women cornered him during the cocktail hour to protest his message. Apparently "sacrifice" is not part of Women's Lib vocabulary.

Katie had selected the first bridal gown she tried on. I was in the dressing room with her and when she turned around, we instantly knew how beautiful it was and we both started to cry. She tried on many other dresses, but at the end, asked to see the first one again. When she selected it, I was thrilled. It was similar to the ivory silk ball gown that Jackie Bouvier wore when she married Jack Kennedy. It had a shirred bodice with cap sleeves and the simplicity made it elegant. Katie was a stunning bride and her joy was contagious.

The reception was at the Drake Hotel in Chicago. Her father's toast made us laugh and cry, but it was their dance that brought everyone to their feet: *Daddy's Little Girl* followed by the *Pennsylvania Polka*. Rich snapped a perfectly-timed photo of the two of them looking at each other while they were twirling around. You could feel the their love.

Katie loves to dance and had everyone on his or her feet. At one point, all her girlfriends and I were dancing together. Then she invited her many cousins who came from near and far to join her on the floor.

In the midst of the dancing and fun, the realization that I was still battling cancer came and went in waves. But I was in some sort of a peaceful emotional cocoon, strangely protected from fear or anxiety. Even though my high heels were killing me, I had energy and a sense of well being that made me feel like I didn't have a care in the world.

But soon the reality would set in: in less than 48 hours I would start radiation for breast cancer.

17

Radiation

Radiation can be a killer ray or a golden beam of healing energy.
—Bernie S. Siegel, M.D., *Love, Medicine and Miracles*

AT MASS ON THE MORNING of my first radiation treatment I realized
that it was the Feast of Our Lady of Lourdes. To me, this was a gift of
divine Providence—one of those synchronistic moments that felt like a
message from heaven saying: *Our Lady will bring you to her Son and ask Him to
heal you.* Or, perhaps she already had.

The Gospel reading was about Jesus healing people on the shore of
Lake Gennesaret. People brought the sick on bedrolls to Jesus, hoping to
touch even the fringe of His garment and "as many as touched it were
made well" (Mk 6:56). I closed my eyes and imagined myself lying on a
kind of bedroll under a big machine that would zap me with radiation. I
asked the Lord to be with me and touch me just like He did those people
in Scripture.

A compassionate male nurse named Joseph marked my abdomen with
black crosses designating the field for treatment. When the big round machine lowered itself over my bare middle, there was a large red cross reflected in the overhead glass. In fact, crosses were everywhere. I think they
pinpointed the areas to be radiated, but to me they were one more sign of
God's presence. I prayed that Jesus would bless the work of the doctors and
empower the machine to destroy the cancer cells. He could heal without

any machines, but I somehow knew that I needed to walk this road using the natural remedies of science and all the other alternative methods to cure me.

I liked Bernie Siegel's approach to chemotherapy and radiation. He was of the opinion that three-fourths of the side effects of radiation and chemotherapy resulted from patients' negative beliefs. In *Love, Medicine and Miracles,* he wrote that negative programming was one reason why a fourth of all chemotherapy patients started throwing up *before* they got to their next treatment. He gave as an example a group of men from England who were given saline and told it was chemotherapy. Thirty percent had their hair fall out.[1]

I decided to take the positive approach.

A glitch with the computer delayed the treatment, giving me a few minutes to reflect and pray. Years ago, when I gave up smoking, I offered my cravings for someone in need. It was like a game of give and take that God honored by blessing someone—and taking away my cravings at the same time. Now, I thought of doing the same thing, offering the uncertainty and physical trauma of each day's radiation for someone in need, a sacrifice of praise so loved by the Lord. This day I thought of Brian, the Confirmation candidate whose name I picked out of a basket after Mass on Sunday for whom to pray.

After the treatment, which was over so quickly it was as if nothing had happened, Tommy and I took Rich to Pottery Barn to look for a writing table for his New York apartment. No sooner did we walk in than he saw a large dark oak table that would make a perfect desk. The floor model was on sale for a quarter of the original price so we bought it, along with a file cabinet to match. We had an early dinner at a nearby Irish pub and enjoyed a long leisurely talk with our son about his new apartment and his life in New York. By the time we got home I was exhausted and went right to bed. The next morning we helped Rich load the new table into the car to drive to New York. After an impromptu lunch with Tommy, Anne and Velma, the mainstays of Witness Ministries, we sent Rich off in a shower of Lourdes holy water.

For the next month, Tommy and I drove to St. Francis Hospital in Evanston every day at 1:00 P.M. for the treatment, and then drove home. Each day's routine was the same. We said the Rosary en route, praying for different people. I liked the fact that the twenty-three days of treatment fell during Lent. It felt like God's perfect timing. After the session on Ash

Wednesday, I stopped in St. Patrick's Church to make a visit. At home I wrote in my journal: *This year I am not empty handed as I accompany Jesus on the Way of the Cross. I can offer Him my struggles—trusting that He has already overcome them for me. It is really comforting to know that Jesus has redeemed our suffering and given it a purpose.*

DRS. CARL SIMONTON AND BERNIE SIEGEL, doctors I had become so enamored of and whose books I was devouring, placed great value on mental imagery and relaxation. They saw them as tools that could effect physical changes, enhance the immune system and even alter the course of a malignancy. In *Getting Well Again,* Simonton explains why he requires his patients to do visual imagery exercises three times a day (between five and fifteen minutes each time). He claims that these techniques enable people to influence their internal body processes and even alter the course of their disease. They teach cancer patients to visualize their cancer, the treatment destroying it, and then to see their body's natural defenses helping them recover.

What convinced me the most about the power of visualization was a story about a patient with advanced throat cancer whom doctors had given only a five percent chance of recovering. Simonton was just developing his biofeedback techniques and decided to teach this man how to relax and do the visual imagery. Like a starving dog that had been thrown a bone, this patient took the imagery and ran with it, missing only one imagery session over the course of many months. He used it during his radiation therapy and, after several months, he showed no sign of cancer. Not only that, he continued using the imagery to help his arthritis. When he succeeded with that, he said he used it to improve his sex life and according to him, it worked.

Based on Simonton's suggestions, I devised my own imagery to focus on during the radiation sessions. After some deep breathing and relax-ation, I saw myself drinking the Precious Blood of Jesus from the chalice at Mass. I felt it traveling throughout my veins and arteries, touching every cell. His Blood, which is Life itself, disengaged what I imagined as crab-like cancer cells (which are deformed life) from their grip on my body and each other, and sent them free floating in pools of weakness and confusion. Then I saw an army of Saint Raphael's healing angels (white cells) travel-ing throughout every area of my body. The white cells, Simonton main-tains, are an important symbol of our own defenses, the part of us that will help us recover. They sprayed the cancer cells with poison. Sometimes I went with them to make sure that they completely covered every area. They even went into the bone marrow, the factories where blood cells are manufactured. When the cancer cells were all dead, the angels sprayed them with powerful water hoses, directing them into a cantilevered bucket system that flushed them through my liver and kidneys to be eliminated through the urine and stool.

The visual exercises gave me a sense of control over my body and the radiation treatments. I saw the imagery as a tool that would help me up-root malignancy and restore health to my body. I actually looked upon the daily treatments as if they were a friend that was helping me heal. Doing the imagery made the time fly.

In a more sophisticated scenario, Dr. Simonton taught his patients to extend the imagery into the future, to see a final, healthy outcome in which they achieved goals and fulfilled their life's purpose. There wasn't enough time to do this extension during the radiation, so I did it at home on a regular basis.

I began my sessions at home by going over the first part of the imagery, then I imagined Tommy and myself sitting in Dr. Cunningham's office listening to his latest report: "Joan and Tom, I have some really good news for you. There is not a trace of cancer left in your body." We hug him and each other, and then plan to have a Mass of Thanksgiving to thank God for His healing. Father Hennessey is the celebrant and the church is crowded with family and friends who have been so supportive along the way. My doctors are all there, and it is truly a Mass of celebration with lots of music. After Mass we have a big party.

Then I saw myself some years down the road at my grandson Tommy's high school graduation (he was 4). I watch him process down the aisle to *Pomp and Circumstance*, the same way my own son did, so tall, so handsome, so full of goodness and life. I shed tears of joy. He's wearing a white tuxedo jacket and when he sees me, he smiles deeply. The final scene is of our 50th wedding anniversary that we celebrate with close friends and our children and grandchildren. Tommy and I dance to *Red Roses for a Blue Lady*, the song we danced to at our wedding. I cry tears of joy—for a lifetime of blessings and gifts beyond measure. God has been true to His promise to reveal Himself to us, especially through the love of our family and friends. We toast each other and then we pray, thanking God for the gift of His constant care and unconditional love that has sustained us through all the trials of our life.

The side effects of the radiation were minimal: fatigue and a slight feeling of nausea on two occasions. People constantly told me that I looked so good and wondered how I could be so sick. My response? *Thank you, Jesus,* a little prayer I said silently and often. I didn't feel sick and I didn't think of myself as sick. I thought, and said, that I simply had a problem with my thymus gland or my stomach or breast.

About three weeks into the radiation routine, my oncologist said he wished his other patients were doing as well as I was. Then he cut back my treatment by three days; that meant finishing on a Friday, leaving the next week free.

After seeing him I stopped by Dr. Cunningham's office, the surgeon who had done the lumpectomy. He was also pleased with my progress. He wanted me to schedule some tests in three months: an endoscopy to check the stomach lymphoma and a mammogram to verify that the cancer was gone. *Did he say gone?*

When the visionary Maria Esperanza told me that I would be "completely healed through a wonderful doctor" (when I first contracted scleroderma), I didn't know who it was. I now think it was Myles Cunningham, M.D., who presented my case of MALT lymphoma of the stomach before two tumor boards at St. Francis Hospital in Evanston. Myles also found the cancer in my breast that was so small, he wasn't even sure he should biopsy it. Myles treated me as if I was a member of his own family, which is what caused him to go the extra mile in caring for me, and, I believe, in healing me.

THANKFULLY, I HAD WEEKENDS off so I was able to accept an invitation from Katie to attend a women's luncheon to benefit a school for autistic children in her community. One of her best friends was running the fundraiser, so we went and had a lot of unexpected fun. I saw so much of myself in Katie ("Mom, I just hate small talk!") and thoroughly enjoyed her companionship and her friends.

The speaker gifted a room full of 600 women with a sidesplitting comedy routine. Loretta LaRoche was a nationally recognized speaker in the area of stress management. A self-admitted class clown who later "got a job doing what I used to get punished for," she used examples from everyday life to show us—sometimes with costumes—how humor can break irrational thought patterns and de-stress us. One of her funniest takes was on the use of "the good towels" and "the good china." We laughed till we cried!

Loretta said that the tears we shed when we cry carry powerful immune boosting enzymes. I had also learned from Norman Cousins and Dr. Bernie Siegel that laughter can reduce inflammation because it increases the production of endorphins, the body's natural opiates. I was reminded of the experience Norman Cousins had when he was hospitalized with a painful autoimmune disease. He wrote that he had less pain and was able to sleep longer after a bout of hearty laughter, and also, that it reduced his SED rate (the amount of inflammation and infection in the blood) by five points.

With all the physical and emotional turmoil in my life, the timing of the luncheon couldn't have been better. I realized what a bore I had become and how the laughter had all but gone out of my life. I once had a great sense of fun and wanted to get it back. My husband has a great sense of play and was thrilled when I wanted to watch reruns of *Candid Camera* one Sunday night. We saw an episode we hadn't seen before. It showed people dropping off their clothes at the dry cleaners. They were told that it would be necessary to take out insurance on their clothes. When the manager explained all the terrible things that could happen to their clothes—fire, damage, stealing—if they didn't protect them, the reactions of the customers were hilarious. We were doubled over in hysterics.

Another way to look at play and laughter is to see it as a catalyst for releasing our inner child. Whatever we do to let our inner child have fun and enjoy himself or herself, will not only relax us and boost our immune system (at least according to science), but it will also bring us inner peace. How? Because when we learn to love ourselves we are more likely to be open and reach out in love to others. And that, I believe, is a worthy goal. When we choose to love and make others happy, our life will change, Bernie Siegel says, because we will find happiness and love in the process. The first step towards inner peace, he advises, is to decide to give love, not to receive it.[2]

EASIER SAID THAN DONE. As well as I was doing physically, I still kept losing my emotional equilibrium. When we were driving to radiation one afternoon, I blurted out some things that had been bothering me that were boiling just below the surface. What put me over the edge was a comment my husband had made to Katie on the phone, a remark which was not entirely accurate and which discredited me. I told him how hurt I felt. He said he did not intend to diminish me and was shocked that I felt that way. I explained about my inner child and how she can't filter things and how, down deep, she believes the lie that she doesn't matter. When we arrived at radiation we hadn't resolved anything, but the air was cleared—at least for me because I wasn't repressing anger and resentment. I felt so much better for being open with my feelings. Sharing negative feelings was new for me; I realized that I was gaining strength in voicing my pain. And, ironically, this was a loving thing to do.

I didn't know if the radiation was bringing me down or if I was in my same old emotional wasteland, but I was feeling distraught. During Mass one morning I asked God to give me a sign of His presence. I felt that it would bolster me and fire my resolve to keep on truckin'. That day two things happened, one after the other, as if they were a direct and immediate answer to my prayer.

First, I took a call in the Witness office from a parish secretary in West Virginia who ordered twenty *Eucharist God Among Us* books. When I asked her what they were going to do with them, she explained that her pastor had received the book for Christmas and was inspired to plan two parish-wide retreats on the Eucharist—one for men and one for women. When I hung up the phone I felt like the Lord had prompted her call to give me a message: "See, in the down times when you think you don't matter, remember this phone call and know how pleased I am with your work." I felt God's love through the heart of the priest in West Virginia.

The second answer to my prayer came during a session with Father Bob. We were discussing where my scleroderma and cancer came from. I was becoming convinced that they originated in my childhood. I had figured out that our bodies know when we're not being authentic and, until recently, I had been playing roles and "performing" my entire life. This constant stress impacted my immune system by suppressing my body's natural defenses, thus making it more susceptible to producing abnormal cells. Without realizing it, I think I invited these diseases to enter my body.

Father Bob suggested holding my stomach and asking it what it wanted to communicate. Because of the deep breathing and relaxation exercises I had been doing, I had become aware of a constant state of tension in my stomach. I think it took the brunt of the stress. "Where does stress come from?" Father Bob asked. "Love is blocked," I said, "love isn't flowing like water through a pipe clearly. Giving and receiving love is blocked."

Father Bob prayed, asking Jesus to take me back to the source and origin of the block. With my eyes closed I saw myself as a young child when something inside of me froze. I saw myself all dressed up in a white organdy dress with patent leather shoes and Shirley Temple curls. My mother valued my appearance and insisted on perfection, probably compensating for her own deprivation. That's when the lie took hold: I told myself that what I do and how I look is important; but underneath I really don't matter.

I wondered if this could be where the stomach lymphoma originated.

In prayer Father Bob asked the Lord to communicate with my inner child. "Is it true that Joan didn't matter?" Then I saw the many ways God cared for my needs throughout my life. He sent Gertrude to our family when I was 6 to give me—and my mother—the love we both craved. While my mother and I couldn't give each other the mother-daughter love we both wanted and needed, God provided us with someone who had enough love to mother the both of us. I knew that I mattered to Gertrude.

As Father Bob prayed asking the Lord to reveal any other blocks, I had an insight that at some very early age I made a decision: if I was not getting the love I needed (from my mother), I would have to get it myself. "You mean you had to be your own savior?" Father Bob asked. "Yes," I said, "I decided that I would have to fill that starving place: myself." "That's the block," he said.

He asked if I were willing to give the decision—to get love myself—to Jesus. I said a prayer letting go of that control, and then Father Bob asked the Lord to release me from that. Before our session ended I asked him if he thought the cancer was coming to me to teach me how to let in God's love. He agreed, but said I first have to let go of those decisions that block love.

From one simple request in the morning for a sign of God's presence, I received two answers immediately. First, the affirmation for my Eucharistic apostolate from the priest from West Virginia, then later that day an insight that helped me dismantle a barrier that was preventing me from loving—myself and others. The desolation was replaced by the consolation of feeling loved. I thought of the Scripture verse, "Thy word is a lamp to my feet and a light to my path" (Ps 119:105). God was lighting my path with truth, showing me that I do matter. I felt it in my bones.

I finished radiation on a Friday, and on the following Monday drove to New Melleray Abbey in Dubuque, Iowa, for a five-day retreat. As soon as I arrived, I headed to the chapel for Vespers (evening prayer). Vivid, joyful memories flooded my imagination. I started to cry, remembering all the people that have loved and cared for me. It seemed like the Lord was filling in all the dry parched areas of my heart with an awareness of His presence in my life—from the time I was very little.

I wrote in my journal: *My life is about gift—one gift after another that God gives me to this day! How could I ever doubt His presence or feel desolate when all I have to do is remember His goodness to me all the days of my life?* I thought especially of Tommy, what a devoted and loving husband he has been. *He has been with me since day one, constantly at my side supporting me in every way. His love is inexhaustible. Thank You Jesus for ordering our marriage. You saw how we needed each other and how we would help each other find You. I see You in Tommy—in his constancy, fidelity, humility, goodness, generosity, wisdom and gentleness. He is Your special son who loves deeply even though he always hasn't been loved in return. Thank You for giving me such a husband, like Saint Joseph, a strong, honorable man to walk with me and father my precious children.*

Listening to thirty male voices accompanying the organ music during Vespers heightened my sense of God's nearness. The monks were Cistercian (Trappist) who followed the Rule of Saint Benedict. When they were not praying they made caskets with wood from their surrounding acreage. The chapel was long and narrow (Romanesque style) with the monks on either side facing each other and guests in the back behind a grill. It reminded me of Saint Bernard's monastery in Fontenay, France. I imagined that being in this monastery was similar to what astronauts experience in outer space—a rarified environment, silence. It was perfect place to find inner quiet, to empty myself and make room for God.

The next morning began early with 6:30 A.M. prayers with the monks, followed by Mass at 7:00. The Gospel was about the man who was ill and who had waited thirty-eight years to be lowered into the pool. Jesus knew he had been lying there a long time and asked him, "Do you want to be healed?" (Jn 5:6). What I heard was, *Do I want to be healed?* For so many years, I said I did, but I behaved just like the man at the pool who constantly blamed others for not lowering him into the pool when the water stirred so he could be healed. I wrote in my journal: *I can see myself in that man, in the unhappiness inside myself that preferred to blame others for my condition. While I said I wanted healing, I resisted it emotionally by all my sorrowing, complaining, and playing the victim, just like the guy at the pool. My unhappiness surfaced early in my marriage, when I blamed my unhappiness either on my parents or my husband. Even though I went to counseling and to healing retreats, my denial was huge and created a wall behind which I hid from everyone, myself included. I sincerely thought throughout most of those years that others were responsible for my problems, saying, "if only circumstances would be different, I could be happy," or, "if only my husband would change, I wouldn't be so upset." I saw the problem outside myself. My unhappiness was due to the behavior of others. If they changed, I could have peace.*

I've spent most of my life asking God to free me from depression that I blamed on others. But my prayer always led me back to myself, as it did now in New Melleray. The Scripture reading might have been the final straw to break the back of my denial. I didn't like seeing myself in the man who blamed and judged others for not putting him in the pool; but that's just who I saw, a pitiful victim. I wanted to change because I didn't want to be like him.

One evening a small group of us who were staying at the Abbey watched a movie about Thomas Merton. I related to Merton because he wrote so candidly about the need to face our inner truth, especially the hidden darkness of our unconscious. He confirmed the path I was following, to face my inner self, to embrace the shadow, the nun who pretended to be dead, the lost child. Merton said that to know God, I must know myself.

If anyone ever met and faced their own inner darkness, Merton did, which he describes in *A Seven Day Journey with Thomas Merton* by Esther de Waal, a book of his essays and poems that I found lying on a table: *All of us who are called to a serious way of life are called to face the blackness of ourselves and of our world. If we have to live the victory of the Risen Christ over death we have to pass through death. Or arise out of our own death. It means seeing death and hell in ourselves. I never imagined when I was a novice and when "His lamp shone over my head" what it would mean to suffer the darkness which He Himself suffers in me.*[3]

I totally related to his struggle to find God, and himself. My quest was identical: to do away with the disharmony in myself, to be the same person on the outside as on the inside. To become who I am. This, Merton says, is the way to sainthood: *What can we gain by sailing to the moon if we are not able to cross the abyss that separates us from ourselves? For me to be a saint means to be myself, because the problem of sanctity and salvation is in fact the problem of finding out who I am and of discovering my true self.*[4]

At Vespers on the eve of my departure from the monastery, the chapel was dark save for a lone vigil light suspended over the altar. The chanting

of the monks was like a lullaby to the Lord. I remained in the chapel to recommend all my loved ones to Jesus, asking Him to bless and heal each one.
I had spent a lot of time interceding for others. I asked God for the grace
of being an open channel of love, so that His healing could flow through
me constantly. This was the whole point of removing the blocks. *This will
be my spiritual priority, to be a worthy and pure vessel of Jesus' love so that He can find
refuge in my heart and reach out to others through me. I must be vigilant not to let any sin
block Him out and prevent His light from shining. This, I feel, is my commission from
the Lord on the eve of my departure.*

I left New Melleray Abbey realizing that healing is a process, not a
one-time happening. It would take time to dismantle lifelong patterns of
behavior—one day at a time. I remembered reading Agnes Sanford, who
wrote the classic best seller on healing, *The Healing Light,*[5] say that healing
is not what God does to you, but *through* you. My job, I felt, was to keep the
pipes clean so His living water could flow through me. This, after years of
having my pipes clogged with the debris of negative thinking and blaming!

On THE DRIVE HOME from New Melleray I didn't feel well physically.
We had planned to go to Florida for a spring getaway, but I could barely
get out of bed, let alone manage the long airport corridors, so we had to
cancel. The signs were all too familiar—my nerves and muscles were pain-
fully strained. I could barely walk or lift my arm without extreme fatigue
and a burning, hurting sensation in my muscles. It was a scleroderma flare.
It felt like I had no protective connective tissue between the muscles and
joints.

I phoned the radiation oncologist, wondering if it could be a residual
effect of the radiation treatments. His first thought was that I might have
myasthenia gravis, a neurological disorder often associated with a thy-
momy. (He was aware that I had had a thymectomy two years before.)
Two hours later we were in the car headed to St. Francis Hospital for an
emergency appointment with a neurologist. He put me through a battery
of rigorous muscle strength testing which I passed. In a follow up letter
to my radiation oncologist, the neurologist said he found "no evidence
of neuromuscular deficit." He described me as a "delightful lady" who
"is stronger than I am." My "appellades" were becoming more flattering
all the time!

Dr. Mercola agreed that the flare was pretty serious. I told him that I had recently eaten a lot of desserts during a retreat at a Trappist monastery. (The monks didn't eat meat or sweets themselves!) Mercola immediately saw the sugar binge as the cause of the flare. Sugar is deadly for this disease, he said, because the bacteria that infest the joints of scleroderma sufferers feast on the sugar and grow in such an environment. He gave me the intravenous antibiotics and once again laid out a nutritional program including juicing a quart of vegetables a day.

I couldn't do much physically because the slightest movement exhausted me, so I stretched out on the couch to watch Cable News. It was downright depressing. A huge scandal was developing over pedophile priests in the Catholic Church. The problem was mushrooming as many of them were realizing they could no longer hide behind the Church. It was incredibly sad and angered me that a lot of the cases had been dealt with behind closed doors so to speak, with quiet payoffs to the victims and hardly a censure to the priests involved.

In the midst of my own struggles, Tommy complained of a tingling sensation in his right arm and face. He kept minimizing it saying that it was nothing, when all I could think of was that he was about to have a heart attack. When he finally called the doctor, he sent him to the hospital immediately. I was in such a sorry state that I could barely walk the halls of the hospital to visit him. After going ten feet I'd have to lean against a wall or sit down to rest. Tests showed that Tommy had suffered a minor stroke, with no apparent side effects. A CT scan confirmed that he had a slight blood clot known as a TIA (transient ischemic attack). Despite all this, we felt so grateful that he dodged a major bullet. Spending an extra day in the hospital "just to make sure" everything checked out all right, he was like a caged animal waiting for a doctor to sign his release papers so he could go home.

In the meantime, Katie and Greg came out to visit. She drove me to Schaumburg for another antibiotic treatment and on the way home we stopped at Whole Foods where she filled up a basket with organic vegetables for juicing. Katie cut up bunches of celery, cucumber, spinach, carrots and red cabbage to put through the juicer to make a big glass of purple juice that actually didn't taste too bad. She then made a meat loaf (using my mother's recipe) for her dad's homecoming from the hospital. Greg arrived in time to help, and when Tommy walked through the door from the hospital, he had a welcoming committee and a wonderful dinner awaiting him. Each of our sons phoned during dinner, worried about their ailing parents.

WITH HOLY WEEK APPROACHING I was feeling the weight of the cross of illness. The physical setbacks really tested my faith because we both had such serious health issues, with no guarantees for the future. Being so incapacitated brought me to a new level of letting go—a deep one, and into another state of desolation. I was physically and emotionally drained, as if I were in a desert without water and with no rescue in sight, as this journal entry shows: *The weather has been overcast and rainy which seems appropriate for Holy Week. I feel disoriented. I've lost my motivation, my energy, and my joy. Maybe I've lost myself. The prayer of my heart at New Melleray was to empty myself to make room for God. It appears that God heard my prayer.*

The one thing that helped me was the realization that I could offer Jesus my pain and unite it to His Cross. It gave me hope. *I offer You my suffering, Lord, and unite it to Your sacrifice of love. Resurrect me, Lord, from all that keeps me from good health—emotionally, physically and spiritually.*

In my ongoing meetings with Father Bob, he suggested that my depression could be a new movement of surrender to God, dying to the old ways as it were. I had tried prayerfully to give over my illnesses, not to mention the worry and fear surrounding them. The process of letting go forced me into a state of detachment so that I lost the sense of what I was about or where I was going. Father Bob said that when St. John of the Cross was thrown into prison, he received the gift of contemplation. He suggested that instead of fighting the emptiness, I should ask the Lord what He would like me to learn through it.

He also said that St. Teresa of Avila went through a troubled time when she didn't have peace. A Jesuit told her to increase her penances and unite them to the Passion of Jesus. When she did that, she found peace. Father Bob said that if I kept fighting the darkness/desolation, I wouldn't find peace because I wouldn't be in tune with what God was doing in my life. This wouldn't be happening to me if God didn't permit it, Father Bob said, and so it is best to ask Him what He wants to teach me through this desert experience. He suggested that I read the prophet Isaiah, who foretold the devastating fears and losses Jesus would experience. If anyone had a reason to be depressed, Father Bob said, Jesus did as this Scripture verse shows: "I have labored in vain, I have spent my strength for nothing and vanity; yet surely my right is with the Lord, and my recompense with my God" (Is 49:4). Jesus surrendered all His hurts and fears, humiliation and abuse, physical and mental torture, betrayal and abandonment to God, because He trusted in his Father's love. He emptied Himself.

Easter Sunday was a joyous day that we celebrated with our family and some extended family. Our oldest son Tommy, his wife Sinead and our grandsons Tommy (4), Ryan (3) and Aidan (almost one year) were there as well as our daughter Katie and her husband Greg, but missing were our son Danny and his wife Pippa and our youngest son, Richard, who were in New York.

Sinead made a delicious honey baked ham and set a beautiful table where we sat for hours, talking, reminiscing, laughing, arguing and just enjoying being with one another. I made Easter baskets for our grandsons with special little toys and some candy. Tommy was amused by the joy I took in this, asking who these were really for—for them or for me? Christmas and Easter brought out the child in me. I saw a reflection of us in our children and a lot of our children in our grandsons. It was such fun feeding Aidan chocolate cake (did I ever allow my own kids to have cake at eleven months?), seeing his initial timidity over the texture, then his growing appreciation for the good taste. Three-year-old Ryan was proud to show me his new big-boy underpants decorated with dragons and announced unabashedly that he was potty trained. Little Tommy presented us with a Grandparents Book that he made in school with drawings of Nana and Papa and our house, really a jumble of blue and green scribbles. When Papa suggested an area that could have been the front door, little Tommy corrected him and showed him not only where the front door was, but also every room in the house!

18

Lung Surgery

> In transcending sickness, your task is gradually to place your mind in
> the service of the Holy Spirit, the true source of healing within you.
> Indeed, your mind can elect to serve God or the world. If you wish to
> transform your thinking from focus on fear to focus on love, then you
> must look inside and change your mind. To change your mind means
> to place it at the disposal of true authority, that power that finds its
> source in heaven.
>
> —Richard P. Johnson,
> *Body, Mind, Spirit: Tapping the Healing Power Within You*

I SCHEDULED AN ENDOSCOPY two and a half months after my last radiation treatment, hoping that the stomach lymphoma would be gone. When I
phoned the nurse for the pathology report, I said a little prayer for strength
to deal with whatever news she gave me. It took her forever to find the
paperwork, and when she finally came back to the phone, her words were
so sweet I could barely take them in: "Your report is good. They found no
sign of gastric lymphoma." THEY FOUND NO SIGN OF GASTRIC
LYMPHOMA, I shouted to my husband in his office. Then five years'
worth of fear and worry tumbled out in sobs. I didn't know I had such pent
up emotions, but the joy I felt was over-the-top wonderful. When I phoned
my children I could barely get the words out without crying. Later that day
I went to Saint Pat's to thank God. I just sat in church basking in gratitude.
Remembering the trip to Lourdes I had a strong feeling that the Blessed
Mother interceded with her Son for my healing. If fact, everything that
was happening to me seemed to have the stamp of a mother's love.

I still had to make the rounds of doctors and tests to be certain that the lymphoma wasn't spreading. In one day I saw three doctors, and had a follow-up CT scan of my chest. The stomach biopsies were negative for malignancy, and each doctor celebrated the good reports. But both my oncologist and radiation oncologist cautioned that lymphoma has a tendency to return, which meant I'd have to be monitored closely over the next several years. All that remained was a routine blood test and I was able to put off another bone marrow test for four months.

Dr. Cunningham said that my recent mammograms looked great and told me that I had nothing to worry about in terms of breast cancer. The lumpectomy "got the cancer," and he thought that the chance of anything else happening was minimal. But because of my scleroderma and all the cancers I've had, he said that the concern is where something will pop up next. He then urged me to stop running on a treadmill of tests. People can become too dependent on tests and doctors, he said, and that is not good. His advice came at a good time as we were hoping to leave for New Jersey to spend the summer. That meant I'd be free of doctors and tests for at least three months.

But there was one more doctor's visit. The surgeon who had done the thymectomy asked to see me to discuss the results of my CT scan. I had a feeling of foreboding. He was concerned about the "infiltrates" in my right lung, and wanted me to have a biopsy. A "little white shadow" was growing and although he thought it was benign, he wanted to be sure.

I worked myself into a state of panic, imagining a long needle inserted between my ribs. This time I prayed to St. Joan of Arc for courage, telling myself that what I was about to endure was nothing compared to her trial by fire. The worst part of it all was a three-hour wait before the procedure. I didn't bring a book and read every magazine in the waiting room twice. It was unnerving.

Finally, a friendly Italian doctor helped put me at ease and the biopsy was tolerable. Once I relaxed, he took three different biopsies because the results kept coming back benign. I was so grateful. I felt like a teenager who passed all her exams at the end of the school year and was now free as a bird. It was June and in a few weeks we would head to the Jersey Shore for the summer.

ON FATHER'S DAY WE went to our usual 8:00 A.M. Sunday Mass. Our good friend Fr. Larry Hennessey gave an outstanding homily on God's love and the gift of fatherhood, witnessing to the love and virtues of his own father who shaped and formed him. Tommy and I looked at each other with tears streaming down our cheeks. I know we were thanking God for our own fathers who loved us in their own ways, giving us their all. I also felt deeply grateful for the way my husband had fathered our children, leading and teaching them with love, gentleness and so much generosity. And last, I thanked God for the gift of my children and for the way I observed Tom Jr. fathering his own sons. He played with them and was their friend, yet was not afraid to set boundaries or correct them when they were out of order. I saw the same compassion and generosity in my son that I saw in my husband. As my dad used to say "The apples don't fall far from the tree!"

Father Larry mentioned how secure he felt growing up in the love between his mother and his father. He said that the respect and love that they shared with each other translated into secure and well-loved sons and daughters, two of whom are priests today. I wondered how many parishioners experienced that kind of unconditional love in their homes.

Father Larry referred to the Catholic bishops who had recently met in Dallas to address the sexual abuse issue among the clergy. He wondered aloud about a lack of security and identity among some of his priest brethren, about an emotional and spiritual instability that somehow leads to deviant and even criminal behavior. Father Larry concluded an emotional tribute to his dad by saying that if these predators had been given the opportunity to grow up in a home such as his, there wouldn't be these problems today. Everyone rose to their feet and gave him a standing ovation.

After Mass our family gathered once again for brunch at our house. The newlyweds, Katie and Greg were there, as well as Tom Jr., Sinead and the boys, Tommy, Ryan, and Aidan, now 14 months. Missing were Danny and Rich who were in New York.

We enjoyed sitting in the warm summer sun on the patio, while the boys ran around on the lawn. After their favorite cheese strata, the dads opened their gifts. I don't know when I felt more grateful, more alive or more joyous. When it was time to leave, Ryan started crying because he didn't want to go home. As they drove away, Tommy put his arm around me. Weren't we just the age of our grown children, piling four kids into the car to go to Scranton to grandma and grandpa's house? Now we were grandma and grandpa—happily so. In less than a week we would pile into our own car for the 15-hour drive to the Jersey Shore.

At the Jersey Shore where I spent every summer until I went to college, I can't tell the difference between my adult and child self. The ocean brings out my inner child. When I swim laps in the saltwater pool at the same beach club we belonged to when I was growing up, I feel 13 again and have as much energy as my little grandsons. In early August I entered the mile swim contest, 72 laps that took me a day to complete. I was giddy with delight when the aquatic director presented me with my prize: a photo button saying, "I did the mile swim."

I looked forward to a slightly more relaxed routine in the summer, although my workaholic habits followed me to the shore where I spent a better part of each day doing research for the book on the Mass, or preparing talks. I began the day with Mass each morning, then worked till mid-afternoon when I went to the club to swim laps. I wanted to get some sun because Dr. Mercola had convinced me of our need for vitamin D. He stressed the fact that people don't get enough of this vitamin, which the skin produces when it is exposed to sunlight. But it was a trick to get enough sun without overexposure to the harmful rays that can cause skin cancer. Vitamin D is associated with bone health but is best known for problems resulting from its deficiency—namely diabetes, heart disease, some cancers, osteoporosis and inflammation. In the winter, I took a vitamin D supplement. But in the summer I soaked up the sun as I had been doing my whole life— only now I was aware of, and grateful to get, the vitamin D.

I had piled boxes of research books into to the car to bring to New Jersey, ones that I would use to establish a timeline of the development of the Sacred Liturgy. One of my goals was to trace its historic development, beginning with its origin at the Last Supper. I also wanted to include an explanation of each rite within the Sacred Liturgy, followed by a reflection on how to enter into the rituals and apply them to our lives.

Mary Higgins Clark, the best selling mystery writer, happened to be a member of our beach club. When I was swimming laps one day, out of the corner of my eye I noticed Mary at the shallow end of the pool, so I swam over to talk to her. My son Danny joined us and the three of us stood in the pool talking about writing. (Danny and Rich are both writers and each has published a book.) She told us that she writes the beginning and end of each chapter before filling it in and does her writing from 5-7:00 A.M. I don't know why I had never thought of that myself, since I am usually awake at 5:00 A.M. and could put in a few good hours of work before starting the day. Now I do some of my best work during those hours.

Mary had recently published her twenty-fourth mystery novel and has more than 85 million books in print worldwide. Mary is a gracious and fun person with an infectious sense of humor. She donates tons of her proceeds to charity and is very generous to the Catholic Church. One evening Tommy and I had dinner with Mary and her husband, John. She gave us a tour of their magnificent restored Victorian home a block from the ocean. I was particularly interested in her office, which was really a porch/sitting room adjacent to their second floor bedroom with a beautiful view of the ocean. Above her desk were framed covers of her books, various awards and copies of the *New York Times* bestseller lists which she had made numerous times. She was particularly pleased that some of her books made it for both hardcover and soft cover at the same time.

Mary impressed me with her disciplined routine, her writing skills and her commitment to publishing wholesome moral novels—rare commodities today. She inspired such hope in me. I wanted to attract people to the Lord in the same way that she drew people into the world of mystery.

IN JULY I WAS working on several talks for prayer breakfasts in the fall, but feeling distracted by a grudge I was nursing. It was at the end of a long weekend of entertaining our good friends, Anna and Robert (she was my roommate at Marymount), and our son Rich and Danielle Donovan, the beautiful girl he was dating. She was born in Chicago but lived and worked in New York. We were always confusing Danie with our son, Danny, so we nicknamed her "Danie D."

That evening we went out to dinner and everyone raised his or her wine glass in a toast. But I didn't have a glass yet. I felt invisible and grew angry. Tommy was unaware that I didn't have a glass and was not able to toast. I inwardly blamed him for being so insensitive. By the time we got home, other instances came to mind in which I felt like I didn't matter, and I blamed him for my upset. Once again, I began to feel trapped—in myself and in my marriage. I wanted him to change and stop that behavior, period. Down deep I knew that the hurts were out of proportion to the actual incidents, and that he really didn't mean to be so insensitive. But I still felt hurt, angry and unforgiving.

I couldn't believe I was getting myself into this sorry state, especially on the heels of our fun weekend. It was such a small thing, but it triggered enormous pain. I felt paralyzed and unable to get out of it. But before we went to bed that night, I forced myself to apologize to Tommy for blaming him for something I knew he didn't do on purpose. I told him that I needed him to be attentive and caring, and when he isn't, I really feel the loss. I was gaining strength in speaking my mind. But early the next morning, my inner conflict came out in my journal: *How can I give a talk on healing when I am back at square one in emotional kindergarten, stuck, unhappy and almost despairing? I am a hypocrite, mouthing inspiring words while I'm ashamed of how I'm living my marriage. There seems to be some block that prevents me from loving my husband as he deserves.*

The next day happened to be the Feast of St. Mary Magdalene. At Mass I prayed for the grace of a repentant heart. Fr. Martin Padovani, a Divine Word Missionary and bestselling author (he wrote *Healing Wounded Emotions* and *Healing Wounded Relationships*), was visiting our parish and said the Mass. During the homily, he said that the only sure way of establishing healthy relationships is to stop expecting the other person to change and to realize that we are the ones who must change. *He was speaking directly to me!* Intellectually, I knew the "what" of change: let go, surrender, and empty myself, but I didn't know *how* to do it. Then Father Padovani said something that I hadn't thought about before: the basic goal of communication is revelation, not resolution. Most people give up trying to communicate because they can't seem to resolve anything, he said. He challenged spouses to consider revealing themselves to one another because that usually leads to understanding, which of course leads to forgiveness and healing. I could feel my heart softening and a new glimmer of hope on the horizon.

This wise priest who was also a family therapist and a clinical psychologist, didn't know it, but he opened a window inside of me where I saw the "how" of change. I wrote down my thoughts as soon as I got home when they were still fresh. *How to change? For me it is to see the onset of my "acting out" which usually starts when I'm tired or overburdened—so that I can nip it in the bud. When I'm tired, my guard is down and I allow negative self-talk and judgments to creep in and stir up trouble. If these negative voices are not stopped, they will paralyze me and cause harm to others, especially Tommy. I feel grateful for this awareness and pray for the grace to love freely and openly without the interference from negative voices that shut me down.*

We resolved things peacefully, but a few weeks later I was back in that same place, feeling trapped and unhappy. It was apparent that I was going through a revolving door that always let me out in the same dark place, and I didn't know why. It felt like there was a lion in my inner basement, a lion that raged and paced in anger. I was anxious and feared the worst, as my journal entry illustrates: *Perhaps the lion should be shot? But if he's part of me then that would mean I should be shot. Sometimes I do think that death would be sweet, it would put an end to my torment. God, is this pain bottomless? Please help me overcome it so it won't rise up from the deep and overpower me. I beg you.*

The next morning I went to Mass and realized that it was the feast of St. Bernard of Clairvaux. Although I wasn't particularly devoted to him, I knew from the research I had done for *My Daily Eucharist* that he was the most celebrated man of his day (twelfth century) by the sheer force of his love for the Church. In one sermon, he could convert hundreds of people, including the most hardened hearts. I asked for his help in softening my heart, and to lead me to the raging beast that was stirring up such anger and fear.

I stayed after Mass to meditate on Psalm 15, which was in a small prayer book I was using.

O LORD, who shall sojourn in thy tent?
Who shall dwell on thy holy hill?
He who walks blamelessly, and does what is right,
and speaks truth from his heart;
who does not slander with his tongue
and does no evil to his friend,
nor takes up a reproach against his neighbor;
in whose eyes a reprobate is despised
but who honors those who fear the LORD
who swears to his own hurt and does not change
who does not put out his money at interest,
and does not take a bribe against the innocent.
He who does these things shall never be moved (Psalm 15:1-5).

I just sat for a long time absorbing its message, when it dawned on me that those words described my husband. The psalm soothed my hurting heart and the festering hurts seemed to melt away. I had come full circle, from wanting to separate, to appreciating my husband's goodness. It was such an immediate answer to my cry for help and I thanked Saint Bernard for pointing me to it. I was always in a rush to get home and get back to work, but that morning I stayed afterwards to pray and reflect. Then I felt inspired to pray the psalm for my husband because it described him perfectly. I ended up thanking and praising God for the gift of my husband

and asking Him to help me see the big picture instead of focusing on the small cracks and faults.

IT WAS A FRUITFUL summer, spiritually speaking. God was answering my prayers, one by one. First, I was learning the *how* of change: revelation, not resolution. I needed to verbalize what was bothering me and share it with my husband. Why it took me so many years to get to this point, I wasn't sure. Perhaps it was because I lost my voice as a child when it came to sharing my hurts. I treated my body like a trash compactor, stuffing every negative painful thing that I couldn't deal with down into myself, until it was full. When it got overloaded, it jammed and kept breaking down. It forced me to face the pain. Finding my voice was a grace from God.

Another valuable lesson I learned that summer was that I had to change my focus, to look at the positives instead of the negatives. That meant silencing the negative voices. It sounds so simple as I write this, but it meant undoing firmly entrenched habits of blame and projection that I had practiced nearly my entire life. I saw how swiftly I changed when I read the psalm that morning in church. What had happened? I looked at my husband through the eyes of God, not through my human, egotistical eyes. And what I saw was truth and beauty, which pumped love into my deflated heart. It was a practical thing. Seeing the giftedness of my husband enabled me to love him.

I learned what I already knew but had forgotten: God made us to be channels of His love, a love that my favorite author on prayer and healing, Agnes Sanford, described as living water or electricity. His love gives us life, she wrote, but in order to keep the current or water flowing through us, we must give it away or it will become blocked or stagnant through selfishness. And as we give, so will we receive. I felt that the Lord was saying to me: *The more you try to reach out and love others, the more I will deliver you from the prison of pain you put yourself in. Bring My life to others and be filled yourself.*

IN THE FALL WE WERE on the road again for Witness, where I gave a number of talks to groups in Ansonia, Bridgeport and Moodus, Connecticut (My Father's Retreat Center). From there we went to Sayre, Pennsylvania, to do a day of reflection on the Eucharist. John Langan and his wife Renee were the parishioners who had invited us to their parish. John was from Scranton, as was Tommy, and when they met they realized that John had gone to Saint Paul's grade school in Scranton with Tommy's sister, Janet.

The day would be comprised of two talks, a slide show, lunch and a concluding Mass. I thought of it as a practice run for the book I was writing on the Mass because it would enable me to test the contents and the visual images of the rituals in the Mass on the group. Their response lit a fire under me to finish the book. When I realized that day that the images heightened their interest in the presentation, I decided to use graphics in the Mass book.

The day after Christmas I was running errands when my cell phone rang. It was the nurse from my thoracic surgeon's office with the results of a second lung biopsy from a few weeks prior. It was a follow-up to the biopsies I had before the summer that were benign. I pulled over outside of Walgreen's and with the motor running, listened to this nurse's matter-of-fact report: "The results show that you have a small cell carcinoma in the right lung and the doctor would like you to schedule surgery as soon as possible."

"What? The biopsy I had six months ago was benign. How could it all of a sudden turn into cancer? Are you sure?"

"Yes," she said. "The doctor is sure. There is a small tumor that must be removed." I couldn't believe it. And I couldn't think of any more questions to ask.

"I'm sorry," she said. And she was gone.

I protested all the way home. *This can't be happening. The last biopsy was benign. How could it turn into cancer so quickly? A tumor? This is impossible. It's a mistake. No, no, no, no, no.* Then I fell into my husband's arms and cried.

I went for what is known as a "pulmonary function test," and found out that my lungs were not diffusing blood as they should or at the right capacity. This was all by way of preparation for surgery to remove the tumor. For several days I was on the verge of hysteria, struggling with a sense of abandonment and betrayal. I felt like I had been standing on a stool that someone pulled out from under me, leaving me flat on my face. Hurt and bruised, I lay there in a pool of self-pity and anger, blaming God and the doctors for this latest cancer. Was it spreading? And, if so, how much and how far? My fear was that the cancerous cells were trying to take over my organs.

After a day of wallowing in self-pity, I snapped out of it and rallied for the fight ahead. I relied on my familiar healing tools and started using them. The first was relaxation. Listening to Peggy Huddleston's tape quieted my jitters and fears and enabled me to pray. But I also knew that deep relaxation boosts the immune system by increasing the number of T cells, killer cells that fight free radicals. Free radicals are molecules responsible for aging, tissue damage, and possibly some diseases. These molecules are very unstable, therefore they look to bond with other molecules, destroying their vigor and perpetuating the detrimental process. If I ever needed to overcome them, it was now. I did the relaxation twice a day.

Another tool was visualization. I imagined myself in scuba diving equipment leading a small army of white killer sharks through my bloodstream. I would lead them to the tumor in my lung, to shine a light on the cluster of confused cells, and then I would watch the sharks devour them. After that I would swim throughout my body and allow them to attack any malformed or weak cells. I also went through my bone marrow and let the sharks feed on any malignant cells. I read in Dr. Siegel's books that in the process of visualization, our bodies don't know the difference between what is real or imagined. I interpreted this to mean that when the sharks are swimming in my system, my body thinks they are actually swimming and devouring the cancer cells.

The third and fourth tools were exercise and nutrition. Exercise boosts the immune system and, according to Dr. Siegel, experiments with animals showed that when they were stressed and not allowed physical activity, their bodies degenerated. But when given the same stresses and the freedom to exercise, Siegel said they remained healthy. The treadmill was hard on my knees, so I rode the bike at the health club about three times a week, doing five miles each time. If I had any energy left over, I exercised on the elliptical machine for about twenty minutes.

I also cleaned up my diet and increased the vegetable drinks because of the nutrition they give to our cells, which strengthens them to fight the cancer cells. The antioxidants (molecules) in the raw fruits and vegetables prevented free radicals from harming healthy tissue. I relied on these resources like a blind woman relies on her seeing-eye dog.

On the eve of another lung test, we sat by a wood-burning fire in the kitchen and I shared with Tommy how frightened I felt, how abandoned and hopeless. After all the prayers, the healing, the trip to Lourdes, the special anointings, and surrendering my life to God, I'd been handed another cancer that felt more life threatening than all the others. His reaction helped me. He said that he saw God healing me, first of scleroderma, then of MALT lymphoma, breast cancer, and now perhaps lung cancer. He reminded me that this tumor had been on the CT scan for a few years and now, in God's perfect timing, it has to come out. "This is another blip on the screen that the Lord wants to heal," he said. Those words made me feel better. But what really changed my attitude was a short admonition he gave me about people who are not as blessed as I am. For many people with cancer, by the time they see the doctor it's too late and the cancer has grown beyond control. With me, he said, the doctors watch every new development in my body, never letting anything surprise me or grow too big. This was true. He reiterated his sense that God is once again healing me, and instead of feeling sorry for myself I should be thankful.

THE FEAST OF THE EPIPHANY fell a few days before my lung surgery in January. This Christian feast celebrates the revelation of God to humankind in the person of Jesus Christ. I was so grateful for my faith in God; it was like a life raft that kept me afloat in the midst of these constant storms. I relied on it now to guide me through the uncertainty of what I might be facing. After Mass on Sunday, Father Hennessey said he would offer Mass for me on the day of my surgery. This was a great gift. His brother died of lymphoma ten years ago to the day, he said, and his sister was facing chemo that week for recurring breast cancer. I told him I would pray for her.

I prepared myself physically, mentally and spiritually for my lung surgery. On the eve of the operation I had a massage so that my body was nicely oiled for the dry hospital stay. We went to dinner with our good friend Brother Bill Tomes, who was a Catholic social worker who actually stood in the line of fire in gang warfare in order to quell the violence in Chicago. (As I write this, Hollywood is making a movie of his life.) We came home and watched a movie and I felt totally relaxed—and ready for surgery.

On the morning of surgery I went to Mass, worked for an hour on my Mass book, and did the relaxation tape one last time. In the early afternoon Katie arrived at the hospital as they were preparing me to go to pre-op. I was ready. Parting from Tommy and Katie was a little tearful, but I felt really peaceful. In pre-op everything was calm. The anesthesiologist said I could keep my earphones on during surgery. This time I had recorded Scripture verses of the healings Jesus performed. Although it was my voice, I wanted the Lord's message to sink into my unconscious during surgery. Stories I read in Dr. Siegel's *Love, Medicine and Miracles*, about unconscious awareness convinced me that people under anesthesia are able hear what is being said to them.

One story in particular really influenced me. It was about an operation Siegel performed on a young man who was so heavy that his weight caused some technical problems during the surgery. When the doctor noticed that the patient's pulse was 130, he said to him, "Victor, I'm having some mechanical difficulties because you're a big guy, but there's no problem with the surgery. This part is a little difficult to do. You're doing well. Don't be nervous. I'd like your pulse to be 83."[1] Within a few minutes, the young man's pulse dropped to 83, where it remained. According to Siegel, these anecdotal stories have convinced many anesthesiologists to speak to their anesthetized patients.

After reading this, and other stories, I got the idea to record the Scripture verses. I always remembered what my good friend, Fr. Bill Byron, S.J., told me one day during lunch. He said that he often repeats the words of Scripture throughout his homilies. "Why?" I asked. "Because there is great power in the Word of God,"[2] he said. Father Bill's comment, together with research on the Liturgy of the Word that I was doing for the book on the Mass, taught me a very important lesson: that God's Word is *living*, meaning that God cannot be separated from His Word.

I think that is why I wanted to listen to the Scripture verses during surgery. It gave me a feeling of empowerment because I believed that Jesus Himself would bring life to my body through His Word.

An epidural they put in my back was tolerable. I only had a few moments to reflect. I thought of all the people who were praying for me and I brought them—and everyone I promised to pray for—into surgery with me. When they wheeled me into the O.R. I was awake, and had about a minute to look around. It wasn't sterile-looking like the countless operating rooms you see on TV. Surprisingly, it was small and cluttered.

On the morning of my third day post-op, I was sitting in a chair struggling with those awful white support stockings that hospitals require to prevent blood clots after surgery. They were impossibly tight and uncomfortable and I was struggling to put them on and began to cry. It was 11:00 A.M. and I wondered where my husband was and why he was so late. I needed his help and was annoyed that he wasn't there. A nurse's aid very kindly assisted me and just as I got back into bed and collapsed in exhaustion from my minor ordeal, in walked my husband with a surprise guest: my son Danny who flew in from New York to surprise me. I did what I always do in moments of great joy or pain: I cry. I felt overwhelmed that he would take time out of his working life to hop on a plane to Chicago just to see his mom. His presence was better than medicine. It cured me.

Four days later when I was at home recuperating from surgery, the phone rang. It was my surgeon. He said, "Lymphoma," and I said, "Oh, it's gone?" "No," he said, "I just took it out of your lung." *The lymphoma had spread to my lung.* I imagined the worst, that the lymphoma was traveling throughout my body going everywhere. I felt like my life was slowly coming to an end.

He said he performed a thoracotomy of my right lung to remove a small portion of a lobe that contained a tumor. It was the same MALT lymphoma that was in my stomach (and which was no longer there thanks to the radiation I underwent the prior year). The doctor said he would call my oncologist to see what treatments she wanted me to undergo. He mentioned a gallion scan and a bone marrow test. Tommy was in South Bend at a Notre Dame basketball game. I hated to ruin his fun but I needed to talk to him. When I finally explained it to him, he was angry at the slowness of my treatment, asking why this tumor wasn't taken out two years ago when it was a "small blip" on the screen. He thought we hadn't been aggressive enough with our approach to all this.

I had trusted the Lord every step of the way to give me new life and healing, which He had done. But now, I felt betrayed. I imagined that is how Martha and Mary felt after Lazarus died. When they heard Jesus was coming, Martha ran out to meet Him saying, "Lord, if you had been here, my brother would not have died" (Jn 11:21). I felt the same way. Why didn't He heal me totally? Jesus told Martha and Mary that Lazarus' death would glorify God, and then He raised Lazarus to life to show God's power. *Lord, do I have to die so that Your glory will be revealed? Will You let me go to the brink and then heal me totally? I sense You want me to put all my trust in You. I thought I had. But I can see by my reaction that I haven't given myself completely to You.*

ON THE NIGHT OF the bad news, I was watching TV, trying not to sink into a depression, when the thought came to me to deal with this, "one day at a time." Actually, that thought lifted me up and gave me hope and a way to manage my anxiety. I wrote in my journal: *If I give myself to the Lord every day and follow the guidance of the Holy Spirit, I will be able to walk in God's light and peace. Please, Jesus, give me courage and hope to steady me, faith to lead me and love to console me. I can do anything if I know You are with me.*

The next afternoon I went to Saint Pat's to sit in the presence of Jesus.

I breathed "Jesus" in and out for a long time. No words, just presence. When I got home I went to my desk to try to work on my book. Words and thoughts came to me: *Empty yourself. Empty yourself every day.* I felt sure this was from the Holy Spirit and I related it to my earlier reading of the first step of A.A.: "We admitted we were powerless over our dependencies— that our lives had become unmanageable." The first step in managing my life was to learn to detach, to empty myself.

I became absorbed with the meaning of "empty yourself," as this journal entry shows: *You "emptied yourself" on the Cross. You gave your all, holding nothing back including your forgiveness. You shared your pain with loud cries. You cried out in anguish to your Father, feeling totally abandoned. You gave of yourself completely and this, I believe, is what you want of us. It means to give until there is nothing more to give. That is what it means to surrender to You and I beg You for the grace to do this daily, constantly.*

I devised a daily plan: to empty myself before the Lord. But what did that really mean? *To give Him any fears, news, worries, new problems, in short, anything that disturbs my peace. Since all is gift, my job is to give it away. In particular, I will not hide any negative feelings but will verbalize my pain, however difficult it will be. God has allowed me to experience this setback—lymphoma—and it is up to me not to try to control everything or anything. My job is to give the control to Him. That, I believe, will bring peace.*

I was finally learning how to give over the control of my life to the Lord: by emptying myself. At Hazelden I learned that Step 1 was to detach, to let go of control by admitting we were powerless over our emotional dysfunction or codependency and that our lives had become unmanageable. I learned the "what" of letting go, but for some reason I was extremely slow learning the "how" of it. Step 1 is basically to become like a little child, vulnerable, powerless and dependent. Little children must reach out to others to get their needs met. It is no wonder that Jesus used a little child to illustrate the way to enter the kingdom of heaven. He wants us to give Him every concern, fear and problem, trusting that He will fill our needs.

I saw that the only "power" I have is to remove any obstacles that prevent the flow of God's love through me to others. The great lesson I was learning was *how* to exercise this power: by emptying myself every day. It is a paradox that when we admit our powerlessness over ourselves, over a sickness, a dysfunction or an addiction, it makes room for God. Then, He fills us with Himself and empowers us to overcome the problem.

19

Finding the Root

It is precisely through the Sacrament of Reconciliation that inner
healing can reach the roots of sin most easily.
                                        —Fr. Emiliano Tardif, *Jesus Heals Today!*

WITH THE LUNG SURGERY behind me, it felt like it was the calm after
the storm. In January we drove to St. Francis Hospital in Evanston for an
appointment with my regular oncologist whose manner was always upbeat
and encouraging. She carried around my medical records in a three-ring
binder that was about five inches thick. Whenever I asked her a question,
she knew just where to look for an answer. I always teased her that if they
had a course in Patient Records in medical school, she undoubtedly got an
"A." Once again she reminded me that the type of lymphoma I had was
very indolent and non-aggressive saying, "People live for years and years
with MALT lymphoma." My CT scan from early December showed no
other signs of lymphoma (which is not to say it didn't exist). It was probably throughout my system but there was no treatment recommended unless it manifested itself somewhere. The doctor suggested that I take some
time off to heal from the surgery, after which she'd order some "awareness
tests" for February and March to determine what was going on in my body.
I always left her office feeling better than when I went in.

I was grateful to God for His goodness to me throughout all these illnesses. He had been at my side, so to speak, steering me to the people and
places that would heal me. I was also thankful for my work, in particular

for the book on the Mass that energized me and gave me a sense of fulfill-ment. Above all I was thankful for the gift of faith that kept me going.

I listed four options in my journal for maintaining a program of health and healing. First, I wanted to spend more time in prayer to practice self-emptying and discernment so that I could more easily recognize the voice of the Holy Spirit. Second, I would continue to do visualization exercises and meditation according to the methods of Drs. Carl Simonton and Ber-nie Siegel. Third, I promised myself that I would exercise in order to boost my immune system and, finally, I would continue to take the vegetable drinks to nourish my cells, strengthening them to fight the cancer cells.

NEXT ON OUR AGENDA was Tommy's long awaited knee replacement surgery. He chose a well-reputed orthopedic surgeon on the North Shore who had a rather cold and abrupt manner. On one of our first visits, he spent about two or three minutes with us—period. I didn't like him and tried to convince my husband to go with someone else, but this doctor's credentials were impeccable (at least as far as we knew) and Tommy had made his decision. After the surgery, on the second or third day post-op, the doctor and his assistant stopped by the room. Leaning casually against the doorframe, the surgeon looked at my husband and said: "It was a perfect operation." Even in his sedated state, Tommy's mental agility was sharp and he retorted, "*What does that mean? Are you implying it was like the 'Perfect Storm'?*" (A movie that was made in the 1990s depicting a real life "storm of the century" in which the skipper and others go down with the ship.) Without acknowledging the jab, the doctor made eye contact with his assistant and left.

The surgery was a traumatic experience and was followed by months of pain. Immediately after the surgery, Tommy spent a week at a rehab center not far from home, which was great for me because I could go and come easily. His leg was wrapped up in a bent position for days, and he didn't receive physical therapy until four days after the surgery. The therapy was grueling and exhausted him.

When my husband returned home, I tried to make life comfortable for him and ease his suffering. He never complained and just kept going to therapy to straighten his leg, which was like torture because it just didn't want to straighten. All in all, he went to therapy seventy-five times, probably setting some sort of a record. The therapist even resorted to sitting on his leg to flatten it. It became apparent to us that the doctor's remark about the "perfect operation" was some sort of a cover up for a botched job. Nothing worked, not even having it straightened under anesthesia. My husband finally switched doctors and had to endure two more total knee replacements.

During this time I underwent more tests: a CT scan, a PET scan (to measure the lymphoma in my system), another bone marrow test and an endoscopy. When my CT scan results came back, there was a new area of low density in the kidney. The radiation oncologist who read the report noted that it could be an infection, or metastasized disease in the form of a tumor, which would likely be lymphoma. The news was hard to take—and hard to live with. I felt real fear, like the lymphoma was systematically trying to destroy me, organ by organ. I wondered where I'd get the strength to face more cancer.

I didn't have the virtues of fortitude and long-suffering that my husband did. With more bad news I fell into a funk. All my good intentions to maintain my health flew out the window. I started feeling sorry for myself saying, "What's the use?" I felt like a sitting duck, not knowing where the cancer would pop up next. I lost hope and didn't even want to work on the Mass book. I cried at the drop of a hat, although I tried to keep up a happy appearance.

In the midst of all this, in the beginning of February 2003, the space shuttle Columbia disintegrated in space with seven astronauts on board. The crew endured six minutes of knowing that they were in trouble before it blew up. I felt the fear that they must have suffered and wondered how they dealt with the realization that they would die in six minutes. I could relate: *I feel like I'm in those six minutes. I'm in trouble and don't know when it will overtake me. I'm deeply upset and inwardly screaming. Why are You dangling me between life and death? One word and I could be healed. What more do I have to do to be healed? I give up, God. I'm out of steam. Empty. Alone. Afraid. I guess You felt that way in the Garden of Gethsemane. Please give me a dose of the blind trust You had to get me through this.*

Maybe I was finally emptying myself.

On Valentine's night Tommy put his arm around me and said, "You've never been a better Valentine." He had a way of saying things in such touching ways. I had been trying to nurse him back to health after his terrible knee ordeal, serving his meals on trays, getting his ice packs, water and newspapers. Actually I enjoyed caring for him and was wondering if the peace that started to settle over me was directly related to my absorption with him. *I'm grateful for the peace that has descended on our relationship like the cloud that used to settle on the Ark of the Covenant. Something profound has happened to relieve me of my negative feelings and judgments that have tormented me for years. Tommy's knee replacement surgery has reduced him to a needy and vulnerable state that has triggered my desire to help him in every way possible. His suffering has enabled me to love him, really love him through my actions. Serving him is a joy. It has called me out of myself and has brought great peace to the both of us.*

On top of this I received good news from my recent battery of tests: the CT scan, PET scan, endoscopy and bone marrow were all negative for lymphoma. *It was gone.* And the problem with the kidney turned out to be nothing. I could not have asked for anything I wanted more in the world than that. To be free of lymphoma, or at least the manifestation of it, gave me my life back. I had been living on the edge for so long; now I could step back unafraid that I'd fall off the cliff at any moment. I was grateful for my supportive husband who carried the burden with me, but if truth were told, he was the one who encouraged me to focus on God's healing graces instead of only looking at the illnesses. I kept getting cancer, but God kept healing me.

On a physical level I was healing, but emotionally I still couldn't seem to hold it all together. "Enough already!" a friend said to me at lunch one day. I had been bemoaning my situation and telling her about the emotional sinkholes I fell into constantly. I agreed with her. Another incident had happened when we were out to dinner with some friends one night when Tommy said some things that really bothered me. He was telling long stories, and, in my judgment, "showing off," which enraged me.

When we discussed it at home, he said that either way, he couldn't win. If he talked too much or too little, I judged him. He felt like a victim, he said, which put me over the edge.

I was beginning to figure out just why these incidents hurt so much. I think there was an unconscious dynamic at play between us that triggered pain from my past. It was really my inner child who reacted to Tommy as if he were—alternately—my mother, or my father. I remembered something that bestselling author and marriage therapist Harville Hendrix had said on TV: the key is to figure out if you are projecting the withholding parent on your spouse. In other words, Tommy's behavior reminded me of my dad's egotistical grandiosity. He often regaled his listeners with the same long, and to me, boring stories, that I could recite by heart because he told them so many times. My dad's controlling behavior bothered me mainly because it rendered him emotionally unavailable. It was all about him, and never about me. I hungered for his caring presence that I continue to look for in my husband.

The hurtful incident that took place when we were out to dinner, happened, I think, because Tommy triggered memories of my dad's storytelling that made me feel invisible. Never mind that my husband's stories were relevant and not repetitive. I had an inner meltdown because I was recycling fifty-year-old buried rage.

At those times, the inner child in me feels trapped and wants to bolt. My adult self says: *If only I had my own condo, I would be happy.* One minute I want to separate to ease the pain, and the next I realize how unfair it is of me to inflict pain on my husband when he is just being himself. I knew that I was looking through tinted glass, seeing his behavior out of my past wounds that made me so intolerant. I had a talk with God. *Jesus, God, please rescue me. Heal my spirit/soul that hurts so much and tries to inflict pain on Tommy. It's not fair to him and eats at our relationship. Lord, I give the whole situation to You: my physical health and my spiritual health. Please intercede for me and show me the lie that is causing me to fall into this sinkhole.*

During Holy Week I decided to go to the Sacrament of Reconciliation. I told the priest in confession that I kept recycling pain in my marriage that surfaced periodically and used it to hurt my husband. The priest who had more wisdom than age suggested that I ask the Lord to lead me to the root of this pain, and then pray for the courage to follow the answer. So I did.

In the meantime I began to feel sick. First, I got a terrible cough, then a malaise came over me that was similar to the scleroderma flare I had a year earlier. My muscles were hurting and once again I was slowly becoming paralyzed. Lying in bed on the first night of this attack, I was thinking of the dream I had about the nun in the casket who pretended to be dead. When I had asked her about her pain, she said she didn't think she could be happy in her marriage so she played dead. She felt totally trapped. Her sexuality was also frozen. I think she came to me in my dream because she wanted to be resurrected—to be brought back to life.

As I recalled the dream, I wondered for the umpteenth time if there was a connection between my emotional turmoil and the physical paralysis that was overtaking me. I felt fear. *I am probably doing this to myself.* I decided to get the antibiotic treatments that brought me out of the flare a year ago, but I also recognized—as if for the first time—how deeply this disease was rooted in my emotions.

When I met with Father Bob a few days later, I told him about the priest in confession who suggested I try to find the root of the pain. I wanted to revisit the dream about the nun in the casket because now I was afraid that I was keeping her in there. I was feeling panicky that if I didn't do something, she might really die.

Father Bob suggested I go back to a memory of something that happened that could have a connection to this deep pain. I thought of the time when I was in a crib, somewhere between two and three years old, when my father came at me with a leather strap. The memories of my childhood are so scant as to be almost non-existent. But this one stuck. I know because I was able to regress and actually feel the feelings of my terrified inner child. As soon as this trauma happened, I think I discounted my own terror and buried my feelings because I needed my father and couldn't bear to upset him.

I told Father Bob that I had already dealt with this memory a long time ago during a retreat, and also through counseling. He suggested that we review it anyway.

I closed my eyes and went back to the scene. I was in a crib in my parent's bedroom. I must have done something really bad to upset my mother so much that she had to have my father deal with me. Daddy went to the closet where he hung a cat o' nine tails (a long leather strap) on a hook, just to the left of the door. I can still see it hanging there. It was two or three feet long and brown. I don't know if he had had a drink or two, but I remember him walking over to the crib while my mother was yelling, "Howard, don't!" at the top of her lungs. It was her fear that terrified me. I don't remember the beating, but I could see and hear her scream, as if I was actually experiencing it. I think I froze in fear. My emotions were raw: *I feel like a bad girl, like I deserve this beating; it is all my fault. Daddy, kill me because I'm so bad. Just beat me till you kill me. I deserve to die.* My emotional pain was intense.

It was a bit unbelievable that a 3-year-old could actually feel such emotional pain. It seems like this thinking didn't just happen on the spot. It had already formed in my mind. Had I suffered some kind of abuse in a prior incident that caused me to hate myself to this degree? I don't know.

Father Bob asked me what would happen if I just lay in the crib quietly. I told him that *if I didn't feel pain, I wouldn't be cared for. If I cried someone would pay attention to me.*

In a matter of a few minutes, two lies emerged which have wreaked emotional havoc for my entire life. The first lie is: "It my fault so he should just kill me," and the second is: "If I don't feel pain, I won't be cared for." My little self was feeling guilty, worthless and no good and in order to get attention, I thought I had to cry and scream.

Father Bob suggested that I imagine Jesus at the scene of the beating. With eyes closed, I pictured Jesus walking towards me. As soon as He came, He covered me with His body and took the blows on His back. I felt protected and cherished. Then Father Bob asked my spirit to go to the place where my cells took in this programming—*that I should be killed*—and ordered them to be transformed in the light of God's truth and love. He said that from the moment of the beating it was recorded in my DNA that I should be killed because "I'm so bad" and that "when I feel pain I will be cared for." Father Bob said that God wants to reverse that and reprogram my DNA to choose life and love and to know that I'm loved and cared for just for myself.

"No wonder you've had so much sickness with that kind of internal programming," Father Bob said.

It was a stunning breakthrough, an answer to my cry for help. It was the root!

My thoughts then switched to my mother. I kept recycling the pain in my relationship with my mother; it was like a bottomless pit. Would it ever end? In all the retreats I attended over the years and in numerous counseling sessions, the subject of our relationship always came up and each time I heaved a sigh of relief believing that the issue was resolved.

I thought I had put the whole issue to bed in the early 1990s when I attended a workshop that psychologist John Bradshaw was hosting on "Loving My Mother." He was the rage then and my son Tom Jr. became enamored of him when he saw him on TV and urged me to watch. Tom Jr. was not usually drawn to things like that and his enthusiasm won me over. When Bradshaw came to Chicago we both signed up for the three-day intensive. Tommy could only attend a few of the sessions, but it was a joy to share this with my son, however briefly.

On the third and final afternoon of the workshop, the lights in the auditorium dimmed and Bradshaw asked us to go deep within to talk to our inner child. Then, with our left hand (or our non-dominant hand) we wrote a letter to our mother. This is what my 2-year-old self scrawled in my notebook: *Dear Mom, I really am a good girl underneath in my heart. I want to be loved. I want you to care about me because I am good and loving. Why aren't you interested in me? Why don't you tell me you love me? Why don't you ask me about what*

I feel or want or need? I know I am a bother to you. I am not important to you. I don't know what I did to cause you to hate me. I feel your hate and I wish you could be happy. I don't like you because you don't like me. I want you to go away and never come back. I don't love you. You hurt me and I don't want to be with you anymore.

I wept as I wrote this. I don't have a conscious memory of feeling that way, so this must have come from the deep unconscious. The pain was genuine and oozed out of me like pus from a wound.

According to Bradshaw, this pain can be generational, handed down from our family tree, and/or we can be born carrying our mother's unresolved grief over her losses. And then, of course, it can be from our lived experience that in my life involved my mother's depression and mental illness. From the intensity of my rage, I think it could have come from all three places.

I revisited the John Bradshaw workshop experience with Father Bob and told him that I think my mother rejected me in the womb. She may have felt burdened and anxious about having another child. I believe that I was born feeling rejected, no good, like I didn't matter. I think I felt her sense of self-rejection and depression and it repelled me. I made a vow, maybe in the womb, to reject her.

Father Bob suggested I ask Jesus to forgive me for vowing to reject my mother. Then I gave Jesus everything I gained by making this vow: control, importance, satisfaction and getting even. Father Bob renounced any spirit that entered in because I made this vow, and then he gave me absolution.

I then offered myself to Jesus to be used in any way He chose for the healing of my mother. I asked Him for the grace to choose my mother and for her to choose me, so that the life and love that God wanted between us would be released. My marriage? "The wound," Father Bob said, "is not the marriage. Marriage triggers the wounds so that we can be healed." In my case, I think Tommy takes the place of my mother, and when something negative happens, I reject "her" all over again.

As I am beginning to understand it, I was born carrying my mother's self-hatred and depression that passed through the umbilical cord to me and covered me like a blanket for most of my life. The beating by my father reinforced my own sense of self-rejection that was so extreme I wanted my dad to kill me because I really wanted to die. I believed that I was no good and that I didn't matter, that I wasn't loveable or worthy to be loved from the time of conception, a belief that passed to my cells. It was a death wish that had a devastating effect on my physical life, causing me to fall prey to so much illness.

As I grew up, I never had the desire to actually kill myself, but I did so symbolically, by putting myself in a casket. Because I couldn't really love myself, I played dead and went about my life denying my real self by acting as if she didn't exist. This was to spare me the pain of having to face the unworthy, unlovable person that I thought I was.

I know it was the Sacrament of Reconciliation that opened the door to my spiritual healing, through the young priest who encouraged me to find the root of the pain. Jesus told St. Faustina Kowalska, a Polish nun who, in the 1930s, received revelations from God about His divine mercy, that this Sacrament is a "Tribunal of Mercy," where "the greatest miracles take place."[1] I believe it because I experienced one.

It was during the session with Father Bob that I witnessed what, to me, was a miracle: to realize that I had been living the lie that I was worthless and no good and deserved to die. Jesus wanted to forgive that sin, to free me from its effects so that I could be me and not have to spend the rest of my life hiding in a coffin, trapped, pretending to be dead.

ABOUT A MONTH AFTER this, I attended a retreat with the Association of Christian Therapists led by Fr. Robert Faricy, S.J., a spirit-filled Jesuit theologian the author of more than thirty books who leads retreats all over the world. In the opening lecture I realized that God was using this endearing, down-to-earth priest to confirm my spiritual walk. "Our goal" Father said, "is to follow the Lord's lead to remove the blocks so that we can grow in our ability to give and receive love." He spoke directly to my experience, saying that if we buy the lie that we're no good or worthless, that is a sin from which Jesus wants to free us. He suggested we pray in this way: "Lord, show me who I really am. Take away my depreciation, the main root of my sins, whatever it is that limits my capacity to love and receive love."

Father's words were like balm for my soul in the sense that they supported my inner work of facing—and embracing—my dark side. When my friend said "Enough already," it unglued me a bit, because honestly, I was tired of the recurring pain. Father Faricy spoke about seeing ourselves as the lost sheep or the lost coin (see Luke 15:3-11) that our Shepherd was searching for. It put everything in perspective. A part of me was lost and it was only through the mercy of Jesus and His redeeming love that I was coming to grips with my brokenness and finding my true self.

20

Good Gifts

Indeed if we consider the unblushing promises of reward and the staggering nature of the rewards promised in the Gospels, it would seem that Our Lord finds our desires, not too strong, but too weak. We are half-hearted creatures, fooling about with drink and sex and ambition when infinite joy is offered us, like an ignorant child who wants to go on making mud pies in a slum because he cannot imagine what is meant by the offer of a holiday at sea. We are far too easily pleased.

—C. S. Lewis, *The Weight of Glory*

IN EARLY MAY WE went to Scranton for Tommy's fiftieth high school reunion at Scranton Prep. I don't know who had more fun, he or I. I enjoyed meeting some of "the group," a bunch of guys he was close to in school whom I had never met. While we were waiting for Mass to begin in the chapel, I struck up a conversation with one of his classmates, John Corcoran, from Lancaster, Pennsylvania. He was an Ob/Gyn who walked with a swagger, carrying a daily Roman Missal under one arm. We hit it off immediately.

At brunch the next morning, John and I talked for quite a while. I felt a kindred spirit in this tall, engaging man, and shared some of my health issues with him. I told him how I had been juicing vegetables after the doctor who treated me for scleroderma explained the benefits to me, how the enzymes in the raw food contained the antioxidants that would boost the immune system. John kept nodding approvingly, then pulled a little orange pill case out of his pocket inscribed with the words, *Juice Plus*. He showed me four capsules, two green and two red, saying: "Seventeen organic freeze-dried veggies and fruits plus a few grains are in these capsules.

If you take four every day, they will give you the required 5 to 9 servings of fruits and vegetables recommended by the American Medical Association." They are, he said, the "next best thing" to actually eating the fruits and veggies. That was good enough for me. I couldn't believe what he was telling me. Juicing so many vegetables and fruits had become very laborious and time-consuming, and the capsules felt like a solution to this task.

I asked John where I could get them. "She is standing right over there," he said, pointing to his wife.

John introduced me to Mickey, a former nurse, who was a distributor for *Juice Plus*. Her understanding of nutrition was impressive, and she was obviously very committed to this program. She told me that it was the most thoroughly researched nutritional product in the world, and that a number of clinical trials showed that antioxidant levels in the blood increased significantly after just thirty days on *Juice Plus*. This one fact alone convinced me to take it. With all the illnesses I had, my immune system needed all the help it could get to fight disease. I also liked the fact that *Juice Plus* was real food, not synthetic vitamins, that could enhance my regular diet.

I ordered a four-month supply, then signed up to become a distributor, because I knew that I wanted to pass on this product to people I met at talks and conferences who struggled with health problems. The rest is history. Since that providential meeting, I've taken four *Juice Plus* capsules every day and have introduced it to hundreds of people similarly concerned about their health. Another bonus is our new friendship with John and Mickey Corcoran.

Before departing for the Jersey Shore for the summer, I had another routine CT scan. When I met with my oncologist, she showed me the good report and was pleased with the overall state of my health. I brought along my *Juice Plus* capsules, hoping to interest her in them for her patients. To get to her office I had to walk past a room where people were hooked up to I.V. machines to receive intravenous chemotherapy. I felt sorry that they had to undergo such harsh treatment and thought that *Juice Plus* could restore their damaged cells and reenergize their bodies. The doctor brushed off my attempt to convince her of the antioxidant power in these capsules saying that she would just as soon eat the actual fruits and veggies. "Yes," I said, "that's great. But I'll bet you can't eat seventeen of them—every day." She just smiled.

A few days before we got in the car for the trek east, we took our grandson Ryan out to dinner for his 4th birthday, a tradition we started a year earlier when we took his brother, Tommy, out to dinner in Chicago. We picked up Ryan and drove him to Sports Authority, where he chose a soccer ball for his birthday gift. Then we went to Ed Debevic's restaurant for a hamburger, a chocolate shake and a round of arcade games. When we drove Ryan home he was sitting in the back seat of the car hugging his soccer ball. Before getting out he said to both of us: "You really have a good time with me, don't you?"

As we drove away Tommy said, "It doesn't get any sweeter than this!"

IN THE FALL OF 2003, I returned to Pecos Benedictine Abbey in New Mexico for a retreat on contemplative prayer with Mother Nadine Brown. Rarely had I enjoyed a book a much as hers: *Interceding with Jesus*. Spending time with a woman who was so on fire with love for God would be a great treat. Her strong faith and her close relationship with the Lord were particularly attractive to me.

Mother Nadine spoke about the gift of the mystery of God within us. The whole Trinity comes to dwell in us, she said, so that we become, in a sense, the Lord's home. She urged us to be as absorbed in prayer as Jesus was, so that we can receive from God. *To receive is the key.* The fruit of contemplation is to know who God is— and who we really are, she said, and to know that we must be healed of who we are not. She described the Holy Spirit as a divine flashlight who helps us see our hidden faults and sins. Surrendering our dark side takes grace, she said, and it is essential that we face the enemy within lest he divide and destroy us. Mother reminded us that Jesus is the light of the world, and we are "children of light," a gift which He gives us, one step at a time.[1]

This humble yet wise nun was one more mentor who affirmed the inner work I was doing. It was really apparent that the Holy Spirit inspired me to go on these retreats to recharge my batteries and give me a spiritual tune up. I learned from her. I was drawn by the ease and simplicity of her prayer life, and by the way she asked the Lord questions and received answers. To her, Jesus was an intimate friend who counseled and consoled her, someone she relied on constantly for guidance and wisdom.

Her example encouraged me to continue my own conversations with the Lord and to try to just *be* in God's presence. After one of her lectures, I sat in the late morning desert sun and wrote in my journal, trying to surrender all my cares to God: my children, my grandchildren (and the ones yet to be born), my friends, the book I was writing on the Mass, my health, and all the people who asked for prayers. *Lord, You have blessed me to overflowing with love and purpose and the means to accomplish things. I want to deepen my relationship with You now by listening more for Your voice, Your direction, and Your desire. Will You speak to me? Also thank You for the healings You have given me, from scleroderma, lymphoma of the stomach and lung, the successful removal of my thymus gland, and healing from breast cancer. Please keep me well so that I can live to see my children's children grow up. Lord, of the many gifts You have given me, I think that faith in You is my number one.*

I reflected on all the years I had been seeking God, beginning in my childhood when as a 3 year-old I became aware of His reality during bedtime prayers with my mother. Then, when I was hospitalized with polio at 6, I cried out to God and began to relate to Him as a loving Father. Reaching out to God was like breathing. I just did it, believing that He would answer me. In high school when I communed with God in the tabernacle, I found joy and meaning for my life through the personal relationship I had with the Son of God. During early marriage, I was drawn deeper into prayer and began to taste the rewards that stemmed from a personal relationship with the Lord. In the chapel of adoration before our trip to Italy in 1992, He promised to deliver me from bondage, a gratuitous gift of love that continues today. It was around that same time during a charismatic retreat that the Holy Spirit reminded me of my obligation to serve the Lord, and that I had new power that came from the heart of Christ, which I was to use to bring His healing love to others. Then during retreats and prayer before the Blessed Sacrament, I felt a deep bond of friendship with the Lord.

These experiences of transcendence which are not unique to me because all people have them, sharpened my awareness of the existence of divine love, within my being and also alive in others. They gave me a desire to be alert and attuned to God's voice that speaks words of comfort and direction for my life. My experiences deepened my faith and trust in God whose presence affirms, leads, loves and heals me. I feel a call to just be with His presence without words or activity.

In addition, I am awed by God's touch that I experience through the Sacraments, namely, the Sacraments of the Sick, the Eucharist and Reconciliation, which I believe heal us at every level of our being. They are, in the words of Fr. Ronald Rolheiser, president of the Oblate School of Theology in San Antonio, Texas, like God's physical embrace. He describes the Eucharist as "the kiss of Christ."[2] Every time I think of the Eucharist in this way, I feel so thankful for such an intimate gift of love.

During the retreat at Pecos, I took long walks and basked in an awareness of God's closeness. I thought of all the blessings that had come my way through faith, the many answers I had found and the lessons I learned by trusting the Lord. One day happened to be Tommy's 68th birthday. During Mass I asked the Lord to bless and heal him. I felt grateful for our years together and was sorry for all the ways I had failed at loving.

I also asked the Lord to tell me how I could love Him more.

Later that afternoon I went to the chapel to prepare for the Sacrament of Reconciliation. While standing in line, I had a powerful insight. The thought came to me that I could love the Lord more by loving Tommy. I began to feel remorseful for my cold heart, for all the ways I had dishonored my husband by putting everyone and everything else first. I saw how I had blocked God's love by blocking him. *Please warm my heart; fill it with Your love for him so I can love him—and You—as You deserve. Please give me new ways to love, to bring life and joy to our home.*

When the retreat was over I was fortunate to be in the same van with Mother Nadine for the two-hour drive to the Albuquerque airport. We had a lot of time to talk and one story she told stuck with me. When she left her cloistered community, she thought that God was calling her to start a new religious order. But after some months had passed, she doubted that she had done the right thing and wondered if she should return. She didn't have a community yet, a center or any money. During Mass at her parish church, the Monsignor interrupted his sermon, looked at her and said: "Don't give up. Do you hear me out there?" It was most unusual. He repeated this five times. Mother Nadine said she got the message: God, it seems, will stop at nothing to communicate with us!

RESEARCHING THE MASS BOOK was a full time job. For a year I parked myself in the library at the University of St. Mary of the Lake Seminary, where I spent four out of five weekdays researching and writing. I kept two tall stacks of books on a library table and made friends with the staff and some of the priests and theologians who were working on their books or doctoral dissertations alongside me. I brought my lunch and ate during breaks with the staff, who were good company, not to mention helpful. Occasionally Father Hennessey popped in and was always able to explain a subtle theological point with great clarity. He is a patristic scholar (having to do with the teaching of the Church Fathers in the early centuries of the Church), who was an invaluable help to me.

At the retreat in Pecos, I asked the Lord why I was having such a difficult time writing the Mass book. Although I felt passionately about the subject matter and enjoyed delving so deeply into the Mass, the writing progressed slowly, painful page by painful page. Although I was doing the writing, I felt as if it was the Lord's book that He was writing through me. He wanted me to cooperate with Him in this work and be open to His voice. I had the idea that He was going to give me images to quicken my spirit so that the writing would flow more easily.

At the time I was researching the origins and meaning of the homily, where I felt more or less stuck—and bored. The homily was less interesting to me than the other parts of the Mass. When I returned from Pecos, I think Mother Nadine's experience of the Monsignor speaking to her during the homily triggered a new interest in it for me. I thought about all the times I had gone to Mass and the priest said something during the homily that directly addressed a problem that was bothering me, especially at weekday Mass. I envisioned the homilist as a locksmith who "carries a master key with him at all times—the Holy Spirit—who can maneuver His way into the rustiest locked hearts!"[3]

I also received some unexpected help from an old friend, Fr. Bill Byron, S.J., who was vacationing near our summer home in New Jersey and gave us a call one day. We invited him to lunch at our beach club and before long the talk turned to writing. Father Bill was in the process of writing, *A Book of Quiet Prayer*. I was still struggling with the homily when he told me a story about a sermon he gave on forgiveness, when he was pastor of Holy Trinity Parish in Georgetown, that turned a couple's marriage around. It was the exact point I wanted to get across about the homily: that a priest, interpreting the words of Scripture, can penetrate the hardest of hearts by the power of the Holy Spirit and call people to a deeper conversion.

At this point, awareness of Witness Ministries was growing, and we received many invitations to give talks in parishes locally as well as in other states. I welcomed the opportunity to test-run the contents of the Mass book on live audiences. Each speaking engagement enabled me to flesh out the message of the book a little more clearly and deeply. I used a power point program to illustrate the rituals in the Mass with stunning images. My goal was to change peoples' perception of the Sacred Liturgy from a "boring" spectacle into a life-changing encounter with the living Christ.

Judging from their positive responses, it worked. Parishioners were eager to be able to enter more deeply into the prayer of the Mass. They really seemed unaware of the enormous spiritual significance of this sacramental ritual: namely, a Rite that Christ instituted to enable us to participate in His passion and death, so that we could experience Resurrection in our own lives. Their comments and questions deepened my own search and helped me perfect the book.

I met some unforgettable people in Sayre, Pennsylvania, Oneida, New York, Ames, Iowa, West Point, Mississippi and McHenry, Illinois. Those are the places that come to mind instantly. There are too many others to mention. In Ames, I gave a talk on the Eucharist to the grade school. Instead of lecturing them, I drew explanations from the children on the meaning of the images. They had been taught well and knew their Bible stories. When Noah's ark and the multiplication of the loaves and fishes flashed on the screen, they jumped to their feet to explain, with great enthusiasm, what they were seeing. It was totally energizing and exciting to teach children because they were so open and eager to learn. I felt like I wanted to do more of it.

EVERY FALL, WINTER AND SPRING, I made the rounds of CT scans and endoscopies. (To date I have had about eighteen endoscopies.) I saw my oncologist every fall and spring for an exam and a review of my file. On this visit, after a routine blood test, for the first time in my nine-year history of blood tests, there was no check in the abnormal column. This doctor, whom I had tried to interest in *Juice Plus*, was very pleased and I was overjoyed. As she was walking out of the office, she turned around and said, "What was the name of that stuff you were taking?" "Juice Plus" I said, realizing that she was making a connection between the fruits and veggie capsules and the great blood test. She gave me a wry smile before shutting the door. She still didn't order *Juice Plus*.

Throughout the fall, winter and spring of 2003 and 2004, new health concerns emerged constantly. First, there was a thickening in the lining of the uterus, which meant I'd have to have an ultrasound and a biopsy. I feared that the lymphoma was spreading. All of these tests took time to schedule, so over a period of a few months, I waited and prayed. In the end, it was negative for cancer and the doctors concluded that the thickening was probably due to the Tamoxifin I was taking for the breast cancer.

At the same time, an ultrasound of my thyroid revealed several small and large nodules that eventually had to be biopsied. One was a cyst that needed to be aspirated, in other words, removed through suction. Before the procedure I was sitting in the waiting room trying to pray and to calm my fears. I asked the receptionist for a piece of paper and wrote words that I felt were from the Lord: *Joan, I am the Technician in charge of you. Be docile to the Spirit of Love deep in your heart. Take charge of your surroundings, especially of the people I put in your path. They will help you and lift you up so the world will know it is I who heal you. I am your Jesus who loves you to death. Be calm my child and open your heart to Me who yearns to love others through you. My power is in your heart. Give it away!*

The thought of the procedure was frightening (a very long needle that I tried to avoid seeing) but because of the prayer, I was completely calm.

The cyst was benign—*thanks be to God.*

Soon after that, when we were visiting friends in Scottsdale, Arizona, in the spring of 2004, and enjoying an outdoor lunch, I bit into a crouton in my salad and two molars literally fell out of my mouth. They broke off at the gum level. Back home in Chicago, doctors explained that it was a bone-loss issue, probably due to my scleroderma. Not only did the teeth fall out, but also another molar had to be extracted because it had become infected. In a matter of a month I lost three important teeth. It took almost three years under the care of a skilled periodontal surgeon to reconstruct my mouth, inserting bone and implanting new teeth. This problem seemed minor when stacked against my preceding health issues, but, in reality, it was not a walk in the park. It affected my eating, not to mention my vanity. When I smiled, there was a gaping hole on one side of my face.

My husband soldiered through two more total knee replacements and months and months of physical therapy. We will never know what the problem really was but personally, I feel that the doctors made mistakes and cut muscles or ligaments that left him with a limp. Complications after the surgeries created bladder problems that he endured for about a year. It was a very rough time that he endured with the patience of Job.

The bright light in the midst of all these problems was our family that was growing at a fast pace. In a matter of two years, we added four new grandchildren and one daughter-in-law to the McHugh clan. Our son Tom, Jr., and Sinead finally had a daughter, Eva, who was followed a year later by Gavin. That brought their total to five. Katie gave birth to Ellie whose sister Erin arrived a year later. Our family was thrilled when Richard became engaged to "Danie D." They had a destination wedding in

Cabo San Lucas, Mexico, that their friends rated as "the most fun wedding they had ever attended." Many of our friends came from home, which made the affair into one long weekend party for us.

At home I was working day and night on the Mass book and going to daily Mass. One morning I felt deep gratitude for my recent clean bill of health as well as for Tommy's recovery from so many serious physical problems. It was as if I were riding a wave on the ocean, and enjoying the ride so much. As the saying goes, God was in His heaven and all was right with the world. My world was all about gift, everything from *Juice Plus*, to my kids and grandkids, to good friends and counselors, retreats with people who shared intimacies of their relationship with God, my apostolate to spread devotion to the Eucharist, and the new work with children. Heading the list was my relationship with the Lord, the source of all this bounty.

I was thankful to God for such largesse and wondered how I could become more centered in Him because I felt pulled in a few different directions. After communion one day I had an impression that was both an image and a thought. Jesus seemed to use examples to tell me how close He was to me. (I had been studying the Eucharist in the Early Church and perhaps that triggered this reflection.) I wrote in my journal: *He is the song and I am the music. He is the perfume and I am the scent. He is the message and I am the words. He is the flame and I am the wick.* These thoughts made me cry.

IN HIGH SCHOOL I kept a holy card tucked into my daily missal that said joy and sorrow follow each other in regular succession. I know it meant a great deal to me because even as far back as adolescence, I bounced between feeling happy and full of life, to sinking into feelings of sadness and desolation. The changing moods were cyclical, almost predictable. During my teenage years, the holy card must have reassured me that the periods of darkness were temporary, and that I would snap out of them.

Fifty-plus years later, these ups and downs were still recurring. *Will they never end?* I wrote one rainy winter afternoon. *Will darkness pursue me and try to envelope me for the rest of my life?* Just when I thought I was getting a handle on things, a trap door opened and down I fell. A disagreement that I had with my husband that I can't even remember now triggered it. I tried to describe the feeling: *Like I am in the cellar of my own home. People are upstairs but no one can see me or hear me. I am alone. Lonely. Trapped with no way out. It is dark and I feel hopeless. Despairing. I have given up. Life is upstairs and outside but not in me. I want to die.*

Once again I turned to Father Bob. He had much to say about depression, having dealt with it in his own life. He said that my depression is the cry of the inner child who is not letting her self be loved. He suggested that I am still clinging to my dad, who cannot solve my problem and I am still trying to alleviate my mother's pain. Father Bob said that I'm blocking myself from being healed because I'm struggling to solve my pain—by myself. I am trying to heal my mother and to heal my father. It is useless because they can't mother or father me. I don't think either of them received what they needed from their parents. "Instead of dying, you are trying not to die" Father Bob said and, "instead of letting go, staying with the emptiness and giving it to God, you try to get love yourself. This is a deception."

"Be willing to learn from desolation," Father Bob said, because "it is showing you that something has to die." He encouraged me to thank the Lord for putting me in the pit because He knows what needs healing. "Ask Him to show you," he said. My tendency was to panic and try harder to get love instead of letting go of it so that I could receive it from God. "Communicate with your inner child," Father Bob said, and "Feel terrible with her." His parting word was, "Do it with Jesus."

This was consoling—and helpful. It was also a path to sainthood that Mother Nadine spoke about during the retreat at Pecos. To be a saint takes a little dying to myself and my need and desires, she said, because God asks that of us. "We have to kind of make room within our heart every day for God's love to fill us because there is a lot of self love in all of us," she said. Then she added, "Once the Lord told me, 'One of us has to go,' and He said, 'It's not going to be Me.'"[4] Her sense of humor was delightful.

WHEN *THE MASS* WAS published in November 2005, we received letters and emails from people across the country who loved the book. One that especially touched me was from a priest in Chicago whom I had briefly met in the 1990s when I gave a slide/lecture on the Eucharist at his parish. Fr. Edward Wilhelm wrote: *Thank you for your wonderful book on the Mass. I am a priest for 60 years. I am thrilled with what you wrote. Thank you for all the research you have done. You are a brilliant writer, Joan. I am still absorbing* The Mass *and it is so wonderful I don't want the book to end!* What an endorsement!

Later that month we were invited to a dinner at the residence of Francis Cardinal George for benefactors of the Chicago Archdiocese. The Cardinal had written the foreword for *Eucharist God Among Us* and had supported our work from the time we first met. We stood in line to greet him and after shaking hands he said quietly to me, "*The Mass* is a great gift to the church. Thank you." We only had a few moments to speak to him while the photographer was snapping pictures so our encounter was fleeting. While driving home I recalled his comment about the Mass book, but I wasn't sure that he actually had said it. So the next morning I faxed the quote to his office saying, "Did you actually say that to me?" The reply came back quickly and in the affirmative. He gave us permission to use the quote in our marketing brochures.

Writing the book on the Mass was an enormously satisfying experience. While my name was on the cover, I have no doubt that the Holy Spirit guided the book from start to finish. It is truly a work of the Lord who uses it to enlighten people, and, in some cases, to bring them back to church. One friend wrote that her daughter-in-law was an evangelical Protestant who recently had converted to Catholicism. "After reading *The Mass*," Bonnie said, "my daughter-in-law said she finally understood its true meaning."

This was a confirmation to me that the book truly was *His* work.

21

Breakthroughs

As I observed myself and received feedback from the public, it became
clear to me that we have within us a place with an infinite dimension
that goes beyond us. Out of respect for the truth I had to speak about
this aspect of the being. I called it the "transcendent dimension." This
Transcendence can be called Truth, Justice, Love or God.
—André Rochais, *When Life Breaks Through*

OVER THE COURSE OF THE next few years, between 2005 and 2008, I
continued having CT scans, mammograms, blood tests and endoscopies.
I also had a colonoscopy. Each time I saw my oncologist, the main doctor who was monitoring my health, I was always on the edge of my seat
in the exam room. When she opened the door, binder and test results in
hand, she'd say, "Well, everything looks pretty good." My body completely
relaxed. I'd say a quick prayer, thanking the Lord for giving me more time,
for giving me back my life. I couldn't stop smiling—on the inside. I felt free
and so happy without any ominous tests, surgeries or problems looming on
the horizon. I couldn't wait to get to the car and call Tommy on my cell
phone.

It was like a miracle. I was like a rubber band that had been stretched
to the max so many times, stressed out from the thought that my days
were numbered. First, there was scleroderma and the panic that it would
disfigure and kill me within the first ten years. Then came the diagnosis
of MALT lymphoma (non-Hodgkin's), and despite what the doctors said
about living a long life with this type of lymphoma, it was still cancer, and
that was unnerving. After that there was the thymectomy in which the doctor removed my thymus gland because it contained a tumor the size of an

egg. That was followed with the diagnosis of breast cancer and a lumpectomy, after which I had radiation for the lymphoma in my stomach. Last but not least, the MALT lymphoma spread to my lung where I had surgery to remove a tumor. It was no wonder the binder containing my medical records was so thick! Throw the emotional black holes and depression into the mix, and you have a rather hard-to-believe testimony of healing.

After one appointment the doctor reduced the frequency of tests, cutting each one back to once a year.

I had one lingering concern. I still felt a general weakness in my legs that made walking difficult. I tired easily and didn't have much strength and wondered if scleroderma, despite the fact that it was in remission, was affecting my muscles. I made an appointment with a new rheumatologist who ordered a battery of tests. Among other things she tested my muscle enzymes. When this young, upbeat doctor phoned a few days later, I fully expected her to say that the scleroderma was progressing and causing my body to deteriorate. Instead, she said something so startling I could barely take it in: "All your tests were excellent. You have zero-problem with your autoimmune system. There is no sign of scleroderma."

My Honda Accord sprouted wings. I drove home in half the time, eager to share this incredible news with Tommy. He was visibly moved and gave me a hug-that-didn't-stop. Seeing his relief and happiness increased my own. "Let's go to Lovell's to celebrate," he suggested. It was our favorite restaurant, a five-star place owned by Jim Lovell of Apollo 13 fame. We used it for special occasions.

The next day I phoned my new rheumatologist's office to clarify exactly what she meant by "zero problem." Maybe it was just in remission, I thought. When she returned my phone call I asked, "Does 'zero problem' mean that the scleroderma is gone?" "Yes," she said, "It is gone. You test negative for autoimmune disease." Every time I think about it, my heart swells with gratitude and praise of God. It is hard to believe, and yet I do believe. I know that the doctors, medicines, radiation, surgeries, spiritual direction, the Sacraments of the Church and alternative healing methods all had, and continue to have, a part in restoring my health. They will continue to play a contributing role in my "undoing," by helping me remove stress and dismantle inner barriers that block the flow of energy—and love.

I could relate to the woman in Scripture who suffered from hemorrhages for twelve years and who reached out to Christ as He was passing by, believing that if she even put her hand on His garment, she would be healed. Her belief in Jesus touched His heart so that power went out from Him and she was immediately healed of her disease. Jesus said to her, "Daughter, your faith has made you well; go in peace, and be healed of your disease" (Mk 5:34). When the love of Jesus Christ touched people in the Gospels they were healed.

Two people whom I trusted had reminded me of that Scripture verse during the course of my illnesses. I was reaping the rewards of what happens when we reach out in faith to Christ. His power goes out to us, just like it did to the woman in Scripture. And while I know that Christ can heal instantly, it has been my experience that healing is an ongoing process that takes place in steps or stages, and will continue until the day we die.

BUT THERE WAS ANOTHER problem. This time it was my knee. The pain had increased over the last ten years to the point that walking or going up stairs was really difficult. In the winter of 2007 when I asked the orthopedic surgeon how bad the knee really was he said, "It's as bad as it gets." It meant that there was bone on bone, and it would only get worse. After so many years of dealing with this bad knee, the decision to replace it was really made for me, because now I had no choice: I had to do it. I scheduled knee replacement surgery a few months out, in the spring.

One morning I was going to daily Mass and Joan, a friend who belonged to another parish in our community, happened to be going to Mass at our church that morning. She could see me limping and asked how I was doing. "Bad," I said, "I just scheduled knee replacement surgery."

I could hear enthusiasm in her voice when she said, "Have your heard about Carmen?" Her husband and I had often compared our bad knee stories at social functions, so I was curious what news she had about his knees. (He had two bad ones.) "Well, last Friday he had a total knee replacement and went home from the hospital later that same day," Joan said excitedly. "Oh my gosh, how was that possible?" I asked. (Tommy had endured three total knee replacements for which he was hospitalized for days.) Joan told me that Carmen went to a surgeon at Rush University Medical Center in Chicago who does minimally invasive full knee replacements and who sends most of his patients home the same day. While trying to wrap my mind around that she added, "Carmen had the surgery on Friday. On Saturday morning he went to Mass."

I wanted to find this surgeon so when I got home I phoned Carmen for details. He sounded like the goose that swallowed the golden egg: happy and relieved that he could get around quite easily, with a minimal amount of pain.

I phoned Dr. Richard Berger's office and spoke with one of his secretaries, who answered my questions to my complete satisfaction. She informed me that Berger was a pioneer in the field of minimally invasive hip and knee replacements, having done thousands of these with great success for a number of years. His patients, she said, recovered faster with less pain than with traditional hip and knee replacement surgery. Apparently Berger's degree in mechanical engineering from M.I.T helped him design specialized instruments, which allow the surgeries to be done without cutting any muscle. These advances enabled most of his patients to walk independently and to leave the hospital the day of surgery. Berger's engineering background also helped him design gender-specific implants that were a great benefit for active people. (I heard anecdotally that he was fascinated as a child watching his father design the mechanical moving sets for Macy's Christmas windows.)

Fortunately, someone on his schedule had cancelled their March appointment, so that slot was available to me, should I want it. But there was a catch. He didn't take Medicare and asked for a hefty doctor's fee up front. I thanked her and then discussed this with Tommy, thinking that it was out of the question. My husband had been through so much and he saw this as a window of opportunity that would hopefully spare me of the agonies he underwent. "Yes, by all means, book the surgery. We will find the money," he said. It was an answer to prayer because I had seen what he had endured and was terrified at the prospect of it. I felt in my bones that this surgery would be simpler and less of an ordeal.

The surgery went well, according to all reports after it was over. I had no bandages or big staples, just a small hand-sown three and a half inch incision. At 3:00 on the afternoon of the surgery, a physical therapist came to the room to take me for a walk. We walked down the hall then up and down a short flight of stairs. "You are good to go," she said, matter-of-factly, "You can tell your husband to go get the car." I was overjoyed. It was pouring rain outside but it didn't matter. I felt euphoric. It was a Friday afternoon and we were heading north on the Dan Ryan Expressway in heavy traffic. I felt well enough that we even talked about stopping somewhere for dinner, but decided against it because we would get home so late. As we inched along in bumper-to-bumper traffic, I needed a seat belt to keep me from flying out the window. The cloud of anxiety that had hovered over the prospect of this surgery for so many years was gone, replaced by an enormous sense of relief and freedom. The thought that I would be able to walk normally again was thrilling, and the fact that I wasn't in pain made me giddy with delight.

Exactly one week later we went to a St. Patrick's Day party at our parish. I put my foot up occasionally to keep the swelling down, but otherwise I felt well enough to enjoy the company and the corned beef and cabbage. It was the music I couldn't resist. When the band played some of our favorite Neil Diamond songs, Tommy knew I wanted to dance. So we did. It was more like stepping slowly and lightly according to the rhythm, but nevertheless we were dancing. It was a fun night that we both enjoyed enormously. But I paid the price the next morning when I could hardly get out of bed. I had overdone it and had to spend the next day icing my very sore—and swollen—knee. It was a minor speed bump and one that, in retrospect, was worth it. I had so much to celebrate, the successful knee surgery being only one victory on a long list. It felt great to be so happy.

In the summer and fall of 2007 and during the winter of 2008 I had a series of disturbing dreams, three of which involved a paraplegic. In the first, a young man who was smiling and very approachable said to me, "What's wrong with me?" In the next dream a young boy had been injured. He was lying on ice cubes and I felt very sad for him. He couldn't move and was just stuck there. Then in another dream a young boy was laying flat in a house overlooking the ocean. His father was standing beside him. He was paralyzed from the waist down but neither the father nor his son seemed to be upset by the boy's disability.

After these came a different dream about the two dogs that we had for years when our kids were growing up. Sam and Snoopy hadn't been fed in a long time; they were forgotten. I was deeply pained over this; it was horrifying and very sad. I felt compassion for them as well as a sense of panic. The poor starving dogs were powerless to speak, unable to defend themselves against such abuse. They were victims in the real sense of that word because they had no voice and were unable to care for themselves.

I knew from studying dreams that the characters and symbols represent the language of the unconscious and have meaning for our life. They gift us with wisdom and insight for our spiritual journey. Did these dream figures represent a part of me that was stifled, abused or stuck in pain? In real life I was still trying to get to the bottom of the pain that I kept recycling. Down deep I was asking, "What's wrong with me?" Feelings of desolation and hopelessness continued to haunt me periodically and I still struggled to come to grips with these feelings. The dreams seemed to point to my inner child who was crying for attention, for emotional nourishment.

AROUND THIS TIME I HAD a "play date" with my 3-year-old granddaughter Ellie. We went to the park and then out to lunch at a local coffee shop. I adored this child—as I do each and every one of my grandkids—but I think Ellie reminded me of myself at that age. One day when I showed her a photo of myself as a toddler in a ballet outfit and asked her who it was, she thought it was herself! She sat in a booster seat across from me and we played a game during the entire lunch. I kept asking her questions such as, "What is your favorite color?" "What is your best toy?" What is the most fun thing that you did recently?" She delighted in each question and answer, after which she would laugh and say things like "Silly, Nana, you know that red is my favorite color!" We laughed our hearts out and had so much fun that time evaporated. Neither of us wanted to stop.

The next day when I took some time to meditate and write in my journal, I recalled my luncheon with Ellie. She was so on top of the world, so simple, so clear, so straightforward, open and spontaneous. Ellie was totally happy with herself and her world—and completely guileless. Her little self was pure and undivided; she was the same person on the outside as she was on the inside. I wrote: *Lord, I love this child. Do I see myself in her, the self who I once was? The me who was bursting with life?*

I wondered if Ellie awakened my own inner child whom I had stifled for so many years. *Is Ellie touching the child in me who is hidden and crying for love? The child who is stifled and fearful of being herself? The child who wants to love and be loved but who stays hidden out of fear? The child who wants to play and create and have fun? Jesus, is Ellie calling out my own inner child who yearns to be free?* I sensed love in her reaching out to me. It was larger than life, it called me out of myself to see, to hear, to taste the world as if for the first time. My own granddaughter was a mirror that reflected God's unconditional love to me. And my inner child responded by wanting to come out to play.

The luncheon was a watershed experience in my spiritual life. It changed me. I think it gave me a glimpse and a taste of my real self, the self who was once free to be truthful, open and unafraid of being true to her thoughts and feelings. After so many years, I was finding my voice.

I wanted to be reborn, to start life all over again. I thought of Nicodemus in Scripture who asked the Lord how one could be born when he is old. Jesus replied, "Truly, truly, I say to you, unless one is born of water and the spirit, he cannot enter the kingdom of God" (Jn 3:3). My understanding of this passage is that we are first "born" into a new and eternal life with Christ through the saving waters of Baptism. What follows is the growth and ever-deepening conversion of our spiritual life in which we are "born of the spirit" (Jn 3:5), which means born to the fullness of life, by being remade in the truth of who we really are. This, from a Christian standpoint, is our goal and purpose: that the image of Christ within us, disfigured by sin, may be restored. To be born into the life of God is to be recreated into His image and likeness: "If any one is in Christ, s/he is a new creation; the old has passed away, behold the new has come. All this is from God . . . ." (2 Cor 5:17-18).

It seemed that everything in my life pointed toward new life. About a month later I had another dream. I was sitting at a table and a lady with glasses was at the other end. She was talking and looking at me. As she talked I became aware that I might know her. I said, "Are you Noni Reese?" She said, "Yes." She was not a close friend but more of an acquaintance who was a year older than I was at Sacred Heart. Noni was an outgoing, fun and happy person who laughed easily. She was gregarious, spontaneous and enthusiastic. In the dream, every time I realized that she was at the table, I started to cry.

I think I was crying because I yearned to be like her. On the morning after the dream, I had a dialogue with her in order to find out why she came to me and what message she had for me. She said that I was a lot like her but that I spent most of my time hiding in my work where I took refuge inside myself. This was true, I said, but I found purpose and joy in my work. Basically, "Noni" said that I was really two people, one who worked and one who enjoyed herself when she was out socially with friends. She came to me in the dream to wake me up to my gifts, she said, to coax me out of hiding and to encourage me be my true self—all the time. She also suggested that I should find an enjoyable outlet that would bring out the best in me, something that was social, engaging, purposeful and fun.

In another dream I had that night the words "Blessed Assurance" kept flashing in the dark. I took at it as a sign that God was watching over me.

The next day I went to confession to my favorite young priest who had helped me so much in the past. This time he said that the pain—the inner sadness and depression—was my sacrifice and suggested that I ask God for the grace to focus on my blessings. Later that day when I took some time for meditation, I saw an image of burning embers in my soul. It seemed like God wanted me to throw my suffering on the burning embers as a way of giving it to Him. This appealed to me because it gave me a way to surrender my pain to God.

IN MARCH, 2008, I FLEW to Worcester, Massachusetts, to spend a few days with Sister Irma Gendreau, who belonged to the Little Franciscans of Mary and whom I had met in Kennebunk, Maine, the previous summer when she conducted the *Who Am I?* workshop. (See Prologue.) Her size was the only petite thing about this lovable woman. Born in Madawaska, Maine, Irma was mighty wise when it came to the spiritual life. She is a trained PRH Educator and one of the most interesting and insightful teachers on the inner life that I have ever met. Irma is a counselor who, in my opinion, has a gift for reading souls.

We first discussed the pain of my childhood. She was of the opinion that I probably felt more pain in my relationship with my mother than I did with my father. This was true. We then reviewed the disturbing dreams and some upsetting incidents that happened with my husband. Irma explained that it was important to stay close to the sensations in the dreams, to feel the painful feelings that they triggered. She told me that she would teach me a way to analyze my disproportionate reactions and to "evacuate" sensations that I've lived with since my childhood. The feelings in the dreams and those associated with my husband were coming from the same place she said: I was reacting as a child to painful incidents that I was unable to acknowledge so many years ago.

This made sense especially when I thought about another recent upset in which I had a disproportionate reaction to a miscommunication between Tommy and me. We were considering buying a TV stand for our house in Michigan. I had seen a few at Best Buy that I was trying to describe to him. At first he didn't hear me so I had to repeat everything. That was strike number one. My mother was hard of hearing and I always had to repeat myself, which I grew to resent. Then we had a confusing conversation about what he thought I said, but I hadn't. He had a totally different idea of what the TV stand should look like that blocked him from hearing me, and we had a complete breakdown in our communication. We might as well have been speaking different languages.

The fact that he didn't hear or understand me made me crazy. Our communication was so garbled that I ended up totally frustrated and in tears.

Irma suggested that the disagreement with my husband was a reaction to my mother not hearing or understanding me. I didn't have a voice back then and was not able to acknowledge how upset I was by her depression and her recurring bouts of mental illness. Recalling my lunch with Ellie, Irma said that I needed my parents to rejoice in me like I did with Ellie because it is our birthright to receive this kind of love gratuitously. Ellie received my gift.

Children have a need for the give and take of love, Irma said, because we have a need for communion, for bonding. When love isn't exchanged, we are wounded in what is essential in us: in our being.

Irma converted the enclosed porch of her home into a small chapel where the Blessed Sacrament was reserved. There were windows on three sides of this long, narrow room, which she made into an inviting prayer space with comfortable chairs that faced a tabernacle at one end where the consecrated hosts were kept. A red hanging vigil light indicated that Jesus was present.

Irma invited me to spend time there, to take all afternoon if necessary, and write an autobiography of my childhood. She urged me to address my parents in whatever way I felt directed and to feel free to say the things I always wanted to say but never did. She hoped I would be able to get in touch with buried anger regarding the emotional presence I craved so deeply and never received.

I was ecstatic, not only to be sitting close to the Blessed Sacrament, but also to have a span of uninterrupted time to commune with God. I wrote in my journal for hours. Literally. *Lord, thank you for leading me here. It is the answer to my cry for help. Please lead me to the source of these deep pains with my mother and heal them. Free me from the prison of this darkness so I can stop blaming Tommy for these pains. Jesus, I place them on the burning embers and offer them to You.*

The reflections that follow came from the deepest part of me. Most of the painful parts were directed to my mother. Here are some excerpts: *I wanted to be loved and held and cherished, but you were always busy. You weren't my friend and I didn't want to be your friend. My little self was very affectionate and I lavished my affection on my dolls. I don't remember ever being hugged or loved, just told "no" and "wait till your father gets home."*

I directed the memory of the crib incident to my father: *I hated myself for being bad and turned against myself rather than you. I thought I deserved punishment and blamed myself. I was whipped into obedience and after that I tried to make you love me. To compensate for not being a good girl, I tried to prove my worthiness for love.*

The following brought tears: *I think I buried my real self. I snuffed her out because she was no good. That's when I lost my voice. I couldn't fight back or speak for myself because I thought it was my fault and I deserved to die. If I could have died I would have. At that moment I tried to be somebody else.*

Mommy you were self-absorbed in all your unhappiness, mentally and emotionally preoccupied with your own depression. You had no time or energy for me because you were always drained by your negative feelings. Your depression frightened me and I recoiled from you.

I was sobbing. *I needed love so much—a friend, comfort, and counsel. But you just weren't there. I often cried myself to sleep. That pain inside of me came out privately, secretly, because I had no one to share it with. Now I'm hurting that I never had a mother who really loved me, who cherished me, who brought out the best in me. You brought out the worst in me. You didn't think about me, you thought about yourself. I was alone and resented your lack of caring.*

My heart was covered over with pretending, denying. I did harm to myself because underneath I thought I didn't deserve love. I thought that I really didn't matter and I gave up on myself and got sick. I denied love to myself and cut off the part of me that craved love. I tried to destroy her by shutting her up, by ignoring her, by rejecting her.

Now I am finding my voice and speaking the truth for the first time. I want to be reborn and, by the grace of God, heal from emotional abandonment that I felt so deeply for so long.

What I wrote seemed so harsh compared to the love I felt for both of them. I said that I had given them power over me for many years, but now I wanted to own my power and speak up for myself. I admitted that I hated the parts of them that didn't or couldn't love me, but I know it wasn't their fault. I could see that they were broken and wounded in their core, a fact of life that hampered their ability to give of themselves unconditionally. Towards the end of the letter I told both of my parents that I forgave them for all the ways they didn't love or validate me. *I release you from the bondage of unforgiveness and tell you that I love you because you gave me life.*

I ended by saying that I was sorry that I didn't honor my life and "gave up" at such a young age. I asked my inner child to forgive me for abandoning her. I wrote, *I want to reclaim her now because I know that I do matter and am loveable. I forgive myself for hating myself and for abusing myself through rejection. I pray to be reborn and give myself the love I never received from my mother or my father.*

When I finished, I read my letter to Irma. It was a real catharsis. I felt purged. Emptied. Cleansed. Relieved. Freed. I got in touch with feelings that I never expressed as a little girl. She said that I have been waiting my whole life for my parents to give me the love that I didn't receive as a child. At some point I transferred that responsibility to my husband.

It has taken me too many years to come to that realization, to get it finally that that my husband—or anyone else for that matter—will never be able to give me the presence I crave so deeply. Irma recommended that I give myself the same kind of love that I gave to Ellie. "Hold your little inner child and welcome her aliveness and her love," she counseled, saying that I need to take care of her because she cannot be left alone. Even though I closed myself off to protect myself, my aliveness and energy was still there. Sister Irma wanted me to encourage her to express her life, her enthusiasm and her energy because "it is at the being level that we give and receive love. Being to being, like Joan and Ellie."

Irma had guided me in my own personal "born anew" experience—by enabling me to reach my little inner child, who was alive and waiting for love. Then she said something that summed up the spiritual meaning of it all: "The deepest core of our being is to experience ourselves as God's child."

"Turn to Jesus," Irma said, "because He is the only one who can reach you in this place, to be present to you in your need." When you are faithful to your being, she continued, to the sensations and the intuitions that come from the being—which is really from beyond you—that is God speaking to you, she said: "It is the Holy Spirit guiding and healing you."

This resonated with my own deepest belief and experience.

Before I left to catch my flight to Chicago, Irma and I sat in her kitchen and had a cup of tea. She told me how to analyze disproportionate reactions. I took notes:

Begin with sensations (feelings) that are alive. Write down what I feel in the situation, focusing on the feeling, not on the incident or on the person. Then describe what you are feeling inside you, not in your head. (There's a difference between and idea and a feeling.) Focus on the feeling. Describe what it is like, using words that rise up from the feeling. When you finish, say, "What is this connected with?" Then let the sensation speak. There may be an incident from the past that rises up. Let is come up. It can come through any of your senses. For instance, you smell bread and you think of your grandmother. If the feeling doesn't come automatically, stop. (Otherwise you'll try to figure it out in your head or try to remember etc.)

Irma continued her commentary on the value of getting in touch with painful sensations. I kept writing:

Don't let your "I" push things away. The "I" created the false self, what we think we are and not what we are in our essence. Stay in the now. Accept pain in the here and now. Let it live. You could never let it live in the past. What heals is the release of the emotion. Drawing life from the heart is what heals it. When you do this, you are living the truth of who you are. You are getting in touch with your being, which is the essence of who you are, the most intimate and deepest part of your personality. It is what makes us unique from other human beings. In Christian language we call it the Soul. The being comes forth with Light, Strength, the force that is within me. When I release the negative energy inside of me, it makes space for the positive energy from the being to come forth, and it comes spontaneously, because the negative energy (coming from my wounds) blocks the positive energy of my being.

When there is nothing left to write, Irma said, stop writing. It is like the manna in the desert. That is enough for today. Tomorrow there will be more.

Irma recalled the teaching Jesus gave when He said that those who lose their life, will find it. Jesus meant losing the ego self, dying to the false self. When we drop the "I" and let our truth emerge from our being, we will find our true self united with God in our soul.

Irma sent me home with two books, written by PRH educators, which contained all this teaching. (See Prologue)

She also gave me two parting gifts. The first was, "Joan, remember that the presence you are yearning for is already inside of you." Second, she said that she thought that my need for presence is also my mission of being present. "Your mission," Irma said, "is to reveal God's presence to the world."

On the flight to Chicago, I wrote in my journal: *Jesus, thank you for bringing me to Worcester, for teaching me, through Irma, how to heal the wounds of my past, especially childhood, to free me from those pockets of pain that literally suck the life out of me.*

Irma confirmed, and continued, the inner work I was doing with Father Bob. Worcester was one more step down the ladder leading me into the depths of my true self.

22

The Problem of Pain

If we become one with suffering and feel it instead of resisting it, the suffering releases and is gone. What is left is connecting with the love that is who we are.

—Peggy Huddleston
Prepare for Surgery, Heal Faster: A Guide of Mind Body Techniques

I LEFT WORCESTER FEELING brand new, empowered to give away the love I had received. No sooner was I out of sight of Irma than my mission became apparent. I listened with empathy to Ed, the driver of the airport van, who was disconsolate that his girlfriend wasn't giving him the attention and love he needed. She didn't return his calls and he was trying too hard to win her love. I told Ed that I understood and suggested that he back off and start to give himself the love he was trying to get from his girlfriend. Ed believed in God, so I urged him to put the matter in God's hands and ask Him to engineer the relationship to work out if it was His will. Then I suggested that he begin to listen to the cry of his inner little boy, who was desperately trying to fill his needs through his girlfriend. I told Ed that if he began to get in touch with the buried wounds from his childhood that were still causing pain, his inner child would eventually stop hurting and stop demanding others to fill his emptiness.

Ed got all choked up. He thought I was some sort of a mystic. He decided not to call his girlfriend and not listen to her voice mail for the umpteenth time. Instead, he thought it a good idea to start taking care of himself for a change and perhaps he would even go bowling again with his buddies.

Under the care of a loving and wise teacher, in a small house in Worcester, Massachusetts, I had come full circle, to finally embrace my inner child who was craving love. I had known *about* her for years, going back to that time in early marriage when I collapsed on the bed at the Carmelite Retreat House and reveled in the memories of chasing sea gulls as a 5 year-old at the beach. When the priest told me that the Lord was speaking to me from memory and wanted me to reclaim my inner child, I cried buckets, wishing that it could happen but not knowing how it could.

That was 35 years ago!

Had I known that it would take so long to find her, I probably would have abandoned the search. Just like I had abandoned her. But something keeps prodding me to knock down inner walls that block my path to peace. That "something," I believe, is Someone greater than I am, the Spirit of Jesus, who drives my search to find love, and to find myself.

When I left Worcester, I felt hopeful that I could love my inner child. I wish I could tell you that getting in touch with her solved all my problems, or that I no longer suffered from periods of desolation. I felt that freedom from pain would give resolution to my search for inner peace, and it would also be a lovely way to put some closure on the journey we have taken together! But, it would not be true. What I can say is that the bumps on the road have become less frequent, and of shorter duration.

Discovering my inner child was one thing. Healing her would be quite another!

ONE OF THE LAST things Irma said to me was, "It is very important that you experience presence." Irma had a way of nailing the truth. The desire to connect, to bond, to experience the emotional presence of my parents and people I loved, was an overriding need that started in my childhood and is still with me today. Hunger for emotional intimacy was certainly behind my devotion to the Eucharist. I think that my connection to God lessened the pain of alienation I felt with the people closest to me, especially with myself.

One afternoon Fr. Bob Sears actually confirmed this. He said that it's probably not an accident that God put it on my heart to spread devotion to the Eucharist. In the Eucharist we connect with the God who bridges all differences, whose love embraces even those who crucified Him, he said. The Eucharist is the Body of Christ. We are the Body of Christ. We are brothers, sisters and mothers to each other, he continued. He reminded me how I've yearned for a deeper sense of belonging throughout my whole life. At some point during my adolescence I "connected" with God in the Eucharist who filled—and continues to fill—a very deep hole in my heart and provides the divine family of which I longed to be part.

It was true. I understood as never before the gift God handed me as a child when He opened my mind and heart to believe in His Real Presence in the Eucharist. God knew my need, and called me out of hiding to find Him.

Now my greatest joy is to share my faith with others, to tell my story, which is really our story. It is the story of God's saving presence in our world and in our life, not a one-time happening, but an ongoing occurrence in our daily lives. I feel called to proclaim from the rooftops what a difference faith can make in our life.

I had an unexpected opportunity to do this in July of 2009 when the Missionaries of Charity invited me to speak to several hundred children who were attending their summer camp in the Bronx. My friend, Colleen, and I drove up from the Jersey Shore to spend the day with Sr. Mary Marta and other sisters of the order, as well as some seminarians, priests and young volunteers who literally came from all over the world for six weeks to help staff the camp.

The neighborhood children were quite poor and many of them had little knowledge of the Catholic faith. I presented a slide show on the life of Jesus, telling the Gospel stories in a way that the children could relate to them. I wanted to plant seeds in their young hearts and minds about the love Jesus has for them, and assure them that no matter what their problems, if they put their faith in Jesus, He would help them.

The children were so eager to learn. They loved the slide of Jesus holding a child on His lap and saying, "Let the children come to me, and do not hinder them; for to such belongs the kingdom of heaven" (Mt 19:14). One little girl volunteered that she never knew that Jesus fed so many people with bread. She then said she learned that the bread of the Eucharist is really Jesus. God was giving these children a gift more precious than gold: faith in Him.

The day concluded when the young, assistant pastor of St. Rita's shared the story of his vocation to the priesthood. He told of his struggles growing up in a family where he didn't get along with his father. He really hated his father's anger and wanted to run away. The children never took their eyes off of him. Many of them probably suffered in the same way he had, coming from broken, abusive homes from which they also wanted to run away.

Slowly, he said, he was drawn deeper into an appreciation for the Catholic Church through a faith community that nurtured his spiritual growth. He repaired his relationship with his father and his whole family reconciled through the love they were experiencing through the Body of Christ. Father Ramon said he fell in love with the Person of Jesus Christ and, at 17, entered the seminary to become a priest. Father Ramon reminded all of us that day about the changes that takes place when we give our lives to Christ: Jesus heals our pain and brokenness and fills us with new love and new life.

That day in the Bronx was deeply fulfilling in several ways. I saw in the priests and seminarians, in Mother Teresa's missionaries, and in the volunteers, people who were living resurrected lives, loving with the love they had received, giving it away, generously, to everyone in need. And my wish to work with children was coming true. By God's grace, He was also nurturing my own inner child.

BASED ON THE GUIDANCE of my gifted mentors, I resolved to spend more time journaling. "When a person enters into her feelings, the depression lifts," Irma had said. This was similar to something that author and psychotherapist Peggy Huddleston said to me over breakfast in New Hampshire: "Suffering comes any time we're resisting feeling and emotion. Any emotion, other than love, that we store, later tries to work its way out of our body, like a splinter. It rises to the surface." Our resistance, Peggy said, causes suffering.

The trouble is, I had programmed myself to *resist* negative feelings. While I know that healing is a process, I didn't know that it would take an earthmover to uproot lifelong patterns of denying negative feelings and projecting them on others.

When I begin to feel needy, or angry, or overlooked, or lonely, or wished that Tommy would change and listen to me or give me what I need, I realize now those are my triggers that little Joanie wants my attention. She knows how to push my buttons. She demands attention and every once in a while, she still wants to run away. She can be bossy, controlling and can ruin my joy. Tommy's behavior can incite rage that is still aimed at her father. But since he's not here, she blames Tommy. Her pain indicates that the adult Joan hasn't fully forgiven either of them for her perceived hurts. I usually get out my journal and follow Irma's guidelines to diffuse the negative energy and get in touch with what is at the bottom of the pain.

But one day I was so upset that I called Fr. Bob Sears for an emergency appointment. As usual, I was reacting to a hurt that I couldn't verbalize. I thought about trying to work through it in my journal, but I decided to reach out to Father Bob instead.

What happened was a miscommunication with Tommy. Same old stuff. He misled me about going to the health club, telling me he worked out that morning, but when I pressed him for details, he was forced to admit that he hadn't gone after all. He told me later that he was too busy, and, rather than disappoint me, he said it was easier just to say that he went.

In the realm of things that trigger pain, this was a minor blip on the screen. But to me, it was gigantic. It was the lie that put me over the edge. I was in a rage. The pain was wrenching, but, as usual, I didn't let on how upset I was for fear of my own anger. So I got in the car and drove an hour to Hyde Park on the south side of Chicago to meet with Father Bob. "I am not going to let Father Bob talk me out of this one," I kept telling myself. "I can tolerate almost anything except dishonesty. This is the last straw."

When I saw Father Bob, I let him have it. No tears this time, just guns loaded.

After presenting my case and without giving me any time to wallow in my anger, Father Bob invited me to go deeper with a simple reflection: "It sounds like the pain of the lie triggered a primal pain."

"What's that?"

"According to Janov, it is something so painful that happened in one's early life (usually womb to six months) that it didn't get to the feeling brain or thinking, or, if it did get there, it got there in a distorted way."

"Oh."

"It would overwhelm you and you'd be in a hospital if you were conscious of it. The fear was paralyzing."

"Oh."

"His lie triggered your rage and the deep hurt of a primal pain, for which you took responsibility. You hid it and denied it. You had no voice."

"Oh. Uh, huh." This was new territory. We had never discussed "primal pain."

"Tommy's lie enraged you because it opened you to your own denial."

I asked him to explain.

"Didn't you lie by hiding your feelings? Didn't your dream show you that you had put yourself in a coffin because you were afraid that if you let out your rage, it would end the marriage?"

I got it. I saw that I had lied too. Not once, but for most of my life, I had engaged in a cover up, hiding my feelings, afraid to say the truth for fear of how my parents or, now, Tommy, would react. I was doing the same thing that I got so upset with my husband for doing: hiding the truth for fear of the repercussions.

Exposing my own dysfunction took the fire out of my fight.

I felt my body relax and thought: *Maybe the problem is where it always is, inside of me.*

"What do I do now?" I asked Father Bob.

"Get in touch with the pain. Tell Jesus you are ready for this to be brought to light. Don't run away. He wants to transform it!"

On the drive home, I made a wrong turn off Lake Shore Drive and got lost in Chicago. I didn't know where I was, but it didn't matter. I felt peaceful, even thankful, remembering another insight that Peggy Huddleston shared with me: "The behavior of the people closest to us acts like a mirror that often reflects things about our selves that we don't want to see, or admit. They trigger old wounds that still need healing. You should thank your husband who triggers your wounds. He is helping you heal." Father Bob had often said the same thing.

They were both right. This was not about Tommy; it was about what God was doing in me. My body was showing me through my feelings that my inner child was pretty hurt. The pain is really an invitation to awareness, Father Bob had said.

Repression of traumatic memories had physiological consequences that, I believe, grew tumors in my stomach, lung and breast. An author and a pioneer in the world of primal therapy, Arthur Janov, whose books Father Bob had recommended, writes that repressed trauma "stays with us as an imprint that is stored in our cells like the India ink stored in the amoeba's vacuole."[1] He goes on to say that, over time, "from its hiding place, the imprint continually disrupts our physiology, perhaps causing colds and allergies during youth, wearing us down physically, making us vulnerable to chronic diseases, weakening our immune functions."[2] Janov states that it can even cause more serious immunological disorders and cancer.

I learned so much from Janov, and I believe his theories. His concepts are not new; they have been around for a long time. Even the author of Proverbs connected the mind to the body when he wrote: "A cheerful heart is a good medicine, but a downcast spirit dries up the bones" (Prov 17:22).

I used to think that the unconscious was like a dark basement filled with scary, horrible demons. After reading Janov, I see it as more of a friendly place, the repository of one's early history.

Whatever else might be lurking down in my inner depths, I don't know, but I'm giving God permission to knock down the walls, because I trust that there is freedom on the other side.

If I had to name one lesson I've learned about the spiritual journey, it is that we are made for love. The core of our being is love. In order to love, we need to receive love. When we are deprived of it, especially early in life, I think we spend the rest of our lives looking for it, trying to fill up the emptiness that follows us through life.

Our path in life is to restore our capacity to love.

This was the theme of another ACT retreat I attended that Fr. Bob Faricy and Cheryl Nguyen gave. In one talk, Father Faricy described people who punish themselves with alcohol, sex and cutting, or who burn themselves with cigarettes. They think that this gives them control over their lives, he said, but in reality they resent their lives and have forgotten themselves in the process; the root of this behavior is low self-esteem and self-hatred.

At first, I felt sorry for "these people," thinking that I really didn't have anything in common with them. But upon reflection I realized that I wasn't so different from them after all. I didn't hurt my body, but I did harm to my soul, by punishing myself through self-hate. I turned all the anger, fear, shame and feelings of loss and betrayal (from the womb and early childhood) against myself, which surfaced as depression. At some deep level I gave up, and spent most of my life unaware of this. "Giving up" is really an unconscious death wish, a reality, Bernie Siegel believes, that affects 15 to 20 percent of all patients. And, ironically, they are the ones, he says, who appear to have it all together even after they are diagnosed with a serious illness.

It took all these years to recognize the harm I did to myself by discounting hurts and negative feelings. It was my illnesses, through the grace of God, that were trying to alert me to this, to help me see that I was unconsciously trying to snuff my life out because I didn't know how to deal with pain. As Father Bob told me more than once, "When we face the pain, we don't need the illness."

For the better part of my life I tried to scapegoat pain, to blame it on someone or something else. It never worked. Even our society tries to dump the fault on someone else. It boggles my mind why people get paid for being at fault. I'm thinking of the lawsuit in which someone sued McDonald's because hot coffee spilled on his or her lap and scalded them. Why they were awarded a ton of money when they caused it to happen defies logic, not to mention morality.

The world deals with pain in one way: by avoiding it, hiding it, deflecting it. Christians are called to a different standard, to stop hiding behind their defense mechanisms and be truthful. And as my good friend, Fr. Larry Hennessey, said in a homily recently when he was describing the life of Christian discipleship, we have to recognize the Adam and Eve inside of us, who scapegoat God and others to deflect our own responsibility.

I still grapple with pain: what to do with it, how to live with it, how to heal it, how to get beyond it. I don't believe that God wills our pain or our suffering; He allows it. I don't think that there is any such thing as freedom from pain. Pain is embedded into the Christian spiritual journey; it has a deeper meaning. Jesus said to His disciples, "Whoever does not bear his own cross and come after me, cannot be my disciple" (Lk 14:27). Jesus died on the Cross in order to save us from sin and death, and asks us to bear our crosses in union with Him. In that way, they are not so heavy, because He has already borne the weight of pain for us. Jesus uses our suffering to heal us—and others—through us.

When I don't run to Father Bob, I sit in my comfortable "prayer chair" and try to dig into the feelings. It is not always easy when you are in deep pain to sort through what is happening. It is a little like taking an elevator to the basement that stops on different floors. There are levels of feeling and it takes hanging in there to plumb the depths of them. What starts out as anger might end up as despair. The point is not to analyze everything, but to feel the feelings until you get to the bottom.

This is deep letting go and surrender, as Irma said. It is about "emptying self" a lesson the Lord has been teaching me for a long time. It is what He did on the Cross, and what He asks us to do with our pain. When we get underneath the surface feelings and get to the bottom, there is truth and love. When we find our truth, we meet Jesus, who is Truth. When we open to the love that is our core, we meet Love.

Jesus didn't scapegoat pain. He carried His Cross and asks us to do the same. Why? To transform our suffering. Much of our suffering arises out of our own inner brokenness, which means out of our sinfulness, our wounds, our addictions and other psychological dysfunctions. Then there is suffering that comes from injustices and accidents, from things over which we have little control.

I have come to view all suffering as an opportunity to grow, to change, to be purified like gold in the furnace, transformed into a new creation that Saint Paul describes in Corinthians: "And we all, with unveiled face, beholding the glory of the Lord, are being changed into His likeness from one degree of glory to another; for this comes from the Lord who is the Spirit" (2 Cor 3:18).

By offering our pain to the Lord, it conforms us to the suffering Christ who endured torture and death in order to free us and give us new life. We are privileged to imitate Jesus by living our crucifixions in our bodies, our minds, our emotions, our relationships, our marriages, our families and our work. It is by uniting ourselves to Him that we are freed from pain. Good Friday leads to Easter Sunday. The Lord went to His death believing that it would lead to life. Our life.

It is through suffering that we are redeemed.

And, although I believe that God doesn't will our pain, I trust that, He is with us in our suffering. As Elie Wiesel, the Jewish survivor or Auschwitz, brought out so powerfully in his best selling memoir, *Night*, we have a God who suffers for us and with us. He told a true story that happened in the concentration camp, when the SS hanged two Jewish men and a youth in front of the whole camp. The men died quickly, but the death throes of the boy lasted for half an hour. "'Where is merciful God, where is He?' someone behind me was asking. We were forced to look at him at close range. He was still alive when I passed him. His tongue was still red, his eyes not yet extinguished. Behind me, I heard the same man asking: 'For God's sake, where is God?' And from within me, I heard a voice answer: 'Where He is? This is where—hanging here from the gallows . . .'"[3]

I think this is one of the most poignant reflections on the Christian meaning and value of suffering.

23

Fruits of the Journey

When we die and when we go to heaven and we meet our Maker, our Maker is not going to say to us, why didn't you become a messiah? Why didn't you discover the cure for such and such? The only thing we're going to be asked at that precious moment is why didn't you become you.

—Elie Wiesel, *Souls on Fire*

I HAD NO IDEA when my body began to break down fifteen years ago and I contracted one illness after another, that I also suffered from an inner brokenness that was impacting me physically. The search to regain my health turned into a quest to find my inner self, the child whom I neglected and abandoned when she was very young, perhaps even in the womb.

When I first came down with scleroderma, it was a disease I had never heard of and couldn't pronounce. Finding out that it is an extremely rare disorder in which the skin and the internal organs thicken, was like waking up after a bad nightmare, only it was real. My curiosity as to what caused the thickening led to more strange information: our cells, which are designed to fight infection, become dysfunctional and attack each other, causing the body to atrophy. In the months following the diagnosis, I learned that my body was mimicking what was going on in my inner life. That insight was like a fork in the road, causing me to take another direction, an inner journey that saved my life.

The only experience I ever had with serious illness was my childhood bout with polio, forty-six years before. The memory of it was as fresh as if it happened yesterday. Even at 6, I was determined to face whatever obstacles were in my path so that I could resume my normal, happy life. I also had faith that God would hear my prayers and get me out of the hospital. I seemed to know that He was not going to miraculously zap me back to health. I was somehow spared feeling sorry for myself and, by the grace of God, knew that I would have to endure hardships that would make me get well: the long needles that crabby nurses stuck me with in the middle of the night, endless pill-taking, hospital food for a very picky eater, and grueling muscle-stretching exercises that were a rite of passage home. I see now that I was endowed with an inner strength and a positive, optimistic attitude that helped me get well.

If polio was a test of how to cope with problems, I passed. It taught me that there is a wider purpose to illness, or to any suffering for that matter. In the hospital I didn't look at sickness as a dead end, as some did. I saw it as a challenge, an opportunity to get better and go home. I knew, at some level, that the choices I made could make the difference between staying sick or getting healthy.

Fortunately, when I was first diagnosed with scleroderma in 1994, those same inner resources kicked in and fired my resolve to find a way to overcome this deadly illness. I had many things going for me. A close family that meant everything to me, and a husband who constantly reminded me that we would beat this thing, and that God would help us find an answer to each problem. I was also blessed with a positive, never-say-die attitude, a deep faith in God whom I believed would guide me, and a ministry of writing and speaking about the Eucharist, which energized me and filled my days with enjoyable, meaningful, work. Chalk it up to God's perfect timing, but when I was very sick and swollen with the effects of scleroderma, I was so busy assembling *My Daily Eucharist,* that my growing incapacities took a back seat to the task at hand. With the gift of hindsight and all that I subsequently learned about the mind/body connection, I now think that the work in which I was so happily engaged poured life-giving energy into the cells of my body, which put the brakes on a growing illness that could have disfigured and paralyzed me.

Initially, I was looking for physical solutions to physical problems. As the crises multiplied, I sought refuge in my faith. At Mass each morning, I asked the Lord for guidance to deal with problems that were blindsiding me. I was groping in the dark, not knowing which way to turn, to whom to listen, what to read, what to think. My faith gave me comfort. In the language of A.A., I had hit bottom, not really knowing how to help myself. There was only one way to go, and that was up. I tried to "let go and let

God," asking for the light of His truth to lead me through the darkness of confusion and uncertainty, back to health.

Like a starving child scavenging for food, I searched the Bible hoping to figure out how to dispose myself for healing. My faith in God already meant a great deal to me, but now I wanted to draw closer to the Lord, and I also was curious to learn about the Holy Spirit.

Scripture passages on healing popped up in my life constantly, either when I perused the Bible, or at Mass during one of the Readings or in the Gospel. What I learned in the early days of my illness was that all healing is related to faith. Jesus repeatedly attributed His miracles of healing to a person's faith, saying on many occasions, "Your faith has saved you" (Mk 10:52). One story really touched me. It was about the centurion who asked for healing for his servant who was lying paralyzed at home. The Lord offered to go to his house, which was a distance away, but this person of authority who had significant police powers said no adding, "only say the word and my servant will be healed" (Mt 8:8). The centurion refused the offer partly because he knew that Jews weren't permitted to go into Gentile homes, and also because he respected the higher authority of Jesus, recognizing that Jesus' "word" carried the power to accomplish whatever Jesus wanted. Scripture records that Jesus "marveled" at this man's faith, saying that in all of Israel, He had not found such faith.

What I heard was that I needed to have the blind faith of the centurion, who was convinced that his servant would be healed with only a word from Jesus. This strengthened the faith I already had, turning it into an *expectant* faith. I think God was tugging at my heart, encouraging me to believe that what He did for the centurion, He would do for me, if I put my trust in Him.

In addition to meditating on Scripture, I wanted to spend quality time in prayer, so I went to workshops and retreats that focused on healing and prayer. I met Fr. Peter McCall, OFM Cap., on retreat in St. Croix. He deepened my understanding of faith, telling me that it is not our faith that heals, but it is the faith of Jesus in us that heals. In other words, the Holy Spirit.

He was also the first to teach me about the mind/body connection, saying that disease can result from negative patterns of thinking and behaving that block the flow of energy—and love. Jesus doesn't only want to take away the symptoms of disease, Father Peter said, He wants to heal the cause. And to do that, he said we have to sort through our inner "garbage," the hurts and angers and resentments we've stored that are toxic and can make us sick. The goal, he said, is to get to the roots of our pain. When we do that, he said, we wouldn't need the illness anymore.

Father Peter was the first in a long line of teachers and mentors whose lessons led me deeper into the inner chaos that was sucking life from me. I see now that I was born with an emotional hole in my heart, believing that I didn't matter, that I wasn't lovable, and that I was no good. Something as simple as not being invited to a party could trigger intense feelings of rejection. I guess my worst fear was being left out or overlooked. Unable to verbalize my pain, I swallowed it.

Fortunately, I had the same determination to face my dark side as I did the physical problems. As Father Peter initially described it, I had a lot of "undoing" to do. First, I needed to break the pattern of denial, because I was programmed to think that others were causing the pain, especially my husband. It took a lot of counseling, retreats, workshops, seminars, and reading to see that the pain was inside of me. Then I had to learn to become accountable for my feelings, which meant getting in touch with them and facing their pain.

The spiritual teachers and mentors who appeared when I needed them, people whom you have met in these pages, walked into the darkness with me, helping me acknowledge the buried wounds. They led me to recognize, and dismantle, the negative core beliefs about myself that prevented me from loving, myself and others. I trusted their skill and their wisdom in leading me into the eye of the storm. Instead of running from pain, which I had been doing my whole life, they taught me to embrace it. I have them to thank for helping me recover my lost, inner child, whom I had silenced and abandoned at such a young age. In finding her, I was finding my true self, or as the late, great spiritual writer, Fr. Henri Nouwen says, the beloved self. That, Father Nouwen writes, is what our spiritual journey is all about: to become the beloved person that we already are.

This is not just my story; it is our story, the story of our salvation, our lived experience in the flesh, as well as in the spirit. They go together. What I've learned is that God is true to His promise to give us more than we can ask for or imagine if we will only have the faith to believe in His love. I've also learned that it is often difficult to feel His love because we don't love ourselves.

Sometimes I am overwhelmed by the love I feel for my children and grandchildren. Then I think that this is a mere reflection of the love God has for each one of us. We are His children, the "King's kids" as one writer described us, who have the run of the castle and who lack for nothing.

Of all the gifts in the kingdom, I think faith is the greatest, because it gives us access to the King. It opens the gate to a new vision of life, one that will lead us to the joy of eternal life, which begins now, *on earth as it is in heaven*. The kingdom is here, it is now, and it is within us. It is the transforming peace, joy and healing love of Christ, which makes us new. As the priest said in his homily at Mass the other day, *we are the signs that Jesus Christ is alive!*

I would stake my life on the words of the Gospel that it is Jesus, through His Holy Spirit, "who will guide us to all truth" (Jn 16:13). I believe He guided my steps, one at a time, to the people and resources that helped me heal. Then He leaves the rest up to us. He wants us to use the gifts we are endowed with in order to become healed and whole. Our mind, imagination, memory, willpower, discernment, intuition, dreams, and the ability to pray and meditate, are like servants at our disposal. They wait on us. They are designed to help us access the place of life and love within our being, the source of Divine Love and Wisdom, that will help us blossom into the unique and beautiful person that God made us to be.

Jesus told us to, "Ask, and it will be given to you; seek, and you will find; knock and it will be opened to you. For everyone who asks receives, and he who seeks finds, and to him who knocks it will be opened" (Mt 7:7-9). I am the poster child for asking. I sometimes think we are afraid to ask, because we don't really believe that our needs will be met. My experience has been just the opposite.

When we first moved to Illinois from Connecticut many years ago, I went to a liturgy meeting at one of the parishes in our community. The priest asked people to raise their hands if they thought that prayer changes things. I was the only one who raised my hand! I believed it then, and I believe it even more now: prayer makes a difference in our life. If we have faith as small as a mustard seed, we can move mountains, Jesus said. Nothing will be impossible to us! (Mt 17:19).

When I was trying to write this chapter, I couldn't sleep one night, so I went to my office and sat in the dark facing my statues. I felt blocked, dry, and even a little sad. I felt like I wanted to cry. "Lord," I said, "why am I sad?" Then it came. First fear. Then anxiety. Doubt. Tears. Down deep, I was hurting over personal problems in our family that I had been trying not to dwell on. I was carrying them on my shoulders, and they were heavy.

I had just received an email from Danny's wife, Pippa, telling me that she was running the New York City Marathon for cystic fibrosis, and for Ellie, our 5-year-old granddaughter who has the disease. In a recent phone conversation with Father Bob, he said that love releases pain. He was right. Pippa's generosity triggered a switch that released a ton of love, for what she was doing, for our family and for Ellie, my adorable granddaughter to whom I introduced you several chapters back. But it also brought up a gnawing fear in the pit of my stomach that stemmed from Ellie's recent visit to Children's Memorial Hospital in Chicago, where she goes for monthly check-ups. For the first time in her young life, we learned that the disease is starting to affect the lungs of this bubbly, beautiful and, until now, healthy little girl. Ellie and her family have a long hard journey ahead. It breaks my heart.

I was also wrestling with some problems close friends had shared with me: Kidney cancer that metastasized to the bone. The break-up of a young marriage, with five children involved. Financial stress after the death of a spouse. There are more. One friend emailed that her 4-year-old grandson was in intensive care with a brain injury after riding on an ATV with his dad. And, I had just received a call from Dorothy, our faithful housekeeper who worked for my mom and dad for many years and who cared for both of them before they died. She could barely talk, telling me that her 22-year-old granddaughter, her great granddaughter and the child's father were killed in a head-on collision. Her pain was too much to bear.

Sometimes, after I give a talk, people will approach to say thanks or to ask for prayers for something in their life. Recently, a woman shared with me that she'd been living with her alcoholic, abusive husband for forty years and was ready to finally end it. And an elderly woman asked me to pray for her 45-year-old son. He was addicted to drugs and alcohol, she said, unemployed and still living at home. The pain was overwhelming.

I learned a way of surrendering these problems to the Lord from Fr. Bob Faricy, S.J., at a recent ACT retreat. He called it "the prayer of the vegetable." "Just put everyone and everything that comes into your mind, even distractions, under the Lordship of Jesus," he said. "Give Him your worries, anxieties and fears, failures, successes, hopes and dreams, for yourself and others, by placing them in His hands, under His loving Lordship," he continued and, to the extent that you do that, you will be cooperating with the Lord in His becoming the Lord of your whole life.

Referring to St. Paul's teaching about Jesus being the focal point of all history, and that all things come together in Him, Father Bob said that

"Jesus is the Lord of all History, He is the Lord of the world, and He is the Lord of me." We are all called to recognize Jesus as our own personal Lord, and, to the degree that I consciously invite Jesus into every part of my life, my whole life becomes a prayer.

This is a wordless prayer. It is a way of just being with Jesus. He knows everything anyway, but praying this way gives me a sense that I'm really connecting with God. So, as images of people or problems float through my mind, I place them in the heart of Christ.

I had recently read a story about the power of surrendering our burdens to the heart of Christ. In a touching memoir that Fr. Jim Willig, of Cincinnati, wrote before he died of renal cell carcinoma, he told about a visit he had from a retired United States Navy admiral, a former prisoner of war in Vietnam, who had been in solitary confinement for seven years. The admiral sought out Father Jim to share this story.

> When I was in prison in Vietnam in solitary confinement, my captor would continually torture me. One day I was tied to a rack. A young soldier was ordered to torture me and break me. During this torture, when I honestly felt I was at my breaking point, a beautiful prayer came instantly to my mind, even though I wasn't praying. The prayer was 'Sacred Heart of Jesus, I give my life to You.' So, I prayed that prayer over and over again. The more I prayed it, the more I felt I truly was giving my life to the Lord. Then this peace came over me like a warm blanket, and I no longer felt pain—only peace. The soldier torturing me saw this transformation in my face and stopped his torture. He went to his commanding officer and said, 'I'm sorry. I can't do this.' And they let me go back to my cell. From that day on, I continued to use that prayer of peace, 'Sacred Heart of Jesus, I give my life to You.'"[1]

Father Jim was so moved by this that he promised the admiral he would pray that prayer every day. The man looked Father Jim in the eye and said, "I know you will. And Father, when you pray that prayer, whether you suffer a little or a lot, whether you live a long or a short life—it will not matter. You will be at peace."[2]

This story moved me deeply. Combining the prayer of surrender with the Sacred Heart of Jesus would be my new way of praying. As images of friends and loved ones came to mind, I placed them in the heart of Christ.

It was deeply satisfying to pray in this way, because I felt like these people and the problems were really under His care. Peace settled over me after my prayer session. I went back to bed and fell right asleep.

YET I MUST TELL you that I still grapple with pain. Even after all the counseling and inner work, I occasionally fall prey to periods of darkness that want to swallow me whole.

My husband can still trigger gut-wrenching pain in me, without even realizing it. Recently a minor disagreement between us set me off. Within minutes I was sliding down a slippery slope, making judgments about him and wishing he were different. His silence and withdrawal enraged me. I began to feel overlooked and invisible. My negative self-talk turned him into a monster. I knew I was being irrational, but I was overwhelmed by feelings of rage that made me want to hurt and abandon him at the same time.

Trying to talk myself out of my feelings was impossible. I couldn't. We had a talk. I tried to make him understand the agony I was feeling. His defensiveness made me more upset. I walked out of his office and wanted to walk out of his life.

I thought about what Father Bob said at the end of our last session when I asked him what I should do now that I discovered this primal pain. He said to tell Jesus that I am ready for this pain to be brought to light. "Don't run away," Father Bob said, "because Jesus wants to transform it."

At Mass the next morning I prayed one of the most earnest prayers of my life: *Jesus, please speak to me like You speak to Cheryl and Father Faricy. If only You would say something to me, it would encourage me not to run from this, but to hang in there to work things out.*

At home I went into my office and sat in front of my statues. I looked at the statue of the Sacred Heart with His arms outstretched, bidding me to surrender my cares to Him: "Come to me all who labor and are heavy laden, and I will give you rest" (Mt 11:28). I thought of everything people had taught me about the prayer of surrender. I remembered Sr. Bea Brennan at our 50th Sacred Heart reunion responding to my question about what to do when darkness overcomes us. "Just sit there with Jesus," she said. "Be in the darkness with Him."

So I sat in the darkness. The feelings rose up like ghouls trying to frighten me into fleeing. I stayed put. I put the pain in the Heart of Christ. I waited for Him to speak to me. Silence.

I thought about Tommy, remembering how smitten I was when we first met. When he took me to Scranton to meet his family, I learned about what his life was like growing up. He had struggles too. He was the last of six. His older siblings were mostly out of the house when he was going to school and his mom was sick a lot of the time. He made the best of things and succeeded in high school and college, winning friends and positions of leadership all through school. He was elected president of his class at the University of Scranton for three years running, and lost the election in his senior year by only one vote.

I was watching an inner video of his early life and it was heartrending. Then I thought of our early years together and what a wonderful husband and father he was to our four kids. Later, at a retreat somewhere, we had to write down one quality about our spouse that we loved the most. It came easily to me: it was "goodness." The scenes of his life and our life together played in front of me like a movie that I didn't want to end. I saw why I fell in love with him, and why I was still in love with him. I also saw that he wasn't a monster, and that I was blaming him for something that was inside of me.

The pain evaporated. It was replaced by warm feelings of love and gratitude. And forgiveness. I released Tommy from every grudge I had ever held against him and any lingering resentments that I might not have verbalized. Whatever barnacles of bitterness that had encrusted them-selves on the walls of my heart just seemed to wash away, cleansing and freeing me from their grasp.

I also forgave anyone who had ever hurt me, including my parents, relatives, close friends and family members. Some of the people I love were not even aware that I held them accountable for behaviors that had hurt me in some way.

And last but not least, I forgave myself, for being constantly disap-pointed and disapproving of myself, wishing that I could be more loving, or more giving, or be like someone else who seemed to have it all together.

Deliberate daily forgiveness was a missing link in my life. Over the years I had exercised forgiveness randomly, during sessions with Father Bob, or through the Sacrament of Reconciliation, or after certain upsetting incidents such as the one with my pastor when I made a deliberate decision to forgive him and to ask his forgiveness for judging and manipulating him. Each time, the act of forgiving released me from a negative bondage with the person, freeing me from painful emotions that held me captive. Or, to use another analogy, it released the poison I was holding, making me feel as if the venom had been drained from a snakebite.

"When we forgive we open a door to heaven, and also open it for those who hurt us," Cheryl Nguyen had often said during our long phone conversations. When Saint Stephen forgave Paul for stoning him, it paved the way for Paul's conversion, Cheryl said. She also brought up St. Maria Goretti, a young uneducated farm girl who forgave her abuser, and, in so doing, prepared her soul to meet her Savior. It was her act of forgiveness that led to her abuser's conversion.

Cheryl equated forgiveness with love and deliverance, which is exactly what our Savior did for us on the Cross. Jesus showed us that love *is* forgiveness in action. His dying delivered us from sin and opened us to our eternal salvation. When we imitate Him and forgive those who hurt us, we are dying to self, detaching, laying down our lives for others. We are losing our life in order to find it.

Marriage Encounter taught us that love is a decision. So is forgiveness. And forgiveness, I believe, is the capstone of my healing journey. Like love, forgiveness has nothing to do with feelings. I *will* to love and I *will* to forgive. As soon as someone or something hurts me or triggers a negative reaction, a negative memory, I will to forgive and let go. It no longer has the power to hurt me.

This is the lesson the Lord has been teaching me for years, through Fr. Bob Sears, the counselors at Hazelden, Cheryl Nguyen and Fr. Bob Faricy during retreats, and through beloved authors such as Agnes Sanford, Bernie Siegel, Fr. Emiliano Tardiff, and so many others. For some reason, it took all these years for me to realize the gift and power of this virtue. It will take practice, but I will strive to live in a spirit of reconciliation, not allowing anyone or anything to rob me of the inner peace and joy that is my Christian inheritance.

Forgiveness, I believe, is the key to the transformation that the Lord wants to effect in each of us. It creates a space in us that Jesus fills with love, which heals and sets us free.

I FEEL JUBILANT! The Lord answered the prayer of my heart, to find His calming, renewing presence in the midst of life's storms that seek to upend me and make me despair. Jesus hadn't said anything to me in words, which is what I had asked of Him that morning at Mass. Instead, He shone the light of truth into my darkness. He gave me new eyes to see Tommy the way He sees him, according to his true identity, and He also reminded me of the secret to lasting healing: forgiveness.

That is the message—and the hope—I leave with you. I pray that you will not be afraid to knock and to seek, because you will find. We all carry burdens that are too heavy to bear. There is so much evil and suffering in the world that we cannot possibly endure it. But there is One who has carried all the sins and burdens of this world on His back, freeing us from its effects. We still may have to endure hardships and afflictions in our life, but like the Navy admiral in the concentration camp, when we open our heart to the Lord, He changes our anguish into strength, our despair into peace, our loathing into love.

Jesus transforms our pain and changes the meaning of our life.

It is a privilege to share my life with you, and especially my heart, so full of gratitude for the Spirit of Love that has guided my steps to healing. My passion, to share God's presence in my life, has become my purpose, to write and speak so that others can taste the love of Jesus, as I have known it. It is ironic, or rather providential, that out of my greatest pain, my need for presence, has come my greatest gift, the desire to be present to others in their need for God. This, I feel, is my mission, to enable others to recognize the love of God that calls them to become fully who they are.

Now it is time to hit the pause button. This book ends here, but the journey continues. In some ways I feel like it has just begun. I hope you feel that way too. The path on which God is leading me is probably different from the one by which He is leading and healing you. Rest assured that my way is certainly not the only way. I have not arrived at some ideal place where I can sit back on my laurels because I have been "healed." I am walking alongside you on the spiritual journey, a person growing and blossoming into the person He created me to be, according to His image, whole and holy.

I hope my story will encourage you to continue to search for the truth of your life and to open up to the transforming power of Love inside your own heart. May you continue your search beyond pain and suffering to know the God-of-Love who wants to heal and transform you—and others through you—into the beautiful, loving, whole and free person that you are.

Endnotes

Prologue

1. Foundation André Rochais du Canada, *"When Life Breaks Through: The Dynamics of PRH Helping Relationships"* (Poitiers, France: 11 Bis, rue des Feuillants 86000), 2004.

   The Foundation published another book, *Persons and Their Growth*, which presents a synthesis of the PRH vision of humanity and its psychological functioning. These books are available at: PRH Institute-USA Center, 8382 Ranch Estates Rd, Clarkston, MI 48348. Tel: 248-391-1383. Or go to: www.PRH-USA.org.

Chapter 3: Inner Disunity

1. Joan Carter McHugh, *Feast of Faith: Confessions of a Eucharistic Pilgrim* (Lake Forest, IL: Witness Ministries, 1994).

Chapter 4: Finding Help—and Hope

1. Henry Scammell, *The New Arthritis Breakthrough* (New York, N.Y. M. Evans & Company, Inc., 1993).
2. *Ibid.*, 60.
3. *Ibid.*, 41.

Chapter 5: Illness and Emotions

1. Andrew Weil, *Spontaneous Healing* (New York: Fawcett Columbine, 1995), 229.
2. *Ibid.*, 227.
3. Anne Harrington, *The Cure Within: A History of Mind-Body Medicine* (New York: W.W. Norton & Company, 2008), 91.
4. *Ibid.*, 95.

Chapter 6: The Roots of Illness

1. Francis Talbot, S.J., *Saint Among Savages* (New York & London: Harper & Brothers Publishers), 336.
2. M. Faustina Kowalska, *Divine Mercy in My Soul: Diary* (Stockbridge, MA: Marian Press, 1987), nn. 687, 1541, 173.
3. *Ibid.*, no. 299.

4. *Ibid.*, no. 796.
5. *Ibid.*, no. 475.
6. *Ibid.*, no. 1543.

Chapter 7: The Gift of Faith

1. Phil Kilroy, *Madeleine Sophie Barat, A Life* (Mahwah, NJ: Paulist Press, 2000), 39.
2. *Ibid.*
3. *Ibid.*,40.
4. *Time Magazine*, October 15, 1979, 15.
5. John Paul II, *The Pope Speaks to the American Church* (San Francisco: Harper, 1992), 64.

Chapter 8: Physical and Emotional Pain

1. Harrington, *op. cit.*, 94.

Chapter 9: Learning to Forgive

1. Charles Osburn with Fred Lilly, *The Charlie Osburn Story* (Pensacola, FL: Good News Ministries, 1986), 85-88.
2. Robert DeGrandis with Linda Schubert, *Healing through the Mass* (Mineola, NY: Resurrection Press, 1992), 32.
3. *Ibid.*, 31.
4. Emiliano Tardif, *Jesus Lives Today!* (South Bend, IN: Greenlawn Press, 1989).
5. *Ibid.*, 109.
6. *Ibid.*, 56.
7. Agnes Sanford, *The Healing Light* (New York: First Ballantine Books/Epiphany Edition, 1983).
8. *Ibid.*, 21.
9. *Ibid.*, 31.

Chapter 10: Cancer Diagnosis

1. John A. Sanford, *The Kingdom Within* (San Francisco: Harper & Row, 1987), 84.
2. George A. Maloney, *Broken But Loved* (New York: Alba House, 1981).
3. Arthur Janov, *The Primal Scream* (New York: Dell Publishing Co., Inc. 1970), 25.
4. Maloney, *op. cit.*, 87.

5. G.K. Chesterton, *Saint Thomas Aquinas, The Dumb Ox* (New York: Image Books Doubleday, 1956), 137.
6. Joan Carter McHugh, *Eucharist God Among Us: Essays and Images of the Eucharist in Sacred History* (Lake Forest, IL: Witness Ministries, 1999).

Chapter 12: A Prayer and a Healing Dream
1. Norman Cousins, *Anatomy of An Illness as Perceived by the Patient* (New York: W.W. Norton & Co, 1979), 39.
2. *Ibid.,* 69.
3. Morton T. Kelsey, *Dreams: The Dark Speech of the Spirit* (Garden City, N.Y.: Doubleday & Company, 1968).
4. John K. Ryan, Trans., *The Confessions of St. Augustine* (New York, Bantam Doubleday Dell Publishing Group, Inc.), 91.
5. *Ibid.,* 91.
6. Louis M. Savary, P. Berne, and S.K. Williams, *Dreams and Spiritual Growth* (New York: Paulist Press, 1984).

Chapter 13: Waking up "Sister Joan"
1. Thomas Merton, *Seeds of Contemplation* (New York: Dell Publishing Company, 1949), 40.
2. O. Carl Simonton, S. Matthews-Simonton and J. Creighton, *Getting Well Again* (New York: Bantam, 1978), 12.
3. *Ibid.,* 44, 45.
4. Bernie S. Siegel, *Love, Medicine & Miracles* (New York: Harper Perennial, 1986), 68-69.
5. *Ibid.,* 80.

Chapter 14: Thymectomy
1. Peggy Huddleston, *Prepare for Surgery, Heal Faster: A Guide of Mind Body Techniques* (Cambridge, MA: Angel River Press, 1996).

Chapter 15: Breast Cancer
1. Joseph Bernardin, *The Gift of Peace* (Chicago: Loyola Press, 1997), 46.

Chapter 17: Radiation
1. Siegel, *op. cit.,* 133.
2. Siegel, *op. cit.,* 146.

3. E. deWall, *A Seven Day Journey with Thomas Merton* (Ann Arbor, MI: Servant Publications, 1992), 47.
4. *Ibid.*, 55.
5. Agnes Sanford, *The Healing Light* (New York: First Ballantine Books/ Epiphany Edition, 1983).

Chapter 18: Lung Surgery
1. Siegel, *op. cit.*, 47.
2. Joan Carter McHugh, *The Mass: Its Rituals, Roots and Relevance in Our Lives* (Lake Forest, IL: Witness Ministries, 2005), 105.

Chapter 19: Finding the Root
1. M. Faustina Kowalska, *op. cit.*, nn. 511, 1448.

Chapter 20: Good Gifts
1. Nadine Brown, *Interceding with Jesus* (Omaha, NE: The Intercessors of the Lamb, 2000).
2. Ronald Rolheiser, "Eucharist: When God Embraces Us Physically," *The Catholic New World*, June 11-24 2006, 13.
3. McHugh, *The Mass, Its Rituals, Roots and Relevance in Our Lives.*
4. Brown, *op. cit.*, 22.

Chapter 22: The Problem of Pain
1. Arthur Janov, *Why You Get Sick, How You Get Well: The Healing Power of Feelings* (West Hollywood, CA: Dove Books, 1996), 25.
2. *Ibid.*, 26.
3. Elie Wiesel, *Night* (New York: Hill and Wang, 1958), 65.

Chapter 23: Fruits of the Journey
1. Jim Willig, *Lessons from the School of Suffering: A Young Priest with Cancer Teaches Us How to Live* (Cincinnati, OH: St. Anthony Messenger Press), 70.
2. *Ibid.*